THE FIFTEENTH CENTURY

VOLUME II

REVOLUTION AND CONSUMPTION IN LATE MEDIEVAL ENGLAND

The essays in this volume focus on the sources and resources of political power, on consumption (royal and lay, conspicuous and everyday), on political revolution and on economic regulation in the later middle ages. Topics range from the diet of the nobility in the fifteenth century to the knightly household of Richard II and the peace commissions, while particular case studies, of Middlesex, Cambridge, Durham Cathedral and Winchester, shed new light on regional economies through an examination of the patterns of consumption, retailing, and marketing.

Professor MICHAEL HICKS teaches at King Alfred's College at Winchester.

THE FIFTEENTH CENTURY

I. Concepts and Patterns of Service in the Later Middle Ages
edited by Anne Curry and Elizabeth Matthew

REVOLUTION AND CONSUMPTION IN LATE MEDIEVAL ENGLAND

Edited by

MICHAEL HICKS

THE BOYDELL PRESS

First published 2001
The Boydell Press, Woodbridge

ISBN 0 85115 832 3

The Boydell Press is an imprint of Boydell & Brewer Ltd
PO Box 9, Woodbridge, Suffolk IP12 3DF, UK
and of Boydell & Brewer Inc.
PO Box 41026, Rochester, NY 14604–4126, USA
website: http://www.boydell.co.uk

A catalogue record for this title is available
from the British Library

Library of Congress Cataloging-in-Publication Data
Revolution and consumption in late medieval England / edited by Michael Hicks.
p. cm. – (The fifteenth century; v. 2)
Selected papers from a conference organized at Southampton on Sept. 3–5, 1999.
Includes bibliographical references and index.
ISBN 0–85115–832–3 (alk. paper)
1. Great Britain – Politics and government – 1399–1485 – Congresses.
2. Consumption (Economics) – England – History – To 1500 – Congresses.
3. England – Economic conditions – 1066–1485 – Congresses. 4. England – Social conditions – 1066–1485 – Congresses. I. Hicks, M. A. (Michael A.) II. Series.
DA245.R48 2002
942.04–dc21 2001035279

Typeset by Joshua Associates Ltd, Oxford

CONTENTS

LIST OF TABLES

LIST OF CONTRIBUTORS

ALASTAIR DUNN has completed his doctoral research on the politics of Richard II and Henry IV and is now Teaching Fellow in Medieval History at the University of St Andrews.

PETER FLEMING is Senior Lecturer in History at the University of the West of England at Bristol and is co-editor of *Regionalism and Revisionism: The Crown and its Provinces in England 1200–1650* (Hambledon, 1999).

JESSICA FREEMAN is currently completing her doctoral thesis on the Middlesex county community in the fifteenth century at London University.

ALISON GUNDY has recently completed her doctorate on the Appellant Earl of Warwick and the politics of the West Midlands at Sidney Sussex College, Cambridge.

JOHN HARE teaches history at Peter Symonds' College, Winchester. He is currently revising a book on the society and economy of late medieval Wiltshire.

WINIFRED HARWOOD is currently researching her doctoral thesis on the bursars' accounts of Winchester College at King Alfred's College, Winchester.

MICHAEL HICKS is Professor of Medieval History and Head of History at King Alfred's College, Winchester and author of *Warwick the Kingmaker* (Oxford, 1998).

JOHN LEE has completed his doctorate on Cambridge and its economic region, 1450–1560, at Corpus Christi College, Cambridge.

SHELAGH MITCHELL has recently completed her doctorate on the Knightly Household of Richard II at London University.

T. B. PUGH is Reader Emeritus in Medieval History, University of Southampton, and has published extensively on the late medieval nobility, marcher lordships and the house of York.

MIRANDA THRELFALL-HOLMES has completed her doctorate on the late medieval obedientiary accounts of Durham Cathedral Priory at Durham University and is training for ordination.

CHRISTOPHER WOOLGAR is Head of Special Collections, Southampton University Library, and author of *The Great Household in Late Medieval England* (New Haven and London, 1999).

LIST OF ABBREVIATIONS

AgHR	Agricultural History Review
AHEW	*Agrarian History of England and Wales*, iii, *1348–1500*, ed. E. Miller (Cambridge, 1991)
BIHR	Bulletin of the Institute of Historical Research
BJRL	Bulletin of the John Rylands Library
BL	British Library, London
BRS	Bristol Record Society
Carpenter, *Locality and Polity*	C. Carpenter, *Locality and Polity: A Study of Warwickshire Landed Society, 1401–99* (Cambridge, 1992)
CCR	Calendar of the Close Rolls
CFR	Calendar of the Fine Rolls
CIM	Calendar of Inquisitions Miscellaneous
CIPM	Calendar of Inquisitions post mortem
CPR	Calendar of the Patent Rolls
DCD	Archives of the Dean and Chapter of Durham
Dyer, *Everyday Life*	C. C. Dyer, *Everyday Life in Medieval England* (London, 1994)
Dyer, *Standards of Living*	C. C. Dyer, *Standards of Living in the Later Middle Ages: Social Change in England c.1200–1520* (Cambridge, 1989)
EcHR	Economic History Review
EETS	Early English Text Society, e[xtra], o[riginal], and s[upplementary] s[eries].
EHR	English Historical Review
Foedera	*Foedera, Litterae, Conventiones etc.*, ed. T. Rymer, 10 vols. (Hague 1745; repr Farnborough 1967)
Given-Wilson, *English Nobility*	C. Given-Wilson, *The English Nobility in the Later Middle Ages* (London, 1987)
Given-Wilson, *Royal Household*	C. Given-Wilson, *The Royal Household and the King's Affinity* (London, 1986)
GL	Guildhall Library, London
Goodman, *Loyal Conspiracy*	A. Goodman, *The Loyal Conspiracy: The Lords Appellant under Richard II* (London, 1971)
Griffiths, *Henry VI*	R. A. Griffiths, *The Reign of King Henry VI, 1422–61* (London, 1981)
Harvey, *Living and Dying*	B. F. Harvey, *Living and Dying in England 1100–1540: The Monastic Experience* (Oxford, 1993)
HPT 1386–1421	*History of Parliament: The Commons 1386–1421*, ed. J. S. Roskell, L. Clark and C. Rawcliffe, 4 vols. (London, 1992)
HRSer	Hampshire Record Series
HRSoc	Hampshire Record Society

KCC	King's College, Cambridge
L&P	*Letters and Papers, Foreign and Domestic, of the Reign of Henry VIII*, ed. J. S. Brewer *et al.*, 23 vols. in 38 (London, 1862–1932)
Liber Albus	*Munimenta Gildhallae Londoniensis*, ed H. T. Riley, Rolls Series, 2 vols. (London, 1860–1)
LRS	London Record Society
McFarlane, *Nobility*	K. B. McFarlane, *The Nobility of Later Medieval England* (Oxford, 1973)
PCFC	*Proceedings of the Hampshire Field Club and Archaeological Society* (now *Hampshire Studies*)
POPC	*Proceedings and Ordinances of the Privy Council*, ed. N. H. Nicolas, 7 vols. (1834–7)
Postan, *Essays*	M. M. Postan, *Essays on Medieval Agriculture and General Problems of the Medieval Economy* (Cambridge, 1973)
PRO	Public Record Office, London
Pugh, *MLSW*	T. B. Pugh, *Marcher Lordships of South Wales, 1415–1536: Select Documents* (Cardiff, 1963)
Reign of Richard II	*The Reign of Richard II: Essays in Honour of May McKisack*, ed. C. M. Barron and F. R. H. Du Boulay (London, 1971)
RO, CRO	Record Office, County Record Office
Ross, *Edward IV*	C. D. Ross, *Edward IV* (London, 1974)
Rot. Parl.	*Rolls of Parliament*, 6 vols. (London, 1767–83)
Saul, *Richard II*	N. Saul, *Richard II* (London, 1998)
SRS	Southampton Record Series
STC	Short Title Catalogue
TBGAS	Transactions of the Bristol and Gloucestershire Archaeological Society
TLMAS	Transactions of the London and Middlesex Archaeological Society
TRHS	Transactions of the Royal Historical Society
Tuck, *Richard II*	J. A. Tuck, *Richard II and the English Nobility* (London, 1973)
VCH	Victoria County History
Walsingham, *Annales*	*Annales Ricardi Secundi et Henrici Quarti*, ed. H. T. Riley, Rolls Series (London, 1866)
WAM	Westminster Abbey Muniments
Watts, *Henry VI*	J. L. Watts, *Henry VI and the Politics of Kingship* (Cambridge, 1996)
WCL	Winchester Cathedral Library
Westminster Chronicle	*The Westminster Chronicle, 1381–94*, ed. B. F. Harvey and L. C. Hector (Oxford, 1982)
Winchester Pipe Roll	*The Pipe Roll of the Bishopric of Winchester 1409–10*, ed. M. Page, Hampshire Record Series 16, 1999
Wolffe, *Royal Demesne*	B. P. Wolffe, *The Royal Demesne in English History* (London, 1973)

This book is produced with the assistance of grants from Isobel Thornley's Bequest to the University of London and the Scouloudi Foundation, in association with the Institute of Historical Research

INTRODUCTION

This volume contains selected papers from the fifteenth-century history conference that I organised at Southampton on 3–5 September 1999. It was the ninth in the series of 'junior' conferences launched by Charles Ross at Bristol in 1978. Southampton '99 adopted the revised Huddersfield format of parallel sessions, which enables a higher proportion of young scholars to contribute. Four plenary sessions featured papers by established scholars, all published here, and a further twenty-eight papers were delivered in parallel sessions, mainly by current and recent research students. Despite generous subvention by the Royal Historical Society, relatively few research students attended who were not speaking, thus depriving delegates and absentees alike of the stimulus and camaraderie that such conferences are designed to afford. The quality of delivery was uniformly high. Reducing so many papers to a volume of reasonable length and balance required a drastic process of selection that cut out many papers of originality and worth. The final selection was made on the grounds of thematic coherence. I thank all those whose papers are not included for their contribution to the success of the conference and in due course I hope to see their work published elsewhere.

That so many papers were delivered by scholars who had not spoken at previous junior conferences is convincing evidence of the amazing vigour and debate of late medieval studies in Britain in an era of continual government cuts and of undergraduate present-mindedness. Twenty universities and colleges were represented at the conference. The balance of the programme, as always, reflects the short-term preferences of a particular generation of research students and their supervisors. That there was little on Europe, warfare, or women indicates not a lack of academic interest in these areas, but merely those projects that were approaching fruition. Where this conference was especially strong was on the sources and resources of political power, on consumption – conspicuous and everyday – and on political revolution and on economic regulation. In focusing on the twin themes of Revolution and Consumption this volume contributes substantially to current historical preoccupations and promotes new insights and methods for others to follow. Even with this narrowed focus, there were complementary papers that unfortunately could not be included.

Richard II, his reign and removal, have never been better known. We have been too long reliant on Victorian editions and Principal Steel's psychological life of 1941. New up-to-date editions of chronicles have appeared from Harvey and Hector, Martin and Given-Wilson, substantial studies from Barron, Goodman, Tuck and Given-Wilson again, a full-length biography from Saul, and, in Richard's sixth centenary year, two further studies by Bennett and a team of contributors.[1] Yet so much more remains to be said.

[1] *Westminster Chronicle*; *Knighton's Chronicle 1337–1396*, ed. G. H. Martin (Oxford, 1995); *The*

What was revolutionary was not so much Richard's downfall, except perhaps with foreknowledge of the Wars of the Roses, but the massive upheavals in landholding of the years 1397–1405: the greatest redistribution, albeit short-lived, between the Norman Conquest and the Dissolution of the Monasteries. Land was wealth and land was power. Its holders were powerful and control of its devolution was important to kings: both an object of policy and the means to achieve it. Richard II, it has been argued, sought both to destroy the territorial units of his enemies and to create new ones for his friends, to wield authority in the provinces, bestow patronage and profit financially. It is not remarkable that such aims conflicted, as Dunn's uniquely detailed analysis demonstrates (Ch. 2), and could not be systematically pursued or effectively realised in the time available to him. That Richard's regime was overthrown encouraged more officials and retainers of proscribed lords to claim to have resisted than was perhaps true. That centuries-old estates, families and loyalties took time to wither cannot surprise. Reversals, revolutions, rebellions and restitutions ultimately restored the status quo. Yet it was not the anger of the dispossessed by themselves that explains Richard's fall. In 1399, as always, we must beware of supposing that what befell was bound to happen and that Richard's new dispositions must inevitably have failed.

The tyranny of Richard's last years rested on those he trusted, above all those of his household, whom he supposedly intruded into the commissions of the peace in a bid to control the localities. Undoubtedly this was his objective, but it was nothing new. It was in the aftermath of the Peasants Revolt, so Mitchell shows (Ch. 3), that Richard turned to his household, appointing them Justices of the Peace even as he resorted, notoriously, to their counsel. She demonstrates convincingly that this was Richard's deliberate strategy throughout. It was made particularly offensive late in the reign by supplanting the precedence of the nobility in a more blatant bid for local control. It is the struggle for control in one key area, the West Midlands, that Gundy explores (Ch. 4), in which it was the king, who was the revolutionary out to destroy the established order, and the Earl of Warwick, in the name of stability and tradition, who withstood him. Royal patronage, such as appointments, were a weapon against the natural ruler, the earl, whose estates had hitherto conferred wealth, local standing, manpower, royal office and royal authority. Though ousted in 1397, the earl was enthusiastically restored in 1399, and his Beauchamp earldom endured thereafter undiminished into its golden age.[2] Perhaps, as Gundy suggests, Richard sacrificed the assumption of allegiance amongst his subjects by making himself into the greatest and most abrasive of bastard feudal lords, but the measure cannot be his overthrow, for that owed so much to contingency and timescale. That 1399 proved revolutionary only in a dynastic sense was

Chronicle of Adam Usk 1377–1421, ed. C. Given-Wilson (Oxford, 1997); C. M. Barron, 'The Tyranny of Richard II', *BIHR*, xli (1968); A. Goodman, *The Loyal Conspiracy: The Lords Appellant under Richard II* (London, 1971); Tuck, *Richard II*; Given-Wilson, *Royal Household*; Saul, *Richard II*; M. Bennett, *Richard II and the Revolution of 1399* (Stroud, 1999); *Richard II: The Art of Kingship*, ed. A. Goodman and J. L. Gillespie (Oxford, 1999).

[2] C. Carpenter, 'The Beauchamp Affinity: A Study of Bastard Feudalism at Work', *EHR*, xcv (1980).

because other potentially revolutionary attributes – the land-settlement and direct rule of the localities – were overturned. Richard could not continue his tyranny and the Lancastrians in practice favoured rapprochement.

The practice of politics was continuously pursued throughout the kingdom, in myriad communities, large and small, rural and urban. Gundy's Warwickshire and Worcestershire, the West Midlands counties, were but two among thirty-seven. Every shire was different in detail and they fall into several distinct political categories. Middlesex, the smallest of them all, belonged to the Church and was overshadowed by the capital and central government. Even so, as Freeman demonstrates (Ch. 6), the stable long-serving elite of about twenty families, who managed its affairs, and the parish gentry identified themselves with the county itself. Almost uniquely, Middlesex lacked significant market-towns and the boroughs to generate the records that illuminate urban life. Borough affairs, it is well known, were run by elite oligarchies, who resisted any self-assertion by the commons, who, however, were freemen scarcely inferior to the corporation and no less politically aware. The oligarchy claimed to rule in the interests of the communalty. Their prevailing political culture or dominant ideology, so Fleming argues (Ch. 11), is depicted in the mystery plays, which frequently both present their propagandist message and mirror contemporary practice. The *sanior pars* permitted to participate in politics were preselected by the corporation. Those taking their disputes to the crown were generally defeated and humbled and were always presented in town records and remembered as wrongdoers.

If Richard II was the revolutionary in the 1390s, it was Richard Duke of York who made it impossible for Henry VI to rule and who contrived another dynastic revolution. Why has been often debated and cannot easily be resolved. Though the greatest and richest of contemporary noblemen, richer not just than his father, as McFarlane long ago remarked,[3] but than all his York and Mortimer predecessors, York had real and escalating financial problems. The collapse of his Welsh revenues – what Pugh (Ch. 5) equates to the end of the Middle Ages in Wales – forced York to sell off the family silver, to dishonour his obligations, to wallow in debt, and die intestate. Here was reason enough to plunder or even appropriate the royal coffers. Whether or not this was his motive, successful protectorates made lavish financial provision for him. How widely known and fully appreciated York's problems were, we cannot be sure, for he kept up appearances. If power was founded on wealth and wealth on land, it was not an accountant's audit of income that mattered, but how much one spent: how conspicuous was one's consumption. Although Duke Richard defaulted on his daughters' dowries, pawned his jewels, sold his lands, and lived off his capital, he remained nevertheless the most conspicuous of consumers and was esteemed as such.

How conspicuous was consumption? Nobody, one might suppose, ever feasted more lavishly than Archbishop Neville at his enthronement feast in 1465. All those swans. Far from it. The quantity of food and drink, though huge, was no more than an aristocrat would expect for ten typical meals of meat. Appearance, Woolgar explains (Ch. 1), was as important as taste: indeed one finds oneself wondering, not just whether the great consumed two

[3] K. B. McFarlane, *England in the Fifteenth Century* (London, 1981), p. 240.

to four times our calorie intake, but whether anybody ate it. After all, it was because not every aristocrat was obese that Edward, the second Duke of York, who asphyxiated at Agincourt, was singled out as fat. Not everyone fared the same in a great household, so Woolgar shows, either in quality or quantity, the greatest dining more sparingly of the choicest cuts, but the sheer quantities, whether measured in pounds or calories, were definitely calculated to impress the most sophisticated observers. Indeed they did. Even metropolitan businessmen were awed by the open-house breakfasts of Warwick the Kingmaker. Such catering was a political statement. The Neville enthronement feast impressed not because of the size of portion – even aristocrats could eat and drink no more! – but because of the numbers attending and the duration of the feast: twice as long as a coronation feast. The Nevilles, it follows, overshadowed any Yorkist king. And what king could allow such space within his schedule?

Such a large-scale event, we can deduce, required not only an army of cooks and a mass of temporary accommodation, but placed a strain on the supply of food not just of a regional capital like York, but far around. We lack the accounts to study that aspect of *this* event, whereas those of the households of Richard Earl of Warwick and Sir Henry Stafford survive. Diet accounts cast light not just on life-style and consumption, but also on sources of supply. Given the absence of systematic sources for inland trade comparable to the customs accounts for foreign trade, they are now the key sources for the study of retailing and market networks. What could Stafford buy in his local market, what from the next large town, and what had he to seek in the nearest port, in London, or at the point of manufacture? The range of trades, crafts and services increased with the size of town.[4] Noble household accounts have their uses here, though they tend to be discontinuous, the households themselves peripatetic, and they illuminate any particular place only spasmodically. Great religious households, of abbeys, colleges and hospitals, are more potentially useful, since they were immobile and thus constantly relate to the same areas. The vast majority have lost their records, but a handful retain them, such as Westminster Abbey, Ewelme Hospital and the Great Hospital at Norwich, which have all featured in past studies.[5] Three such pioneering analyses appear here, in each case as tasters of larger projects, by Threlfall-Holmes on Durham Cathedral Priory, by Harwood on Winchester Cathedral Priory and by Lee on Cambridge (Chs. 8–10). It is such projects that, in due course, will enable historians to reconstruct patterns of consumption and trade across late medieval England as a whole.

Patterns of consumption, retailing and marketing inevitably illuminate local and regional economies. The traditional context is one of depression and contraction, as set out in Postan's classic article of 1938, the most cited work in this volume.[6] More recent historians have drawn attention to

[4] J. Patten, *English Towns 1500–1700* (Folkestone, 1978), chs. 4 and 6.

[5] Harvey, *Living and Dying*, pp. 34–71; J.-P. Genet, 'Économie et societé rurale en Angleterre au XVe siècle d'après les comptes de l'hôpital d'Ewelme', *Annales*, xxvii (1972), pp. 1449–74; C. Rawcliffe, *Medicine for the Soul: The Life, Death and Resurrection of an English Medieval Hospital* (Stroud, 1999).

[6] Postan, 'The Fifteenth Century', *Essays*.

chronological irregularities, such as the mid-fifteenth-century depression,[7] and to regional variations. These studies indicate just how extensive were the services available locally. Durham Priory, for instance, no longer needed to seek imported wine or spices at York or Hull since Newcastle could meet the demand, and Winchester Priory obtained many non-local commodities off the shelf in Winchester. New crops, such as saffron, were being developed. Such studies, in short, indicate that much more was happening than decline. So, too, does Hare's study of Wessex (Ch. 7). The flight of cloth-making to the countryside, where smaller towns flourished, and investment in houses, inns and churches indicate regional prosperity. The relaxation of demographic pressure, rising productivity and living standards, what Bridbury dubbed *economic growth*,[8] permitted diversification and expansion in crops, crafts and occupations that anticipated those of the late seventeenth and eighteenth centuries. Although great institutions stopped farming the demesnes, they did not cease to be *farmed*. Leasing did not replace large-scale commercial farming with peasant subsistence smallholding, for often demesnes were leased in large blocks and always substantial rents had to be paid. Leasing stripped out the heavy management overheads justifiable in the era of high-farming and ever rising prices and placed the demesnes in the hands of practical farmers anxious to identify and satisfy market needs. If regrettably the decline of institutional agriculture has deprived us of our best sources for who was farming the demesnes and what they were producing, yet they emerge once more as suppliers of specific products from stated locations in the records of King's College Cambridge and other institutional households. How well they prospered we may judge from surviving houses at Mells in Somerset or on the Winchester bishopric estates, now regularly discovered and dated by carpentry or dendrochonology,[9] from the churches they patronised, and the monuments and brasses they commissioned. *Pace* Postan and Huizinga, the Middle Ages were adapting and expanding rather than waning.

Nor were these developments of purely economic and social significance. If manpower and wealth, the ultimate sources of political power, derived from land and that land was increasingly exploited commercially by non-aristocratic capitalists, what implication did this have for the rule of the shires? The great religious institutions were surely already on trajectory for their post-medieval centuries as rentiers of effectively secularised estates, in which even the tenants were counted as military resources by laymen. What of the aristocracy? No longer directly involved with their estates, were they increasingly reliant on the authority bestowed by royal commissions? Rather than wrong, was Richard II merely premature?

A conference of this complexity cannot be a one-man band. I owe particular gratitude to John Hare, who conducted the tour of Bishops Waltham Palace on which he is the acknowledged expert, and to Sarah Lewin, who chaired a

[7] J. Hatcher, 'The Great Slump of the Mid-Fifteenth Century', *Progress and Problems in Medieval England*, ed. R. H. Britnell and J. Hatcher (Cambridge, 1996), pp. 237–72.

[8] A. R. Bridbury, *Economic Growth: England in the Later Middle Ages* (London, 1962).

[9] For example E. Roberts, 'Overton Court Farm and the Late Medieval Farmhouses of Demesne Lessees in Hampshire', *PCFC*, li (1996).

parallel session all Saturday subtitled *Recent Research in Late Medieval Wessex*. George Bernard kindly read T. B. Pugh's paper in his unavoidable absence and a dozen chairpeople ran the sessions. Richard Brown, Winifred Harwood, Toby Purser, and Carrie Smith manned information desks, directed car-parking and generally ensured that everything ran smoothly. I pay grateful tribute to them all.

Michael Hicks
Winchester, December 2000

Fast and Feast: Conspicuous Consumption and the Diet of the Nobility in the Fifteenth Century

Christopher Woolgar

The enthronement feast of George Neville as archbishop of York is one of the most quoted examples of conspicuous consumption in late medieval England. While it may be among the best known, it is not at the same time among the best understood. The volume of consumption has impressed many commentators. The list of the 104 oxen, 6 wild bulls, 1,000 sheep, 304 calves, 304 pigs, 400 swans, 2,000 geese, 1,000 capons, 2,000 piglets and more makes it otiose to enumerate the categories that are more unusual to our eyes, the bitterns, heronsews, curlews and egrets that formed the provision for the feast, that is, the bulk purchases made especially for it.[1] For all that feasts – and, paradoxically, abstinence – on this scale are discussed as an integral element of the way of life of late medieval England, there is a surprising lack of context that might provide more illumination of this celebration. Was it typical of the level of consumption, or something that was employed for a special occasion? How long did the feast last? When exactly was it held? What was distinctive about its composition? How (and why) did abstinence feature in this abundant celebration? Who was there and why?

This paper aims to move forward the understanding of medieval aristocratic consumption in two directions and then to return to the Neville feast. Firstly, there is a good deal of evidence which can be analysed to establish individual levels of consumption and nutrition, against which the consequences and significance of fast and feast can be set. Secondly, the notion of conspicuous consumption – and how it might or not reflect medieval priorities and consciousness – needs examination. Here it is important to establish where the balance of consumption lies: what makes it conspicuous? Is it quantity, quality, decoration, presentation, taste or smell?

[1] For example W. E. Mead, *The English Medieval Feast* (London, 1931), pp. 32–4; D. Brewer, 'Feasts in England and English Literature in the Fourteenth Century', *Feste und Feiern im Mittelalter: Paderborner Symposion des Mediävistenverbandes*, ed. D. Altenburg, J. Jarnut and H.-H. Steinhoff (Sigmaringen, 1991), p. 13; A. Emery, *Greater Medieval Houses of England and Wales 1300–1500*, 3 vols. (Cambridge, 1996–), i, p. 293. The account of the feast is most usually cited from *Johannis Lelandi Antiquarii De Rebus Britannicis Collectanea*, ed. T. Hearne, 2nd edn, 6 vols. (London, 1774), vi, pp. 2–6. For the history of this text, see below.

Patterns of consumption and the diet of the nobility

Over the last thirty years, historians have established the broad outlines of the patterns of consumption in different groups in medieval society. At the same time, there have been both some detailed studies and European comparisons.[2] Few will not know of Barbara Harvey's analysis of the diet of the closed community at Westminster Abbey at the end of the fifteenth century and start of the sixteenth, based on a series of accounts that not only recorded the commodities acquired and their consumption, but also – and most unusually – effectively gave menus meal by meal. This enabled her to estimate what an individual might eat over a long period of time and to follow through the consequences for that individual.[3] Professor Dyer's analyses of peasant diet and that of harvest workers within this group were based on a range of more disparate sources, and have traced the growing element of meat in peasant food, alongside a diminishing contribution made by cereals.[4] He defined the general characteristics of aristocratic diet, a generous provision of meat and fish, with a calorific intake of around 4,000 to 5,000 kcal per person per day, suggesting that there was comparatively little development in the diet of the aristocracy between the thirteenth and fifteenth centuries.[5] This conclusion may now be modified in the light of evidence for an evolution of aristocratic diet in the fifteenth century, with a concentration on lighter meats for the highest echelons, those that might be subject to routines of carving and display, at the expense of staples like beef, mutton and especially pork; a significant diminution in fish-eating; and the possibility that defined groups within the aristocratic household fared differently in terms of consumption.[6]

This paper focuses more closely on the diet of the aristocracy during the fifteenth century, to isolate diets of individuals, or groups of individuals, from a small selection of accounts. For these purposes two sets of accounts have been selected. The first is for the 'intrinsic' or 'inner' household of the Earl of Warwick for the year starting at Michaelmas 1420 – unusually named in that, instead of

[2] The literature has grown enormously in this period, starting with the series of preliminary papers in *Annales* in 1961, encompassing the proceedings of conferences: *Manger et Boire au Moyen Âge*, ed. D. Menjot, Publications de la Faculté des Lettres et Sciences Humaines de Nice, 1st series, 27–8, 1984; detailed studies by e.g. L. Stouff, *Ravitaillement et alimentation en Provence aux xive et xve siècles* (Paris, 1970). While there are surveys of agricultural production and marketing (e.g. *AHEW*, pp. 324–525), there is a lack of in-depth regional studies of consumption in England; for an attempt to frame the discussion on a regional (and seasonal) basis, C. M. Woolgar, 'Diet and Consumption in Gentry and Noble Households: A Case Study from around the Wash', *Rulers and Ruled in Late Medieval England: Essays Presented to Gerald Harriss*, ed. R. E. Archer and S. Walker (London, 1995), pp. 17–31.

[3] Harvey, *Living and Dying*, pp. 34–145, 216–30.

[4] C. Dyer, 'Changes in Diet in the Late Middle Ages: The Case of Harvest Workers', *Everyday Life*, pp. 77–99; C. Dyer, 'Did the Peasants Really Starve in Medieval England?' *Food and Eating in Medieval Europe*, ed. M. Carlin and J. T. Rosenthal (London, 1998), pp. 53–71.

[5] C. Dyer, 'English Diet in the Later Middle Ages', *Social Relations and Ideas: Essays in Honour of R. H. Hilton*, ed. T. H. Aston, P. R. Coss, C. Dyer and J. Thirsk (Cambridge, 1983), pp. 191–216. S. Mennell, *All Manners of Food: Eating and Taste in England and France from the Middle Ages to the Present* (Oxford, 1985), p. 40, also argues that there was little change between the twelfth and the fifteenth centuries.

[6] C. M. Woolgar, *The Great Household in Late Medieval England* (New Haven and London, 1999), pp. 91–2, 132–5.

recording the costs of the lord's immediate household, it is effectively for the establishment of his wife, Elizabeth Berkeley, and their three daughters, as the earl was absent much of the time. This document gives both the daily (or diet) account of expenses and the bulk purchases of the household, residing at Berkeley, journeying to Walthamstow and London, and travelling on to Warwick and Salwarpe, near Droitwich.[7] The second group of accounts is for the household of Sir Henry Stafford and his wife, Lady Margaret Beaufort, Dowager-Countess of Richmond and mother of Henry VII, at the palace at Woking. For the late 1460s there survives for this household both a daily account for consumption (a diet account) and a journal of purchases for the household. The volume of information in these Stafford accounts is such that the analysis has been restricted to a five-week period in the summer of 1469, 9 July to 13 August.[8]

The aristocratic great household does not provide the same closed community as the monastery, nor the same body of records. With the comings and goings, it might easily be imagined that it is not possible to say much about the diet of household members. The evidence, however, is that food for each meal was prepared to a consistent pattern of rations, that there were more general assumptions about what constituted an appropriate amount of food to set before each person.[9] Anyone who looks at the *Northumberland Household Book* of *c.*1512 will see in operation the planned economy of the great household, the calculation of the annual costs and needs of the household in terms of foodstuffs, which was built up from an understanding of these standard rates of allowance.[10] This principle is borne out where accounts can be analysed in detail, indicating regular amounts per person, effectively a system of portion control. It is therefore possible to work out a typical allowance per person, although this is not necessarily what he or she consumed. It is less satisfactory as an overall indication of nutrition: a household member would not have spent his whole life in the establishment in quite the same way that a monk would have done.

In the fourteenth century, with the appearance in diet accounts of records of *fercula* – portions of food – it is possible to demonstrate in some cases that these represent the numbers of persons present to whom food was served. By the end of the century some of these accounts make it clear which meals are being eaten and by how many individuals. At the same time, the recording system in the account makes more and more explicit what was consumed, as opposed to what was purchased.[11] These figures can then be used as the basis for a calculation of rations per person per meal.

[7] Longleat MS Misc. IX, described by C. D. Ross, 'The Household Accounts of Elizabeth Berkeley, Countess of Warwick, 1420–1', *TBGAS* 70 (1951), pp. 81–105. The dating of this account is slightly erratic: it never satisfactorily resolves giving thirty-one days to November, but it almost certainly belongs to the years 1420–1. I have followed the dates for days given in the manuscript, except for obvious slips of the pen.

[8] WAM 12186 ff. 81v–89v; WAM 12188 ff. 1–11r; in general, M. K. Jones and M. G. Underwood, *The King's Mother: Lady Margaret Beaufort, Countess of Richmond and Derby* (Cambridge, 1992), pp. 137–42.

[9] For rations of bread and ale, Dyer, 'English Diet', pp. 192–3.

[10] *The Regulations and Establishment of the Household of Henry Algernon Percy, the 5th Earl of Northumberland*, ed. T. Percy, new edn (London, 1905), pp. 4–5, for the supplies of cattle and mutton. In this case, however, it is not known precisely how many portions were represented.

[11] *Household Accounts from Medieval England*, ed. C. M. Woolgar, British Academy, Records of Social and Economic History, n.s. 17–18 (Oxford, 1992–3), i, pp. 28–30.

The resulting picture is no more than a general guide. In an acutely status-conscious household, not everybody ate the same foods. There were typically three main dietary regimes – and possibly five or six – in operation simultaneously. The diet of the household member who was not of gentle rank accounted for the bulk of food consumed (as they were the most numerous in the household). The diet of those of gentle rank was different, as was the diet of the lord. A fourth category, the diet of the lord's family, particularly of the female members, may possibly be further differentiated; and the diet of religious in the household was equally separately characterised. At the same time, the poor who might be supported by the household had a distinctive diet: some categories of poor, if not maintained within the household itself, may have been exempt from regimes of abstinence and fasting.[12] That said, an underlying pattern of consumption can be demonstrated, that is, what went into each portion.

To use household accounts for this purpose quickly demonstrates their limitations. In order to look at the general picture, it has been necessary to exclude those days which had distinctive or anomalous dietary practices. Those days when both meat and fish were eaten have been omitted from the calculations: in neither the Warwick nor the Stafford accounts can one work out who ate how much on days when both meat and fish were present, nor what was served at each meal. Likewise, Good Friday in the Warwick account has been omitted, as bread and ale alone were consumed – the nearest that household came to absolute fast. Equally, in the same account, on the three days immediately preceding Lent (2–4 February), at 242 meals (excluding breakfast, which accounted for another 23 meals), a thousand eggs were consumed, an average of just over four per person per meal, a pattern of consumption quite unlike the rest of the account.

There are also difficulties with other contents of the account. In the Warwick account, beyond the daily consumption of the staples of saltfish, dried fish and herring, the document records fish, particularly fresh fish, in much less detail than the Stafford accounts. Further, there is some evidence that the purchases of fresh fish recorded in the Warwick account were consumed over several days, rather than solely on the day of purchase.[13] Another restriction has come from the need to focus on the food placed on the table at particular meals. Of the three daily meals, breakfast (*jantaculum*) was only eaten by a minority of the household and was generally, at the start of fifteenth century, not a meal at which much meat or fish would have appeared, although that was a position that had changed by the end of the fifteenth century.[14] Because of its changing content and its restriction to the lord and his close circle, it has been set aside from this analysis. Also excluded thereby is the political breakfast, its use to secure favour and advantage, from the entertainment of chancery clerks to the hospitality offered by Warwick the Kingmaker recorded in the *Great Chronicle of London*, with six oxen for breakfast – that is, approximately 1,920 portions.[15]

[12] C. Walker Bynum, *Holy Feast and Holy Fast: The Religious Significance of Food to Medieval Women* (Berkeley, California, 1987), p. 41, on Thomas Aquinas.

[13] For example 18 February, Longleat MS Misc. IX f. 69v.

[14] Woolgar, *Great Household*, p. 87.

[15] For the use of breakfast as a douceur, Woolgar, *Great Household*, p. 87; *Great Chronicle of London*, ed. A. H. Thomas and I. D. Thornley (London, 1938), p. 207; for the calculation of portions of beef, below.

For convenience, too, the regular drinking sessions, in the afternoon and probably the morning, at which bread and ale would have been available, have been ignored: it is not really possible to indicate who in the household may have benefited from these, nor the quantities each individual might have received. Likewise the availability of wine in the chamber during the day and liveries that would have been available in rooms during the night have been discounted – as well as any additional amounts a servant might have received in terms of rewards and liveries. Information about consumption at these times is in the accounts, for example the bread, ale and wine given by the Staffords at drinkings, or at the gate of Woking palace, or to workers making hay there – but it cannot be directly related to particular individuals in the household.[16]

The focus has therefore fallen on two main meals, lunch (*prandium*) and supper (*cena*). As the regime of abstinence meant that on some days it was customary for the second meal not to be taken – particularly on Friday – the results are expressed in terms of food that was put on the table per person per meal. This does not, however, equate with consumption – the subtractions of almsgiving, of food distributed from the table, need to be taken into account,[17] but it does provide a picture of what was available for the aristocracy and their households to consume. A further point to note is a difference between the two households in their weekly pattern of consumption. Warwick's household had a pattern of abstinence which normally meant that fish alone was eaten on Friday and Saturday, that there was a single meal on Friday, and that on Wednesdays both meat and fish were consumed. The Stafford household differed from this in its abandonment of fish consumption on Wednesdays, giving them over wholly to meat.[18] To facilitate comparison, the propositions made by others about the size of medieval livestock and fish, edible proportions, meat weights and calorific values have been accepted.[19]

Henry Stafford's household at Woking in 1469

Lunch and supper in the household of Henry Stafford were constructed on a fairly strict basis of allowances per person dining. In terms of cereals, each person received a ration of bread and ale that varied little from meal to meal. At each meal, anyone present could expect half a loaf of bread. The loaf in this household was comparatively small, baked at thirty-five loaves to the bushel of

[16] WAM 12188 f. 2r.

[17] For example BL Harley MS 6815 f. 35.

[18] For an analysis of patterns of medieval fish consumption, C. M. Woolgar, '"Take this penance now, and afterwards the fare will improve": Seafood and Late Medieval Diet', *England's Sea Fisheries: The Commercial Sea Fisheries of England and Wales since 1300*, ed. D. J. Starkey, N. Ashcroft and C. Reid (London, 2000), pp. 36–44, 247–8.

[19] Outlined in Harvey, *Living and Dying*, pp. 226–30; Stouff, *Ravitaillement et alimentation*; and other work on cattle and sheep sizes, e.g. A. J. S. Gibson, 'The Size and Weight of Cattle and Sheep in Early Modern Scotland', *AgHR*, 36 (1988), pp. 162–71. I have also used McCance and Widdowson's *The Composition of Foods*, ed. B. Holland *et al.*, 5th edn (London, 1991); *Dietary Reference Values for Food Energy and Nutrients for the United Kingdom: Report of the Panel on Dietary Reference Values of the Committee on Medical Aspects of Food Policy*, Department of Health, Report on Health and Social Subjects, 41 (London, 1991); and the Ministry of Agriculture, Fisheries and Food, *Manual of Nutrition*, 10th edn (London, 1995).

wheat, producing about 0.4 lb bread per person per meal, the equivalent of 390 kcal.[20] The product of each baking was consumed in its entirety before new bread was obtained and it was not therefore uncommon in this household for bread to be up to a week, or even a fortnight old. The ration of ale was almost invariably a quarter of a gallon per person at each of the two main meals, that is 363 kcal at each.[21] This rate of issue is the same as in the household of Edward IV set out in the household ordinance of 1478.[22] The calculation in the account was based on all members of the household receiving a ration of ale, even if in practice the gentle members had wine.[23]

The bulk of the consumption at each meal was meat or fish. There were two principal meats, beef and mutton, with the addition of veal, a little pork and poultry. Aside from the head, chine and entrails, carcasses of mature cattle were butchered into four quarters, each of which was then divided into four rounds. In this household beef was divided up approximately on the basis of twenty portions per round.[24] This pattern of butchery and size of portion – 320 portions per carcass – had a much broader and longer-term currency. A mess for four monks of Westminster at the end of the fifteenth century was one-eightieth of a carcass.[25] In the early fourteenth century, the standard may have been larger. The estimates of rations for the garrisons of Berwick and Edinburgh divided a carcass of beef into forty messes (*fercula*), each to feed two soldiers or workmen at two meals, that is about twice the amount of meat per person per meal allowed in the fifteenth century.[26]

Between 9 July and 13 August 1469, there were twenty-two days when meat alone was eaten. At 2,784 individual meals on these days, a total of seven cattle, three quarters and one round were consumed, along with forty-three sheep; or 1,876 lb edible carcass of beef and 1,039 lb edible weight of mutton, an uncooked weight of meat per person per meal of 0.67 lb of beef and 0.37 lb of mutton: that is, at each meal on average each person would have had set before them 1.04 lb of meat. The beef would have produced 475 kcal per meal per person and the mutton 293 kcal.[27] The other meats in the account – veal,

[20] WAM 12188 f. 3r, 13 July; f. 6v, 28 July; f. 9r, 5 August; f. 10v, 11 August. Loaves are measured in this account by the short hundred. Compare Woolgar, *Great Household*, p. 124.

[21] Calorific value based on pale ale. On Friday 14 July, the rate was 0.48 gallons per person, that is double rations of ale on this Friday, sufficient for two meals even though only one was eaten; but on Friday 21 July and Monday 24 July, when one meal only was eaten, the ration remained 0.25 gallon.

[22] *The Household of Edward IV: The Black Book and the Ordinance of 1478*, ed. A. R. Myers (Manchester, 1959), p. 214.

[23] Wine consumption was restricted to a small group in the household and has been left out of the calculation. In addition to consumption at meals, there was consumption in chambers, at the gate and as 'singingwine': WAM 12188 f. 6v.

[24] The word used is *rond*. Calves were divided into four quarters and a breast: WAM 12188 f. 6v, 27 July; and I have assumed the same pattern for cattle, with the addition of the head, chine (the area immediately around the backbone after the sides of beef have been taken off), entrails, hooves, etc., which appear separately in accounts. The cattle were butchered in the household, however, whereas the veal arrived ready jointed.

[25] Harvey, *Living and Dying*, pp. 228–9.

[26] M. Prestwich, 'Victualling Estimates for English Garrisons in Scotland during the Early Fourteenth Century', *EHR*, lxxxii (1967), pp. 536–43. It is possible, however, that more men had a share of this ration on a regular basis.

[27] Gibson, 'Size and Weight', p. 165, n. 17, each cooked ounce of beef, 44 kcal; p. 170, n. 51, each cooked ounce of lamb, 49 kcal.

piglets, capons, pullets and squabs – were probably consumed by a small proportion of the household, those described as *gentiles*, the gentle members of the household, who made up just under a quarter of its numbers. Thus on the twenty-two meat days there were consumed a total of 6.5 calves, 27 piglets, 22 capons, 235 young chickens, 5 geese, 69 squabs and 3 stockdoves, and 4 other poultry. The gentle part of the household accounted for 766 of the 2,784 meals served in this period. This would have given the gentle members of the household a further 0.3 lb of pullet or young chicken (294 kcal), 0.34 lb (239 kcal) of veal and 0.44 lb (663 kcal) of piglet per person per meal: that is, a gentle member of the household could expect on average probably a further 1.08 lb of meat per meal.

In practice some of these meats, such as capons, may have been reserved for a very few people – here, for example, there was an average of one capon a day – and, conversely, the lord would not have eaten much of the mutton and beef. The lord's diet would have been more varied: he had access to all dishes, and there may have been a significant element of fruit. Whether what was set before him contained less calories is an open question, particularly as he had access to a range of dishes made with sugar and cream.

The general ration of fish available to all household members was reasonably substantial, although not on the same scale as the meats. In the Stafford household, there was a good deal of variety in terms of fish, particularly in fresh fish. The everyday staples, principally cod, or cod-like fish – ling, haberdine (which was almost certainly salt cod at this date),[28] and stockfish, that is, dried fish – are the best for comparative purposes. There was no, or very little, herring at this time of year in this household. Ling, and either haberdine or stockfish were served at every meal. To these staples, fresh fish were added, but not so consistently that the amounts placed on the table might be predicted (the document does not present the regularity of Westminster Abbey in the preparation of fish meals and this may suggest that the supply of fish was not as regular or reliable). There was a total of 1,048 fish meals in the period at which 360 lb of cod or cod-like fish were served, or 0.34 lb per person per meal. Of the fresh fish that were served at meals, plaice appears in most quantity. For example, on a typical Friday, 21 July, there was food for sixty-seven people: two ling and six haberdines, with fifty-seven plaice, one conger, thirteen small eels, one brill, one butt (or flatfish) and four chub. The plaice were probably small, to judge by the price.[29] When they were served they would have produced on average just under one fish per person, that is most people would have had one and others would have had something else. To the cod, this might add 0.84 lb of plaice, giving more than 1 lb of white fish per meal, or in terms of calories, 258 kcal from cod and 355 kcal from plaice.[30] No eggs or milk were used here on Fridays, in accordance with stricter traditions of abstinence, but butter was. Eggs and milk were present, however, on Saturdays.

[28] Compare Harvey, *Living and Dying*, pp. 226–7. At an earlier date it may have included sun-dried fish (later called stockfish), referring to the area of origin of the trade in this foodstuff, from Bayonne and the Basque region: see OED, s.v. haberdine.

[29] WAM 12188 f. 3r: the 49 on 14 July were bought along with 1 butt, 5 soles and a gurnard for 5s. Compare Harvey, *Living and Dying*, pp. 50, 226–7, for the size of plaice.

[30] A ration that is very similar to the allowance for the monks at Westminster Abbey: Harvey, *Living and Dying*, p. 64.

Rye, peas and oatmeal appeared every day in the journal of purchases, but they did not appear each day in the diet account, the daily account of consumption. The documents mention about one peck of rye each day; possibly a similar amount of peas on seven days; and two bushels of oatmeal over the whole period. How it was consumed is more difficult to say: a proportion may have been used for feeding poultry. While most poultry was purchased and consumed immediately, some may have been kept alive in the household. A payment for the construction of a dog-kennel in the poultry suggests a guard for fowl, rather than a hunting establishment.[31] Some of the peas and oatmeal would doubtless have been for human consumption, in pottage and soups.

There is very little mention in the account of either vegetables or fruit. Onions appeared on 8 and 12 August; and there was a purchase of either pears or leeks on 9 August.[32] Fruit was more in evidence at other times of the year, for example in the pears (wardens) and apples purchased around the time of the visit of Edward IV to the hunting lodge at Brookwood in December 1468.[33]

Although we know how many people ate lunch and supper, the accounts do not provide a figure for those eating breakfast or any indication, beyond bread and ale, of what was served at that meal. What is apparent, however, is a ratio of bread and ale served at that time. If the breakfast ration was also half a loaf per person, that is, just as at the other two meals, then accompanying it was quarter of a gallon of ale. As loaves did not appear in fractions smaller than a half, this was the most likely amount to have been served. The accounts also mention further distributions of ale and bread. On average this would have produced a livery of ale equivalent to about a half pint more per person per day. There was a direct relationship, however, between the livery of ale and the liveries of bread: if eight loaves were given out in this way, then there were eight gallons of ale as well; if it was seven and a half loaves, then seven and a half gallons. It is not clear whether this was a proportional addition to everyone's ration, or something else. There was, for example, no diminution on Fridays or on other days with one main meal.

The journal of purchases is particularly valuable evidence for the dependence of the household on the market. Purchases were made each day.[34] At least twelve trips to Guildford were made or organised by John Clement (a local merchant), probably with a packhorse, that is, every two to three days. Guildford supplied most of the fresh foods entered in the poultry account: capons, young chickens, rye, peas, butter, eggs and milk; a lot of the sea fish, including plaice, haddock, whiting, sole, sea bream, crab, shrimps, besides oysters and eels; some freshwater fish, chub, tench and trout; as well as mustard.

The household was supplied with livestock from Richard Machoun. On 14 July, he supplied twenty-eight shearlings (sheep that had been sheared once), of which twenty-five and a quarter were consumed between 14 July and 5 August, when he supplied a further twenty. He also supplied the cattle for the household: on 31 July, two bullocks and three oxen were bought from him for 68s. A

[31] WAM 12189 f. 1v, *c.*1469–70.

[32] *Piris* in the journal of purchases, WAM 12186 f. 88r; *poris* in the diet account, WAM 12188 f. 10r.

[33] WAM 12186 f. 42r.

[34] The direct relation between the number of eggs bought and that consumed each day is indicative of this system.

further three oxen were bought from him on 12 August, for 51s. Between 31 July and 12 August consumption of beef totalled two carcasses, two quarters and two rounds. The household was thus not overstocked, was resupplied in step with consumption, and consumed this meat, probably butchered within the household, as fresh as possible. Although there is little reference to salting, contemporary expectation was that meat would not last fresh for more than two or three days, decaying rapidly thereafter.[35] Veal, on the other hand, came from a different supplier, John Manchester. It was purchased already butchered – by the quarter, half and breast – and was consumed immediately. John may have been related to Thomas Manchester, an official in other Stafford households, who, in 1465–6, was also responsible for supplying livestock to the household of Anne Stafford at Writtle.[36]

Freshwater fish, an expensive commodity (the cost of trout ranged from 4d. to 7d. in this account, and one chub was bought for 10d.), came from several sources and was possibly specially caught.[37] Henry Terell made journeys to the Walton and Shepperton area for freshwater fish, on 26 July specifically stated as being 'for the lord'; and John Clement acquired some at Guildford. Sugar and wine came from London; beer from Staines. Richard Machoun, who had supplied the livestock, also provided ale and substantial quantities of wheat and oats. The only foodstuffs that were not supplied in this way were the staple preserved fish, the ling, the haberdines and stockfish.

This gives a picture of a very substantial household, well supplied with fresh products from the market, with generous provision for household members and visitors. But were all aristocratic households alike? While that may broadly have been the case, closer examination shows marked differences between establishments. Some of these are apparent from the account of the intrinsic household of the Earl of Warwick, for 1420–1. In this household there were also significant differences in consumption over the course of the year that had an effect on the quantities available per person.

The intrinsic household of the Earl of Warwick, 1420–1

Warwick's household had a greater emphasis on cereal consumption. Loaves were baked at the rate of 30 per bushel of wheat: the ration was one loaf per person per meal, that is, a loaf of 0.93 lb, or 908 kcal. The ale allowance was also larger at ¼ gallon per person per meal, or 726 kcal.

The pattern of meat consumption was similar to that of the Stafford

[35] *Peter Idley's Instructions to his Son*, ed. C. D'Evelyn, Modern Language Association of America, monograph series, 6 (Boston, 1935), p. 196: Book 2, on the Seven Deadly Sins, lines 2,276–82: 'A man may kepe mete and holsomlie preserve/ Twoo daies or thre in right good savour;/ But when it is yet, no thyng may it conserve – / That was swettest in taast is most bitter in savour;/ No man may abide the stynke and the odoure./ For in half a day it is foule, rotten, and mowled;/ To orrible it is to speke how sone it is defouled.'

[36] M. Harris and J. M. Thurgood, 'The Account of the Great Household of Humphrey, first Duke of Buckingham, for the year 1452–3', *Camden Miscellany*, xxviii, Camden, 4th series, 29 (1984), p. 52; BL Add. MS 34213, e.g. ff. 20r, 22r, 44v. John Manchester also supplied a barrel for grease and may therefore have been a butcher as well as a livestock supplier.

[37] C. Dyer, 'The Consumption of Freshwater Fish in England', *Everyday Life*, pp. 101–12.

household and was derived from fresh meat, butchered in the household throughout the period of the account. Using the days on which meat alone was eaten, two periods have been selected for the analysis of meat consumption. In the first, 1 October to 31 October 1420, there were 1,077 meat meals, at which were served 0.92 lb of beef (647 kcal) per person per meal, along with 0.64 lb of mutton (502 kcal) per person meal, that is 1.56 lb of meat or 1,149 kcal per meal. On top of this the gentle members of the household probably had about 1 lb of poultry and 1.25 lb of pork (largely from piglets), or another 2,864 kcal per meal, producing a total for meat alone of 4,013 kcal per person meal. The quantities were lower both in weight and particularly in calorific value in the second period, 7 January to 4 February 1421: 0.74 lb of beef per person meal (522 kcal); 0.4 lb of mutton per person meal (314 kcal), or 1.14 lb of meat per person, giving 836 kcal. Ordinary household members may have had 0.2 lb of pork as well; gentle members, the piglets, producing 0.77 lb per person meal (1,160 kcal) and 0.54 lb of poultry (529 kcal), that is another 1.31 lb of meat per person meal. While the gentle members may have had as much as 2,525 kcal of meat set before them at each meal at this time of year, the portion was nonetheless 37.5 per cent less than the amount in the early autumn.

In October 1420, the staple fish provided were 0.31 lb of white fish (cod) per person meal, giving 232 kcal; and 0.33 lb of herring or 309 kcal per person meal, a total of 541 kcal per person meal. This was about the same as the ration of fish that was served in the household of Henry Stafford, but it is necessary to add to it unspecified amounts of fresh fish and salt salmon, ten of which were consumed over this time. In January 1421, the ration on fish days was more than twice as high: 0.64 lb of white fish (cod) (479 kcal) and 0.64 lb of herring per person meal (591 kcal), together making 1,070 kcal per person meal. To this fresh fish must be added, as well as butter and cheese. In Lent 1421, the portion was about 10 per cent smaller (and would have been reduced further on the additional fast days in this season) – 0.58 lb white fish per person meal, or 440 kcal; and 0.59 lb herring per person meal, or 548 kcal, a total of 988 kcal per person meal. Quite a lot of other fish were consumed in Lent, but it is difficult to quantify them.

This examination of the detail of consumption (Table 1) confirms Professor Dyer's view that there were very substantial provisions of food in the great household, that they represent a substantial supplement over the amount that is today estimated as the daily average energy requirement for a reasonably active man (2,550 kcal) or woman (1,940 kcal).[38] The excess is particularly striking on meat days, when the average energy requirement would have been exceeded in the provision at a single meal; and if there were two meals, and breakfast, very considerably exceeded. On a fish day, there was a much closer equation to this figure; and on a day of reduced intake, such as Friday, consumption might fall under this value. In a prolonged period of abstinence, for example in Lent, there would have been a cumulative effect of some significance; but it would not have offset the cumulative effect of over-provision at other times.

There were, however, substantial differences between the households in the quantities of food set on the table per person, besides seasonal differences and distinctions of status. A gentle member of the Earl of Warwick's household would, with breakfast, in October 1420, have had set before him on a meat day

[38] *Dietary Reference Values*, p. xix.

Table 1. Consumption in aristocratic households

	Earl of Warwick			Henry Stafford
	Oct 1420	Jan 1421	Lent 1421	Jul/Aug 1469
Meat meal				
Ale	726	726		363
Bread	908	908		390
Beef	647	522		475
Mutton	502	314		293
TOTAL	2783	2470		1521
Gentle members				
Other meats	2864	1689		1196
TOTAL	5647	4159		2717
Fish meal				
Ale	726	726	726	363
Bread	908	908	908	390
Cod	232	479	440	258
Herring	309	591	548	
Other (plaice)	?	?	?	355
TOTAL	2175	2704	2622	1366
Gentle members				
Probably little additional				
TOTAL	2175	2704	2622	1366

Note: All figures are given in kcal.

at least 12,928 kcal of food; an equivalent ration in Sir Henry Stafford's household would have reached no more than a nonetheless impressive 6,187 kcal. The ration on fish days also shows the allowances in the Stafford household running at about half those in Warwick's household.

These allowances can be compared with those of the monks of Westminster at the conclusion of the fifteenth century.[39] A gentle member of the household of Sir Henry Stafford would have had more meat, perhaps 4 lb per day; a monk would have received about 3 lb a day in the misericord, about 1 lb per day in the refectory. Lesser members of the Stafford household may have had about 2 lb per day. In terms of fish, the ration was similar overall. The cereal component of the diet, however, was markedly larger for the monks. Bread for ordinary members of the Stafford household totalled about 0.8 lb (Westminster 2.25 lb); for the gentle members of the household, including breakfast, probably 1.2 lb. The ration of ale for the Stafford household members was again smaller: 0.5 gallon per day for ordinary members; 0.75 gallon for those eating breakfast. A monk at Westminster would have expected about 1 gallon. Like the monks of Westminster, the allowance per person per meal was well in excess of what was needed. There was, however, a general difference between the two groups overall, with the emphasis on meat, as opposed to cereals, in the aristocratic setting.

[39] Harvey, *Living and Dying*, pp. 64–5.

The lord had a diet that differed from this norm. It might eschew, on the whole, the huge quantities of red meat that others had set before them. The purchases that were almost certainly destined for the lord's table can be traced: high quality poultry and fowl; freshwater fishes, particularly those of high quality; fruit; and wines. In the Warwick account, the effects of the presence of Earl of Warwick were immediate, as were those of the household's most distinguished guest, the Duke of Bedford. In 1421, during Lent, the Earl of Warwick was present in his household from 3 March until 12 March, leaving after breakfast, returning on the night of 15 March and departing again after lunch on 17 March. His presence was marked by the purchase of a succession of lampreys[40] and two trout brought from the earl's estate at Chilton, at a cost of 20d.[41] For the visit of the chancellor of the Duke of Bedford on 7 July 1421, a capon was bought for 20d. – they were normally priced at around 4d. each.[42]

This was one of a number of visits made by the chancellor, besides those by others of the duke's servants, in anticipation of the entertainment of Bedford himself on 4 August (at Goodrest, in Wedgnock Park, near Warwick).[43] There were two capons *de hautegrece* bought at Coventry for 3s. and another eight for 4s.; two herons for 4s. and one cygnet for 5s. 6d. There was also a reward of 13s. 4d. for the duke's cook, Bett (who had come with him), along with two grooms of the duke's kitchen, who may have been designated to look after the duke's breakfast.[44]

How does one account for the difference between what was laid on the table and what might be a reasonable level of consumption? To accept that some would have been given away in alms is a reasonable explanation. In both the Stafford and Warwick accounts, however, hospitality and alms were to a large extent included: visitors were given the same rations as the others in the household. At Woking, in July and August 1469, there were numbers of individuals 'whose names are not known' recorded as guests.[45] There was a note each day of wine, ale and bread disbursed at the gate and food must more generally have been available there. Likewise the pilgrims, hermits and prisoners who featured in the Warwick account were included in the main part of the household for consumption, although some were fed at the gate.[46] It is difficult not to conclude, therefore, that household membership was for stalwart trenchermen.

[40] For example Longleat MS Misc IX f. 73r, 3 March, 1 for 6s. 4d.

[41] Ibid. f. 73v.

[42] Ibid. f. 112r.

[43] Ibid. f. 120v.

[44] The cook, Bett, is probably the same individual as John Bec, the duke's master cook, a master of the Cooks' and Pastelers' Company, who was paid by Bedford's executors probably between 1438 and 1442, and who died in 1453: *The Bedford Inventories: The Worldly Goods of John, Duke of Bedford, Regent of France (1389–1435)*, ed. J. Stratford (London, 1993), pp. 157, 180, 260, 406. For other expenditure associated with this visit, Longleat MS Misc. IX ff. 16v, 17r, 25v.

[45] WAM 12188 e.g. f. 2r, 9 July, ten in this category; f. 6r, 25 July, six others; f. 6r, 26 July, four others.

[46] For example Longleat MS Misc. IX f. 45v, 16 Nov 1420, two pilgrims; f. 46r, 17 Nov 1420, one hermit; f. 46v, 19 Nov 1420, two pilgrims; f. 49r, 29 Nov 1420, one pilgrim at the gate; f. 50v, 1 Dec 1420, three valets, prisoners, at the gate; f. 51v, 5 Dec 1420, one pilgrim at the gate; f. 52r, 7 Dec 1420, two pilgrims at the gate; f. 52v, 10 Dec 1420, one pilgrim at the gate.

Conspicuous consumption

In all this, the most striking aspect of the evidence of consumption is that it is conspicuous to us by its quantity. This notion needs to be set alongside other factors in the presentation of the food, in terms of social competition. In all aspects of consumption, 'nobility' had a consequence. The volume of foodstuffs set on the table might be one aspect, certainly one that was regarded by contemporaries; but its concomitants were equally important. In an aristocratic context, these might manifest themselves in the precious vessels, tablecloths and other fine textiles, the rituals of serving that accompanied the food and the quality of the servants.[47]

Food was equally a part of spectacle. On the one hand, there was a political purpose to a great feast, underscored by the iconography of its subtleties – the decorative set pieces served with many of the courses at a major feast. At the same time there were undertones of morality associated with food, from the condemnation of drunkenness and lechery associated with feasts, the beneficence resulting from alms, to the virtues of abstinence and the appropriateness of gifts of food. There were direct associations between gentility and foodstuffs, in terms of sumptuary tradition, the use of foods from hunting, or reserved classes of food. Morality and gentility were at the same time important dimensions to the space or stage where the food was eaten.[48]

In looking at the evidence for food as spectacle, the characteristics of the foods and their presentation need further consideration. How did late medieval cookery, at the apogee of its profession, consider the taste and smell of food, its colour, decoration and garnishing, its texture and its shape; that is, how it could be formed and sculpted? The visual impact of medieval food in particular is important to its interpretation. Late medieval texts tell us directly comparatively little about how food tasted and almost nothing about how it smelled, but they do tell us a good deal about how it was supposed to look.

Late medieval cookery books largely contain recipes that must, from their ingredients, have been reserved for those of the highest status – the references to swans, cranes, peacocks, to high status fish, such as turbot, and among the earliest mentions of carp in England indicate this.[49] Many of the dishes presented in these texts were not what they seemed, from the replumed peacock, served 'as he war a quyk pekok', with his tail displayed;[50] to the apples, sometimes golden, sometimes green – meat-balls made of ground beef

[47] Woolgar, *Great Household*, pp. 136–65; for some continental examples, F. Robin, 'Le luxe de la table dans les cours princières (1360–1480)', *Gazettes des Beaux-Arts*, 86 (1975), pp. 1–16.

[48] Brewer, 'Feasts in England and English Literature', pp. 22–4; Woolgar, *Great Household*, pp. 133–4; G. Walker, *The Politics of Performance in Early Renaissance Drama* (Cambridge, 1998), pp. 53–9.

[49] *Two Fifteenth-Century Cookery-Books*, ed. T. Austin, EETS, o.s. xci (1888), p. 21, using trout, roach, perch or carp; for a date of *c.*1430–40, C. B. Hieatt, C. Lambert, B. Laurioux and A. Prentki, 'Répertoire des manuscrits médiévaux contenant des recettes culinaires', *Du manuscrit à la table: essais sur la cuisine au Moyen Âge et répertoire des manuscrits médiévaux contenant des recettes culinaires*, ed. C. Lambert (Montreal, 1992), p. 335.

[50] *An Ordinance of Pottage: An Edition of the Fifteenth Century Culinary Recipes in Yale University's MS Beinecke 163*, ed. C. B. Hieatt (London, 1988), p. 109; also *Two Fifteenth-Century Cookery-Books*, p. 79.

or veal, bound with egg, 'endorred' with a glazing of egg yolk[51] or coloured green with a parsley batter.[52] The authenticity of the urchins, or hedgehogs, was not conveyed by their smokey-bacon flavour, but by appearance: the ground pork, encased in a pig's stomach (maw), had for spines almonds chopped into long, thin and sharp pieces, fried in fat and sugar, some coloured white, some green and some black.[53] 'Eggs in Lent' was how a rubric marked an equally bizarre substitution for the forbidden item, the recipe describing how the whites and eggs should be blown out, the shell washed, and the inside replaced by almond milk, half coloured with saffron and some canel (cinnamon), the other half kept white.[54] What was essential here was how the dish looked, not how it tasted: and some of the dishes were fantastic, such as the cockatrice, endorred with egg yolk and saffron and gilded with silver and gold foil.[55]

The recipes are often not specific about the meats and fish: it is apparent that a range of similar flesh and textures could be employed to do the same job. There were thus dishes on fish days that aimed to look like meat dishes. On a flesh day, 'Vyaunde Cypre' was made with pork or chicken, with sugar from Cyprus; on a fish day, salmon was used, coloured with alkanet, to produce a red dish.[56] Almond milk was similarly used as a substitute for dairy products. The tastes would have been very different; but the main purpose was to make a visual substitution, not one of taste or smell.

The texture of food in these dishes was very similar. The cook aimed to prepare something from a plastic medium, that could be shaped, sculpted and coloured at will.[57] Instructions for food preparation aimed at a uniform consistency of meats and fishes, with the removal of sinews, bones, fins, etc. Much was therefore reduced to a common form, or medium, with meat and spices ground down, and then consolidated with a binder such as egg yolk or wheat starch, leaving the mix to be shaped at will. Thus 'Leche Lumbard', a pork dish, had the meat ground up and cooked, shaped like a peasecod, coloured with saunders and saffron.[58] The exception to this pattern were those foodstuffs which needed to be kept together, for example for roasting; but stuffings for these meats followed the same pattern.

It is well known that the use of spices was a hallmark of cookery at the highest level, a use imitated elsewhere on special occasions, or using cheaper flavourings;[59] but it is quite legitimate to wonder what the effect of all these spices was – and wonder is a particularly appropriate word. In skilled hands, they were used to construct something marvellous, that is, it was something to be wondered at, or astonishing. The 1420–1 account shows that the Earl of Warwick was particularly partial, as were many of the highest aristocracy, to

[51] *Curye on Inglysch: English Culinary Manuscripts of the Fourteenth Century (including the Forme of Cury)*, ed. C. B. Hieatt and S. Butler, EETS, s.s. 8 (1985), p. 70.
[52] *Two Fifteenth-Century Cookery-Books*, p. 14.
[53] Ibid. p. 38.
[54] Ibid. p. 41.
[55] Ibid. pp. 115–16; *Curye on Inglysch*, p. 139.
[56] *Curye on Inglysch*, pp. 119–20.
[57] M. Pelner Cosman, *Fabulous Feasts: Medieval Cookery and Ceremony* (New York, 1976), pp. 61–4.
[58] *Curye on Inglysch*, p. 112.
[59] Woolgar, 'Diet and Consumption', pp. 29–31.

lamprey. A recipe for a fresh baked lamprey expected it to be spiced with cinnamon, powdered galantine, Lombard powder, powdered ginger, saunders, sugar, saffron and salt. 'If you want it to be a colour between brown and yellow, add more saunders.'[60] This last injunction is an important clue to the overall intention.

One area associated with spices – and an important element in visual impact – was colour. It is referred to in recipes at least as often as taste, probably more frequently. Some spices have little effect on taste: their use is much more to do with colour. A particular exception is saffron, which has an effect on taste as well as colour. It was used extensively in recipes, though, for colour – those requiring it were especially numerous. Other ingredients were much more like modern food colouring, with little effect on taste. But whether it was yellow (and a large quantity of food was coloured yellow if one follows recipes, perhaps less so if one looks at accounts), white, red, black or brown, green or a disconcerting blue, it is less clear what the significance of the colour was.[61]

Some colours had inherited important associations from Antiquity, for example, purple for imperial or monarchical dignity, or red for light. The hue and density of the colour and its lustre or shine were all relevant. The shine of cloth, for example, produced by shearing closely (*retonsio*), was particularly prized, just as it had been in the ancient world and in Byzantium.[62] The use of colour in medieval cookery can in the first instance appear odd, occasionally alarming. A number of definite trends, however, can be discerned. Some dishes were known by their colour alone and the purpose of other dishes can have been little more than to add colour to the table. 'Lete lards' (a custard of milk and eggs, with lard, served cold, sliced) were to be made yellow with saffron, white with amydon (wheat starch), red with saunders, purple, blue and black with other spices and processes.[63] 'Brawn ryal' could be made as bright as amber with saffron, or green, or brown, or blue with other colourants.[64] Fish dishes were frequently coloured green, perhaps a reflection of their watery origin: such was gynggaudy; mackerel in sauce to be boiled with mint and other herbs, to be coloured green or yellow; plaice in 'cyvee' (normally an onion sauce, but an ingredient lacking from this recipe) was coloured a yellowish-green with weld.[65] Red was also a popular colouring. Most dishes called 'Saracen' – 'sawse Sarzyne', 'pylets yn Sarcene', 'bruet Sarcenes' – were red, coloured with alkanet or saunders.[66] A popular dish of eels – sore – was, as the name suggests, red. Some dishes changed colour over time. Mawmenny (minced meat, usually poultry, in a sauce of wine or almond milk, with

[60] *Ordinance of Pottage*, pp. 82–3.

[61] The suggestion that colouring so much yellow represented an alchemic translation of this material to gold is perhaps not improbable: Pelner Cosman, *Fabulous Feasts*, p. 63.

[62] The use of colour is a long and complex subject, but for a view that in the medieval period 'colour provided imaginative embellishment, rather than expressing any notion of objective truth', J. Gage, *Colour and Culture: Practice and Meaning from Antiquity to Abstraction* (London, 1993), p. 87; generally, pp. 39–91.

[63] *Curye on Inglysch*, pp. 113–14.

[64] *Ordinance of Pottage*, p. 66.

[65] *Curye on Inglysch*, pp. 119, 122, 124.

[66] Saracen sauce: *Curye on Inglysch*, p. 117; *Two Fifteenth-Century Cookery-Books*, p. 30; *Ordinance of Pottage*, pp. 41, 53.

spices) was probably indigo in the first part of the fourteenth century, yellow by the late fourteenth century, and had become an orange-red by the 1420s.[67]

Another aspect of colour, its lustre, was important. A great many dishes were glazed with egg, to give a shine. Gold foil was used as decoration for a whole class of foods.[68] Colours were mixed to provide a parti-coloured effect, for example in stuffing for venison or boar (white, yellow, black and green).[69] Flowers were used for colour and possibly also for taste and perfume, although these latter two uses are less explicit: hence dishes such as 'rosee' (a fritter using roses and rose leaves for colour); 'spiney', using hawthorn; 'pyany', using peony flowers; 'primerole', using primrose; 'violet', using violets; and 'heppee', using rose hips.[70] Elsewhere there are instructions for shaping images, made, for example, of sugar and for colouring them, for gilding, silvering, using red, green (using a blue and a yellow dye), and making the green lighter with more saffron.[71]

This evidence indicates that colour was employed to make a point, that it was a decorative point, rather than one of deeper meaning, but nonetheless one that might override taste and smell. One noteworthy feature is that the palate of food colours matches almost exactly the tinctures of heraldry.

What was the main point of the cook's craft? Was he primarily a painter and decorator? The recipe books do not neglect taste entirely and there are also directions in some of these documents for the preparation of food. These include practical instructions for preparing the more unusual birds, the swans, bitterns, herons, quails and the like.[72] There are a few references to tasting: for pies of meat, capons and pheasants, a powder was to be made, that is, a preparation of spices, mixed here with vinegar, saffron and salt 'and take hit in thy mouth, yf hit be welle sesond'.[73] 'Hare in talbut' was to be seasoned with powder and salt, a quantity of wine and a little sugar, that is, it was to be adjusted for taste.[74] Some recipes took days to prepare, particularly the sweets, or where meats needed to hang.[75] Charcoal was used for cooking the more delicate dishes, for the control it gave.[76] Along with these directions are further instructions for the final preparation of dishes at the dresser, focusing on presentation. For example, white mortress, of pork, was to be strewn at the dresser with powdered ginger mixed with almonds.[77]

Recipe books have largely been the preserve of culinary historians, but they need to be considered more widely.[78] In terms of taste, a culinary analysis

[67] *Curye on Inglysch*, pp. 9–10, 200–1.
[68] *Ordinance of Pottage*, p. 90, for instructions for putting gold foil on walnuts.
[69] *Two Fifteenth-Century Cookery-Books*, p. 49.
[70] *Curye on Inglysch*, pp. 70–1, 83, 90–1.
[71] Ibid. p. 153.
[72] *Ordinance of Pottage*, pp. 91–9, 'For to sle al maner of foules & roste hem & serve hem forth'.
[73] Ibid. p. 85.
[74] Ibid. p. 46.
[75] Ibid. p. 65.
[76] Ibid. p. 63.
[77] *Two Fifteenth-Century Cookery-Books*, p. 28.
[78] See both the comments of C. B. Hieatt, 'Making Sense of Medieval Culinary Records: much done, but much more to do', *Food and Eating*, ed. Carlin and Rosenthal, pp. 101–16; and B. Laurioux, *Le Règne de Taillevent: livres et pratiques culinaires à la fin du Moyen Âge* (Paris, 1997), pp. 5–6.

misses the point that this may not have been what mattered most in food preparation, that colour, shape and presentation were more important.[79] For it is in terms of spectacle that these foods should be evaluated and it is here that recipe books are a crucial support for an understanding of the place of food in conspicuous consumption, in an order of the senses in which taste and smell were less important than the visual impact.[80] The view of Aquinas that smell, touch and taste were not foremost in the appreciation of beauty, that it was sight and hearing that should be given prominence, may be a philosophical explanation of a more generally accepted cultural phenomenon.[81] Recipes are crucial for understanding the significance of food as an element in social competition and the magnificence of the result.

This is perhaps an appropriate point to return to the Neville enthronement feast. The Neville feast is most often cited from Hearne's edition of Leland's collectanea. Its source, beyond this, as Hearne acknowledged, is a unique printed copy in the Bodleian Library, which is associated with a series of separate items published around 1570–1, including the Warham enthronement feast of 1505 (of which part of another printed copy exists in Lambeth Palace Library); and a note about a feast in 1520, in honour of Charles V, the Holy Roman Emperor, met by Henry VIII at Dover, and received by Wolsey. This last feast was given at Canterbury by Archbishop Warham for Charles V in Whitsun week.[82] Hearne thought the texts might have been collected together and printed at the instance of Matthew Parker – and his connection with the repair of the hall in the archbishop's palace at Canterbury is particularly noted.[83]

The Neville enthronement took place on Sunday, 22 September 1465.[84] Hearne's account of the feast has three elements. It starts with the 'provision', that is, the list of bulk purchases. Then there is a listing of the officers and personnel taking part, who was seated where and how many there were. Thirdly there is 'the order of certaine dynners, as they were set foorth in course', which gives menus for three meals.

Both the list of quantities of food – particularly of food in reserved categories – in the provision and the description of what was eaten at the meals give an important indication of the levels of consumption. The document mentions between two and three thousand participants and servants, those eating in the

[79] Wider reasons may induce people to use or imitate particular foods and techniques of preparation. 'The overwhelming evidence is that people come positively to like foods which developing social standards define as desirable': Mennell, *All Manners of Food*, p. 53.

[80] A viewpoint also summarised by Walker Bynum, *Holy Feast and Holy Fast*, pp. 60–1.

[81] D. McQueen, 'Aquinas on the Aesthetic Relevance of Tastes and Smells', *British Journal of Aesthetics* 33 (1993), pp. 346–56; N. Campbell, 'Aquinas' Reasons for the Aesthetic Irrelevance of Tastes and Smells', *British Journal of Aesthetics* 36 (1996), pp. 166–76.

[82] Hearne, *Collectanea*, vi, pp. 2–40, 'out of an old paper roll' (Bodleian Library, Oxford, MS Bodl. Rolls 8), with the Neville feast on pp. 2–6. For the Neville feast, *The Great Feast at the Intronization of the Reuerende Father in God George Neuell, Archbishop of Yorke* (J. Cawood?, 1570?), STC 18482.5; the Warham enthronement, *O quantum in rebus inane. Intronizatio Wilhelmi Warham, A.D. 1504* (J. Cawood, 1570?), STC 25073.

[83] Hearne, *Collectanea*, p. 34.

[84] The date given by Hearne, 6 Edward IV, has gone awry in transmission: J. Le Neve, *Fasti Ecclesiae Anglicane 1300–1540*, vi, *Northern Province* (*York, Carlisle and Durham*), ed. B. Jones (London, 1963), p. 5.

low hall, in the gallery, officers and servants of household officers, cooks and servants of other men. Between them they probably had approximately 25,000 lb of beef and just over 24,000 lb of mutton, along with about 15,000 lb of pork. This is about 21 lb of meat per person (based on 3,000 people), or what a member of a great household might have expected to be set before him over a period of ten typical meals of meat.

Hearne's account does not state how long the feast lasted. The record of 'the order of certaine dynners, as they were set foorth in course' does, however, provide some information. The first listing is for a meat day (but it does have one item of fish); the second, a mixture of meat and fish; and the third, of fish alone. The presence of this pattern suggests that there must have been a Wednesday (when meat and fish would have been consumed) and a Friday or Saturday (when fish was consumed to the exclusion of meat). Given that the enthronement took place on a Sunday, the feast probably continued through to at least the following Friday. It is unlikely to have commenced much before the Sunday: the Earl of Warwick, the steward for the feast, was at Topcliffe on Thursday, 19 September 1465, about twenty-five to thirty miles from York.[85] With feasts of this scale, there is evidence that participants may have eaten only one meal each day. Even if they ate two meals a day, it is not unreasonable to expect the event to have lasted a week: this would have given ten meals predominantly of meat, with a mixture of fish for some on Wednesday and fish alone on the Friday, on a scale not dissimilar to the underlying level of consumption in aristocratic households.

Support for this view of the length of the feast comes from another account of the meals served. Published in 1500 by Richard Pynson, the king's printer, as preliminary material to *The Boke of Cokery*,[86] the text gives a fuller version of the three courses of the feast for the Sunday, followed by two further meals of three courses for meat days, and the first course of fish for a meal on either a fish day, or one on which both meat and fish were eaten. These may, together, be an account of the main feast meal day by day from the Sunday through to the Wednesday, the first part of a longer description.

The foods that were marked out for the great were a distinctive, but not an unusual expectation. The menus themselves were not out of the ordinary for a feast of this nature, with their array of fine foods, the birds and game that would normally have been reserved for the foremost in the household: cygnets and swans, peacocks, plovers, bitterns, pheasants, egrets, quails, heronsews, curlews, plovers and redshanks. The celebration of abstinence with an array of freshwater fish – the tench, trout, chub and perches – high quality sea fish, such

[85] *The Plumpton Letters and Papers*, ed. J. Kirby, Camden 5th series, viii (1996), p. 37.

[86] *The Boke of Cokery* (London, Richard Pynson, 1500), STC 3297, aii, ff. 4–5, unique printed exemplar at Longleat, partial description in E. G. Duff, *Fifteenth Century English Books: A Bibliography of Books and Documents printed in England and of Books for the English Market printed abroad*, Bibliographical Society, Illustrated Monographs, 18 (Oxford, 1917), p. 14: 'The fest of my lorde chaunceler archebysshop of Yorke at his stallacion in Yorke the yere of our lorde MCCCClxv'. Pynson probably published this at the same time as he was working on the Privy Council's orders for the reception of Katharine of Aragon, *The traduction & mariage of the princesse* (London, Richard Pynson, [1500]), STC 4814, and a part of the text, listing those who were to meet and accompany her, not present in the only copy of *The traduction* (BL, C.21.b.29), concludes the Longleat *Boke of Cokery*. For earlier manuscript versions of the cookery book and feasts, Hieatt, Lambert, Laurioux and Prentki, 'Répertoire des manuscrits' in *Du manuscrit à la table*, pp. 331, 341.

as turbot, and crustacea, also marked out the foods reserved for the diners of the first rank – and was again typical.

Subtleties are noted by the *Boke of Cokery* at four of the six courses on what was probably the Monday and Tuesday of the celebration – but without any detail. The subtleties in the menus recorded by Hearne for two of the days (they do not appear at the fish meal) were comparatively straightforward dishes raised up for the occasion, with extra decoration. The three that accompanied the courses of the meat menu – a great custard, planted; chestons ryall; and chamblet viandier – were probably of this type. On the meat and fish day (probably Wednesday 25 September), there was more variety: a dolphin, in foil and a hart; Sampson; a tart; gilt leche Lumbart, a coloured jelly, and a subtlety of St William, with a coat armour between his hands. Aside from St William's antecedents as archbishop of York, the Earl of Warwick and Archbishop Neville were licensed in 1461 to found a college of chantry priests at York, with landed endowment of up to £100 p. a., which was dedicated to St William. The college was under construction in 1465–7 and those at the feast would have known well the Neville patronage that had brought this particular endowment to fruition.[87]

In conclusion, these subtleties do not tell much about the design of the event and its iconographic programme. Rather the principal feature of the Neville feast that needs remark is its magnitude in another sense – its duration. A feast on this scale was much more than a monarch might arrange for his coronation. The future Richard III was present at the Neville enthronement, yet the record of the feasts for his own coronation festivities does not encompass more than three consecutive days.[88] If the Neville feast lasted a week or more, its key point was its political importance, a celebration underscoring the position of the Nevilles in England[89] – but that and a reconsideration of the texts describing the feast are subjects enough for another paper.[90]

[87] J. L. Flandrin, 'Structure des menus français et anglais aux xive et xve siècles', *Du manuscrit à la table*, pp. 189–90; M. Hicks, *Warwick the Kingmaker* (Oxford, 1998), pp. 237–8.

[88] *The Coronation of Richard III: The Extant Documents*, ed. A. F. Sutton and P. W. Hammond (Gloucester, 1983), pp. 283–302.

[89] Hicks, *Warwick the Kingmaker*, pp. 227–34, especially 230–1.

[90] *The Boke of Cokery* is being republished under the direction of Professor Hieatt.

Exploitation and Control: The Royal Administration of Magnate Estates, 1397–1405

Alastair Dunn

I

In the decade between the inception of Richard II's so-called tyranny, and the defeat of the last Percy rising, in 1408, the higher nobility of England endured a remarkable phase of tenurial instability and insecurity. Few of the greatest magnate estates of this period avoided some form of forfeiture or confiscation, or an intrusive royal wardship. Although the political context of these tenurial changes has received considerable attention, the details of administration, finance and personnel have, in many respects, been neglected. First, some of the assumptions that have been made about the control and disposal of estates by Richard II and Henry IV merit reappraisal.

In the autumn of 1397, Richard II rewarded his allies with many of the estates that had come into crown hands following the Parliamentary forfeitures of the Duke of Gloucester and the Earls of Arundel and Warwick. Given the scale of the land transfers which Richard II orchestrated, it is tempting to impose on the pattern of his grants a preconceived template for the reordering of the balance of territorial power. However, the facts do not support this construction. The disposal of estates in the autumn of 1397 was a ragged affair, the tell-tale signs of cancelled and diverted grants betraying royal indecision and strategic hesitancy. For example, on 9 August 1397, Thomas, Lord Despenser, was granted the custody of the former Beauchamp marcher lordship of Elfael. However, in the following month, Richard II changed his mind, and granted this lordship to his former chamberlain, William Scrope, the newly created Earl of Wiltshire. Scrope himself lost out in 1399, when Richard II deprived him of the custody of the forfeited Fitzalan Shropshire castle of Dawley, in favour of the sheriff of the county, Sir Adam Peshale.[1] Similarly when Richard came to dismember the Beauchamp empire, no single royal favourite was allowed to step into all the shoes of the dispossessed Earl of Warwick. The prized castle and lordship of Warwick went to a newcomer to the county, Thomas Holand, Earl of Kent, whilst the remaining components of the Beauchamp empire were divided among a number of Richard II's favourites, including Thomas Mowbray, Thomas Despenser, John Beaufort and Edward, Earl of Rutland.[2]

Richard II's disposal of the Beauchamp properties poses important questions

[1] *CPR 1396–1399*, pp. 186, 269, 540; PRO E 159/175, Hilary 22 Ric. II, m.3.
[2] *CPR 1396–1399*, pp. 200, 201, 211.

about the broader objectives of his patronage in the final years of his reign. Professor Tuck has identified an essentially negative priority behind Richard II's actions:

> In making his grants, Richard deliberately divided up each of the three inheritances [i.e. those of Gloucester, Arundel and Warwick] so that they ceased to exist as social or economic units . . . . Richard's purpose was to ensure the creation of a new territorial order so different from the old that restoration to the forfeited lands would be impossibly complicated.[3]

However, Professor Given-Wilson discerns a more positive objective in Richard II's grants:

> The logic of the 1397 grants is thus to be found not in the desire by Richard to destroy forever the possibility that the three great inheritances of his opponents might be re-united . . . but in the desire to re-inforce the existing regional strengths of his friends.[4]

These two interpretations of Richard II's actions are far from incompatible. The evidence from the patterns of dismemberment and alienation supports a synthesis of these two views, as Professor Saul has suggested.[5] It is clear that Richard's grants served the twin objectives of fragmenting his fallen enemies' inheritances, and granting them out so as to complement the existing territorial strengths of his allies.

We should also remember that patronage was not just a top-down process, and that the pattern of Richard II's grants may owe much to pressure from royal favourites. The surviving petitions submitted by Richard II's favourites for grants from the spoils of forfeiture surely represent only the tip of the iceberg.[6] One of the most significant grants of 1397, that of the castle and lordship of Arundel to John Holand, followed his repeated petitions for this valuable trophy.[7] The petition of John Montagu, Earl of Salisbury, in March 1399 for a grant of the custody of the Wiltshire lordship of Trowbridge, following the death of John of Gaunt, met with similar success.[8]

Given the obvious significance of these petitions, and the royal grants which followed, it is possible that the impetus for the division of the spoils of political victory lay as much in the expectations of the counter-Appellants of 1397, as in any preconceived royal scheme for the redistribution of forfeited lands. Perhaps, therefore, we should regard pressure for reward from Richard's allies as being of equal importance to his own designs, in shaping the patterns of his patronage.

[3] Tuck, *Richard II*, p. 191.
[4] Given-Wilson, *English Nobility*, p. 137.
[5] Saul, *Richard II*, p. 473.
[6] J. A. Tuck, 'Richard II's System of Patronage', *Reign of Richard II*, pp. 4–5.
[7] PRO SC 8/269/13406, /12421; *CPR 1396–1399*, pp. 280–1 (28 Sep. 1397).
[8] PRO C 81/1394/118/48; *CFR 1391–1399*, p. 296 (22 March 1399). For the Montagus' efforts to wrest these properties from the duchy of Lancaster, see *VCH Wilts*, viii, pp. 128–9.

II

For the first decade of his reign, Henry IV faced repeated and sustained challenges from a number of his most powerful subjects, the failure of which brought many great aristocratic estates into his hands. Throughout these years of most acute peril, Henry IV's freedom of manoeuvre was circumscribed by contending political pressures. The costs of resisting the Glyn Dŵr revolt and other rebellions, combined with those of policing the Scottish marches, maintaining the English possessions in France, and meeting the other regular expenses of the crown, stretched Henry's resources to breaking point. For parliament, the solution lay in a more efficient and intensive exploitation of the immense territorial resources that Henry controlled – which included his paternal inheritance, and that of his deceased first wife, Mary Bohun, as well as the lands forfeited by his enemies.[9] Allied to this were repeated demands for the resumption of crown annuities, and estates that had been alienated from the royal demesne.[10] Thus, Henry was trapped between the spiralling costs of containing rebellion and warfare, and the political imperative of rewarding those who had upheld his rule at the greatest periods of crisis.

In February 1400, the royal council recommended that all of the forfeited lands of the Epiphany conspirators be retained by the crown 'to maintain his honourable estate . . . without charging his people'.[11] This advice was soon translated into official policy, as, on 24 February 1400, the crown entrusted the keeping of all lands of deceased tenants-in-chief to the custody of Sir Thomas Rempston and Thomas Tutbury, steward and treasurer, respectively, of the royal household.[12]

In the majority of cases, the lands of the leading Epiphany rebels were gradually restored to their widows and other dependants, after a few years in the custody of the crown, or its allies. The systematic alienation of forfeited estates to royal allies, as practised by Richard II in 1397, was prudently avoided by Henry IV, in 1400. However, there are at least two significant examples of royal efforts to derive permanent benefit from the forfeiture of the Epiphany rebels. On 20 February 1400, the duchy of Lancaster annexed the great Leicestershire, Derbyshire and Nottingham estates of the lordship of Castle Donington, worth over £100 annually, which Thomas Holand had forfeited through his leadership of the Epiphany Rising.[13] The justification offered was that Castle Donington lordship had been held by Thomas of Lancaster, at his execution in 1322, and that it had thus belonged, rightly, to his descendants, following Earl Henry's restoration in 1324.[14] Thus Henry IV was able to strip the Holand family of lands which they had held, peacefully,

[9] Wolffe, *Royal Demesne*, p. 73.

[10] A. L. Brown, 'The Commons and the Council in the Reign of King Henry IV', *EHR*, lxxix (1964), pp. 1–30; A. Rogers, 'Henry IV, the Commons and Taxation', *Medieval Studies*, xxxi (1969), pp. 44–70.

[11] *POPC*, i, p. 109.

[12] *CPR 1399–1401*, p. 245.

[13] PRO DL 29/728/11988 m.11 (account of the 'north parts' of the duchy, 1400–1).

[14] PRO E 357/14 (escheators' account rolls) m.8d.; *CCR 1399–1402*, pp. 59–60; *CIPM 1399–1405*, p. 333, no. 975.

for almost seventy years. A similar assault was made on the estates forfeited by John Montagu, Earl of Salisbury. The Dorset manors of Canford and Poole were claimed by the duchy, on the same grounds – that they had rightly belonged to the earldom of Lancaster since 1324. Although Henry later relented in the case of Canford, it would seem that Poole was retained by the duchy of Lancaster.[15]

In at least one case, Henry had not needed the pretext of forfeiture to strip one of his enemies of substantial estates. During the 1380s and 1390s, Richard II had committed the custody of several duchy of Cornwall properties to John Holand, his half-brother. These grants conferred on Holand considerable power and influence in the south-west, and he came to assume the role of an unofficial viceroy in the region.[16] As he had inherited little in the way of land, Holand relied very heavily on this portfolio of manors for his income, and had even made his home at Dartington Hall, in Devonshire.[17] On 22 December 1399, Henry IV stripped Holand of eleven of his manors, on the grounds that they were inalienable from the duchy, according to the instrument by which it had been created in 1337.[18] Although it is likely that Holand's decision to rebel against Henry predated this massive blow, it surely confirmed him in his course of action.[19]

Should we regard these annexations as a systematic effort to augment the territorial holdings of the duchies of Lancaster and Cornwall (and, by extension, the crown)? The lands already controlled by Henry, which included the duchy of Lancaster, half of the former Bohun estates, and the custody of a number of noble inheritances, dwarfed these transfers. Moreover, they also seem fairly inconsequential compared to Richard II's short-lived annexation of the Arundel marcher lordships to the Chester palatinate. Although Castle Donington was a valuable property, it could make only a negligible contribution to the crown's landed income. Rather, we should regard these dispossessions as acts of opportunism, inflicted against politically weakened and marginalised enemies. Although it is understandable that Henry IV should flex his muscles against families who, a matter of months before, had profited from his own exile and the persecution of his friends and allies, this was nevertheless a dangerous game, given the fragility of his tenure of the crown.

By 1405, Henry IV's commitment to retain all forfeited estates to fund his private expenses had become politically unsustainable. The extreme difficulty with which he contained the multiple crises of the years 1403–5 illustrated the degree to which he relied upon his family, retainers and other allies. Moreover, he had also been hardened by the treachery of the Percies and their extensive

[15] *CCR 1399–1402*, p. 60; *1405–9*, p. 445; R. Somerville, *History of the Duchy of Lancaster*, i (London, 1953), p. 173.

[16] In 1384, Richard II had granted Holand a reversionary stake in the Audley of Heighley estates, which, by right, should have descended to the abbey of St Mary Graces, in accordance with the directions of Edward III's will: C. Given-Wilson, 'Richard II and his Grandfather's Will', *EHR*, xciii (1978), p. 328.

[17] A. Emery, *Dartington Hall* (Oxford, 1970).

[18] *CIM 1399–1422*, p. 58, no. 100.

[19] M. M. N. Stansfield, 'The Hollands, Dukes of Exeter, Earls of Kent and Huntingdon, 1352–1475' (unpub. Oxford Univ. D.Phil. thesis, 1987), p. 129.

affinity, many of whom sought his pardons repeatedly, only to rebel again within a matter of weeks.[20] He was thus less reluctant to alienate the spoils of forfeiture, than he had been at the beginning of the reign. Princes Henry and John, Ralph Neville, the Beauforts, and many other royal allies, profited from the spoils of Henry IV's victories of 1405.[21]

No less than Richard II, Henry IV was faced with considerable pressure for reward from those who had supported him at times of most acute crisis. However, the key distinction between the practices of these two kings was Henry's realisation that the perpetual disinheritance of the heirs of lords who had challenged his rule threatened to build up lingering resentments of perceived injustices. It was the practice of rehabilitation through service that enabled Henry IV and his successor to build up a store of goodwill among the heirs of many of their bitterest enemies. Names such as Holand, Montagu and Mowbray figure prominently in the battle honours of the Lancastrian campaigns in France.[22] By offering their greatest subjects an active and rewarding stake in the spheres of governance and warfare, the first two Lancastrian kings repaired much of the damage to crown–noble relations caused by the feuds which had raged during Richard II's tyranny and in the aftermath of his deposition.[23]

III

The transfer of the custody of magnate estates was not merely an exercise in the redistribution of territorial power. Money was the essence of these tenurial changes. Even the business of sending out escheators, surveyors and serjeants-at-arms to seize estates was an expensive undertaking. Over four days (16th to 19th) in October 1397, the wages of twenty-three royal servants engaged in the confiscation of forfeited goods and chattels totalled £110 – a sum exceeding the income of many wealthy knights.[24] The physical implementation of forfeitures was a massive logistical exercise, the bulk of which was carried out by the established royal authorities in the counties – the sheriff and escheator.

One of the most efficient – and ruthless – agents of Richard II's tyranny was Clement Spice, escheator of Essex. Spice's patch included the castle and lordship of Pleshey, the principal residence of Thomas, Duke of Gloucester, which he held by the inheritance of his wife, Eleanor Bohun. From the moment of Gloucester's arrest at Pleshey, on the morning of 10 July 1397, Spice was placed in control of the liquidation of his Essex estates. It is possible that Clement Spice supervised the production of the well-known published inventory

[20] For the case of Sir Henry Boynton, see M. H. Keen, 'Treason Trials under the Law of Arms', *TRHS*, 5th series, 12 (1962), pp. 85–103.

[21] *CPR 1405–1408*, pp. 40, 50, 105; J. H. Wylie, *History of England under Henry IV*, ii (London, 1894), pp. 280–4.

[22] C. T. Allmand, *Henry V* (London, 1992) pp. 370–1.

[23] C. Carpenter, *The Wars of the Roses. Politics and the Constitution in England, c.1437–1509* (Cambridge, 1997), p. 71.

[24] PRO E 403/556, mm.2–5.

of the duke's goods.[25] This inventory was probably composed to enable the crown to value the duke's moveables for the purposes of auction.

The proceeds of the sales from the Gloucester inventory soon mounted up, so that, by the winter of 1397, very substantial cash sums were passing into Spice's hands. Between the end of December 1397 and the end of January 1398, twenty-eight men in the employ of Clement Spice accounted to him for cash totalling £620, from sales of Gloucester's chattels.[26] On one day alone (19 January 1398), Clement Spice accounted to the exchequer for a lump sum of £939 of proceeds from these sales.[27] Faced with the prospect of having her household stripped bare, Duchess Eleanor bought back large amounts of her late husband's property. In 1398, she redeemed goods worth a total of £1,136. Her expenditure included £260 at an auction conducted in London by Richard Whitington, and she also spent £436 on buying back silverware from Clement Spice.[28]

Although Duchess Eleanor received livery of her Pleshey estates on 30 November 1397, Clement Spice stripped her of all the agricultural profits, totalling £227, that had accrued since her husband's arrest in July of that year.[29] The speed with which the crown succeeded in laying hands on Gloucester's wealth was remarkable, and owed much to the zeal and efficiency of its servants. We can, however, only speculate as to the amount of cash, ornaments and other precious items that never made their way onto the inventory, and lined the pockets of Clement Spice and his servants.

The pattern of frantic asset stripping by the crown at Pleshey Castle was replicated on a massively increased scale on the forfeited marcher estates of the Earl of Arundel, following their annexation to the newly created principality of Chester, on 25 September 1397. Both the executed Earl of Arundel, and his father, had used their marcher castles as repositories for their enormous liquid wealth. Given-Wilson has noted that the elder Earl of Arundel, who died in 1376, had nearly 9,400 marks deposited at Holt, and 4,900 at Clun, in 1371.[30] Richard II adopted these castles as ready-made safe deposits for his own burgeoning wealth, in the last two years of the reign. In 1402, John Ikelington, an exchequer clerk, received acquittance from Henry IV for £43,500 of cash which Richard II had lodged with him for deposit at Holt castle.[31] Richard II's obsessive concern for the security of the newly annexed Arundel marcher estates was not without justification, as a number of opportunists had exploited the vacuum of authority between the earl's arrest and the take-over of royal officials, to liberate £720 of coin from Oswestry castle.[32]

The newly installed royal administration at Bromfield, Yale, Chirk and

[25] 'Inventory of the Goods and Chattels Belonging to Thomas, Duke of Gloucester . . . [etc.]', ed. Viscount Dillon and W. H. St. John Hope, *Archaeological Journal*, liiii (1897), pp. 275–308; for an analysis of this inventory, see Dyer, *Standards of Living*, pp. 77–8. Dr J. Stratford has kindly drawn my attention to Clement Spice's inventories in PRO E 364/35, rot. id, m.9, and PRO E 372/246.

[26] PRO E 401/608, mm.20–2.

[27] *CCR 1396–1399*, p. 241; PRO E 401/608, mm.21, 25; *CIM 1392–1399* p. 223, no. 372.

[28] PRO E 357/13, m.11d.; *CCR 1396–1399*, p. 182.

[29] C. Given-Wilson, 'Wealth and Credit, Public and Private and Private: The Earls of Arundel 1306–97', *EHR*, cvi (1991), p. 8.

[30] Given-Wilson, *Royal Household*, p. 181.

[31] *CIM 1392–1399*, p. 112, no. 235.

[32] See below.

Oswestry embarked upon a massive and systematic campaign of asset-stripping. Between 20 April and 29 September 1398, the royal administrators collected a total of £2,765 of receipts from these estates.[33] That even the most humble local receiver owed his position to the crown was an incentive to maximise the collection of revenues. The pattern of expenditure by the Chester administration confirms the grossly exploitative character of the royal control of these estates. In Michaelmas term of 1398, £2,576 of receipts from these estates were disbursed to 758 royal retainers. If we can assume that a similar disbursement was made for the second half of the year 1398–9, then the total outflow of cash from these estates to Richard II's Cheshiremen would have been £5,150.[34] It thus appears that over 90 per cent of the income generated by the former Fitzalan marcher estates flowed out of the region to bankroll the royal affinity. Given the enormity of this exploitation, it should come as no surprise that the northern Welsh marches did not raise a finger to uphold Richard II's cause at his hour of need in July 1399.

Richard II's efforts to exploit the wealth of other estates which came into his hands during his 'tyranny' produced varying results. Four days before the death of Margaret, Duchess of Norfolk, on 24 March 1399, Richard II had entrusted the control of her lands, and those of her exiled grandson, Thomas Mowbray, to a committee of administrators, headed by the Bishops of Salisbury and St Davids, Sir John Bussy and Sir Henry Green.[35] For the following seven months, until Henry IV wound up their operations on 18 November 1399, this committee was entirely responsible for the administration of the Norfolk lands.

The limitations of the crown's capacity and ability to profit from the Mowbray estates in 1398–9 is clear from the evidence relating to the Lincolnshire lordship of Axholme. Of the £135 of receipts collected at Axholme, over £80 was disbursed on wages and administrative costs, whilst £38 went as dower to Elizabeth Fitzalan, Duke Thomas's wife. Only £8 – or 6 per cent – of the total issues were paid to the crown receiver.[36] The crown's performance in the administration of the other Mowbray estates was extremely variable. Whereas the royal receivers were paid 90 per cent of the issues collected on the Yorkshire lands, they received only 40 per cent of those collected in Sussex.[37] Although some of this discrepancy can be accounted for by differences in the administrative and wage costs on each of the Mowbray estates, it would also appear that there was no concerted effort by the crown to maximise their income-generating potential. By the time of the Lancastrian revolution, the committee of royal administrators had accounted at the exchequer for the rather disappointing total of £367 from the Mowbray inheritance.[38] When Henry

[33] PRO SC 6/1234/7 mm.1, 1d (account of lordships annexed to the principality of Chester, 1398).

[34] PRO SC 6/1234/7, m.11d.; R. R. Davies, 'Richard II and the Principality of Chester', *Reign of Richard II*, p. 269n.

[35] *Rot. Parl.*, iii, p. 372.

[36] PRO SC 6/909/20 mm.1–3 (account of receiver-general of Axholme, 1398–9).

[37] PRO SC 6/1087/14 (accounts of ministers, Thirsk, Hovingham and Burton-in-Lonsdale, 1398–9); SC 6/1020/10 (collector of Beeding, 1398–9); SC 6/1021/3 (keeper of Brembre bailiwick, 1398–9); SC 6/ 1021/4 (Robert Cook, bailiff of Brembre burgh, 1398–9); SC 6/1022/26 (beadle of Grinstead, 1398–9).

[38] PRO E 401/614 m.12.

IV terminated Richard II's committee of administrators, in November 1399, he ordered a comprehensive audit of all the Mowbray estates. This revealed the extent of the Richard II's failure to realise the full value of the Mowbray inheritance, as over £1,500 of cash receipts were found to still be in the hands of local officials.[39]

Why did Richard II's administrators enjoy such limited success in the financial exploitation of the Mowbray lands? One reason may be that the Mowbray officials – all of whom were left in place – had colluded to minimise the effectiveness of the royal administration. Another possible explanation for this apparent failure can be found in the crown's concern to avoid an oppressive tone of management, and to retain the sympathies of men attached to Thomas Mowbray. By the 1390s, many of Mowbray's retainers, such as Sir William Bagot and William Rees, sheriff of Norfolk, also enjoyed strong connections with the crown.[40] The extent to which estates could be squeezed financially may have owed as much to political as to economic considerations.

After the Lancastrian Revolution, the administration of the Mowbray lands proved to be an exercise of nightmarish complexity. Although the aggregated lands of the Mowbrays and the earldom of Norfolk were worth in excess of £4,500 annually, it was an uphill task for the crown to realise a significant fraction of this potential yield.[41] Not only was the geographical distribution of this inheritance as disparate as that of the Mortimers, but its wealth was also subject to the competing claims of the Mowbray annuitants, the widowed Duchess Elizabeth, her children, and a horde of disgruntled creditors.[42] This task was made all the harder by the outbreak of revolt in Wales in 1400, which threatened the family's valuable estates at Gower and Chepstow.

The records of the Mowbray estates for this period reveal the complexity of the task which faced the crown in meeting its dower obligations to Elizabeth Fitzalan, widow of Duke Thomas. When Henry IV's faithful friend and servant, Sir Hugh Waterton, took over control of the Mowbray lordship of Gower, on 6 December 1399, the financial workload was so demanding that he brought in a professional auditor. Robert Eggerley was a member of a burgeoning class of professional bureaucrats whose significance grew with the size and complexity of the estates which they managed.[43] Eggerley had established his reputation in the service of the Earl of Arundel, and is credited with the authorship of the immense surveys which the Appellant earl had commissioned for his marcher lordships in 1391–3.[44]

The work of Eggerley and Waterton was further complicated by the rapid escalation of the Glyn Dŵr rebellion. By 1401, Swansea was a heavily militarised town, and the castle had become an important link in the royal

[39] PRO E 101/511/31 (audit of Mowbray lands, 1399–1400).

[40] For Bagot and Rees, see *HPT 1386–1421*, ii, pp. 99–103; iv, pp. 187–9.

[41] R. E. Archer, 'The Mowbrays, Earls of Nottingham and Dukes of Norfolk, to 1432' (unpub. Oxford Univ. D.Phil. thesis, 1984), p. 75.

[42] For the payment of £960 of debts, and for additional outstanding sums owed by Thomas, Duke of Norfolk (d. 1399), see BL Add. MS 16556 (account of John Lewis, receiver-general, 1401–4), m.17 and roll of creditors attached to m.21.

[43] PRO SC 6/1202/15 (keeper of Gower, 1399–1400).

[44] BL Add. MS 10013 (survey of Bromfield and Yale); *Extent of Chirkland, 1391–3*, ed. G. P. Jones (Liverpool, 1933); *Lordship of Oswestry, 1393–1607*, ed. W. J. Slack (Shrewsbury, 1951).

defences in south Wales. The accounts for this period convey a palpable sense of fear that Glyn Dŵr's men would fall upon the lordship from the Brecon hills.[45] Whatever the fears of the garrison for their own safety, the crown was more worried by the vulnerability of the cash in transit from south Wales to London. The men who escorted £130 from Swansea to Hugh Waterton's Herefordshire home of Eton Tregose, and thence to London, in July 1402, were well aware how tempting a target their chests and cash-bags were for Glyn Dŵr's men. In spite of these difficulties, the Lancastrian officials succeeded in collecting and delivering a respectable proportion of the sums due to Duchess Elizabeth and her son, Earl Thomas.[46]

Royal efforts to control and exploit the Mortimer inheritance were similarly bedevilled by political and financial difficulties. In the autumn of 1398, the keeping of those Mortimer estates that were not assigned as dower to Countess Eleanor, were divided among a number of Richard's closest favourites, and the profits were earmarked as a contribution to the endowment of the new Queen, Isabella of France.[47] Although insufficient data is available to put an accurate annual valuation on the Mortimer lands, they may have yielded in excess of £4,500 annually in the 1390s. In the year between Earl Roger's death and the Lancastrian Revolution, the royal keepers of the Mortimer lands accounted at the exchequer for almost £1,000 of issues.[48] Over £800 came into the hands of John Holand, Duke of Exeter, keeper of the Mortimer lands in south Wales, although only £450 of this sum was accounted to the exchequer before the 1399 Revolution.[49] As in the case of the Mowbray lands, Earl Roger's widow had a major stake in this inheritance, and the disintegration of Richard's rule in the summer of 1399 prevented a full year's accounting of receipts at the exchequer. A more specific explanation for the limited success of this exploitation may lie in the failure of royal officials to recover substantial arrears of rents and farms, which, on the Kent manors alone, ran to £500.[50]

In November 1399, the Earl of Northumberland, and his son, Hotspur, gained control of the management of the Mortimer inheritance as a reward for their massive contribution to Henry's usurpation. The two-thirds of the inheritance that Northumberland controlled was worth about £2,500 net, annually, which, after the deduction of the £1,063 farm, left him with a surplus of over £1,400.[51] Hotspur controlled the lordship of Denbigh separately, for which he owed the crown an annual farm of £667, which meant that, of the £1,270 of receipts collected in 1401–2, he could have expected a profit of at least £600.[52] Therefore, Northumberland and his son could have made a private annual profit of about £2,000 from the Mortimer inheritance. Moreover, the

[45] PRO SC 6/1202/17, m.2 (Gower lordship, 1401–2).
[46] PRO SC 6/1202/15–18; BL Add. Roll 16556.
[47] *CPR 1396–1399*, pp. 408, 429, 431, 514. However, Thomas Holand, Duke of Surrey, was granted the keeping of the Mortimer lands in Ireland, free of rent, for three years.
[48] PRO E 357/12 m.40 (10 Nov. 1398); E 401/611 m.16 (8 Jan. 1399); E 357/13 m.31 (26 May 1399).
[49] PRO E 357/13 m.8.
[50] PRO SC 6/1112/9 (Mortimer Kent and Essex manors, 1398–9).
[51] *CFR 1399–1405*, pp. 22, 38–9; C. D. Ross, 'The Yorkshire Baronage, 1399–1450' (unpub. Oxford Univ. D.Phil. thesis, 1950), p. 331.
[52] PRO E 401/617 m.9 (17 Dec. 1399, payment of £667 as the moiety of Denbigh); SC 6/1185/4 m.8 (total receipts of Denbigh, 1401–2: £1,270).

Percies and their officials were less than efficient in paying their exchequer farm, as, by the time of their rebellion in 1403, they had accounted for only £1,300.[53]

The deteriorating relationship between Henry IV and the Percies, which centred on the latters' claims that they were owed large and mounting arrears of payment for the defence of the Scottish marches, and their military responsibilities in Wales, had serious repercussions for the administration of the Mortimer inheritance.[54] Moreover, the outbreak and intensification of the Glyn Dŵr revolt meant that the crown wished to exercise a much more direct control over the material and financial resources of the Mortimer marcher lordships. On 7 March 1401, Henry IV ordered a general resumption of the Mortimer estates, and, in the ensuing redistribution, the Percies' authority was diluted considerably.[55] It is possible that the erosion of their control of the Mortimer inheritance was as important a cause of the Percies' rebellion as their disagreement with Henry IV over arrears of wages, and his failure to support their territorial ambitions in southern Scotland.

Richard II's seizure of control over the duchy of Lancaster estates in 1399 has been regarded, rightly, as the most dramatic act of his 'tyranny.' Although the political repercussions of this act are well known, little effort has been made to understand its financial dimensions.[56] In his history of the duchy of Lancaster, Somerville asserted that Richard II and his allies 'drew little benefit from their occupation of Lancastrian estates', and that 'no accounts could have been rendered to the new masters; their tenure proved to be too short'.[57] Royal and duchy records for this period however tell a different story. In June 1399, over £1,500 of duchy receipts were paid into the exchequer by the royal controllers.[58] The subsequent movement of some of this cash can be traced by the efforts of the duchy officials to obtain its recovery. In the middle of August 1399, shortly after Richard II had been taken as a captive to Chester, clerks of the royal chamber, and of the exchequer, restored over £1,700 of receipts to the duchy of Lancaster officials.[59] It is clear from this that substantial sums of duchy revenue were in the process of being digested by the royal financial organs, and that a significant proportion had been earmarked for the use of Richard II's chamber. This evidence adds some weight to the suspicions that one of the principal motivations behind Richard II's confiscation of the Lancastrian inheritance was his greed for its wealth-generating potential.

Although less blatantly avaricious than his predecessor, Henry IV enjoyed some success in milking the estates of his enemies to his own advantage. Perhaps the most valuable estates that came into Henry's hands following the

[53] PRO E 401/617–19.

[54] J. M. W. Bean, 'Henry IV and the Percies', *History*, xlix (1959), pp. 221–7; P. McNiven, 'The Scottish Policy of the Percies and the Strategy of the Rebellion of 1403', *BJRL*, lxii (1980), pp. 498–530.

[55] *CFR 1399–1405*, p. 142.

[56] For a discussion of the political background to the seizure of the Lancastrian inheritance, see C. Given-Wilson, 'Richard II, Edward II and the Lancastrian Inheritance', *EHR*, cix (1994), pp. 553–71.

[57] Somerville, *Duchy of Lancaster*, i, p. 136.

[58] PRO E 401/614 mm.11, 13.

[59] PRO DL 28/4/1 f. 4v (account of receiver-general of Henry of Lancaster, Feb. 1399 to Feb. 1400).

Epiphany Rising were those of Thomas Holand, Earl of Kent. In the year 1400–1, the crown made a profit of £920 from its control of his Yorkshire estates alone.[60] Similar success was achieved, although on a smaller scale, on the forfeited estates of John Montagu, Earl of Salisbury. By May 1400, the crown had extracted £127 of profits from a parcel of his Somerset and Dorset estates.[61]

The financial exploitation of confiscated estates proved to be a complicated business, with mixed results, for both Richard II and Henry IV. Although both kings derived some profit from the lands which they controlled, only the annexed Arundel marcher lordships yielded their full potential. In most other cases, estates were fragmented into uneconomical portions, with high administrative costs and a diminished potential for profitable exploitation. The political imperative of rewarding allies, which faced Richard II in 1397, and Henry IV in 1405, resulted in a massive diminution of the stock of forfeited lands at the crown's disposal. Once the carcasses had been picked clean by widows, heirs, feoffees and creditors, the remnants often failed to yield their anticipated value.

IV

Although exploitation and enrichment were the sinews of violent tenurial change, these processes also touched the lives of a large number of officials, servants and retainers – and others with a more nebulous connection to a fallen lord.

Richard II's most hated enemy, the Earl of Arundel, had ruled his Welsh marcher estates through a large and capable bureaucracy. The tradition of long and competent service on the Fitzalan marcher estates was best represented by Alan Thorp, who had served as receiver of the lordship of Chirk every year, bar one, between 1383 and 1397. Like his colleague, Robert Eggerley, rector of West Felton, Thorp also enjoyed a Shropshire benefice, at Clungford, which, naturally, was in the gift of the Earl of Arundel.[62] During the 1393 Cheshire gentry revolt, Arundel had demonstrated his power through his spectacular non-intervention, as he had been content to observe, from the security of Holt Castle, the struggle of Gaunt and Gloucester to restore order.[63] Richard's enduring hatred for, and mistrust of, Arundel, combined with his ambitions for the palatinate of Chester, found expression in his annexation of the earl's marcher lordships to the new principality in September 1397.[64] Alan Thorp was one of more than thirty officials who were ejected in a wholesale purge of Arundel's marcher administration. The castle constables were prime targets for

[60] PRO E 159/177, Hil. 2 Henry IV mm.49–9d.

[61] PRO E 357/14 m.55.

[62] National Register of Archives List 10568, Chirk Castle MSS and Docs., i, receivers' rolls, 38–44; *CPR 1396–1399*, p. 199.

[63] J. G. Bellamy, 'The Northern Rebellions in the Last Years of Richard II', *BJRL*, xxxxvii (1965), pp. 254–74; P. J. Morgan, *War and Society in Medieval Cheshire, 1277–1403*, Chetham Society, 3rd series, xxxiv (1987), p. 196.

[64] *Rot. Parl.*, iii, pp. 353–4.

this purge, and Arundel men were ejected in favour of leaders of the royal Cheshire retinue, such as Sir Robert Legh, Thomas Beston and Peter Dutton. This wave of sackings extended beyond the stewards and constables, and touched minor local office holders and tenants.[65] Richard II's clear-out threatened the tenurial security of a much broader cross-section of society than any of the other forfeitures of this period. The scale and vindictiveness of this purge has more in common with Edward II's persecution of the Contrariants and their gentry adherents in the 1320s.[66]

Robert Parys and William Scrope represented the twin faces of the royal control of the annexed Arundel marcher lordships – bureaucracy heavily reinforced with coercion. A civil servant par excellence, Robert Parys should figure more prominently in our understanding of the administrative architecture of Richard II's tyranny. Although born into a Cambridgeshire family, Parys inherited a strong connection to the earldom of Chester, as his father, also Robert, had served as chamberlain of the palatinate, for the Black Prince, for twenty years, from 1353. After an apprenticeship as sheriff of Cambridgeshire in the 1380s, our Robert Parys was called to fill his father's chamberlainship in May 1394. From the mid-1390s, he was at the very centre of Richard II's increasing interest in the western peripheries of his kingdom.[67] Vast quantities of cash and munitions, and royal armies, passed through his Chester administration, en route to Wales and Ireland. His appointment as principal surveyor and receiver of the Earl of Arundel's forfeited lordships, in April 1398, represented the only truly systematic effort to exploit forfeited lands in this period. This was a truly professional administration, as Parys was supported by his deputy, Roger Brescy, and the escheator of Chester, Hugh Knutsford. Although Richard II's principality of Chester was dissolved in the aftermath of the 1399 Revolution, its most capable servant made an easy transition to Lancastrian service. His new challenge, as chamberlain of north Wales, was to marshal the resources of the principality against Owain Glyn Dŵr. Parys' son, also Robert, became the third generation of his family to serve in north Wales, and was slain in the fighting at Caernarfon, in March 1407.[68]

Although Parys and his colleagues presided over the civil structures which controlled the Arundel lordships, their authority was ultimately dependent on the military strength of the Chester palatinate. From 28 January 1398, the full coercive apparatus of the principality of Chester was concentrated in the hands of one man, William Scrope, Earl of Wiltshire.[69] In the early 1390s, he had risen as the eminence grise of Richard II's court, discharging the vital role of underchamberlain from 1393.[70] However, Scrope was primarily a coercive agent, who had begun his career soldiering in France – a natural transition

[65] PRO SC 6/1234/6–7 (forfeited Arundel marcher lordships, 1398–9).
[66] S. L. Waugh, 'The Profits of Violence, The Minor Gentry in the Rebellion of 1321–1322 in Gloucestershire and Herefordshire', *Speculum*, 52 (1977), pp. 859–866.
[67] M. J. Bennett, 'Richard II and the Wider Realm', *Richard II: the Art of Kingship*, ed. A. Goodman and J. L. Gillespie (Oxford, 1999), p. 188.
[68] *HPT 1386–1421*, iv, pp. 20–2; R. R. Davies, *The Revolt of Owain Glyn Dŵr* (Oxford, 1995), pp. 26, 48, 221, 245.
[69] PRO CHES 2/71, m.3d (account roll of chamberlain of Chester, 1397–8).
[70] Given-Wilson, *Royal Household*, p. 283.

from his hot-headed early years on his father's northern estates.[71] His appointment to Chester followed a three-year spell as justiciar of Ireland – a portfolio to which his character seems to have been well-suited.[72] By the end of 1398, Scrope had monopolised the judicial and military power of the crown from Anglesey to Macclesfield, and his court at Chester kept a careful eye on local men who had been connected to the Earl of Arundel.[73] At one point in 1398, Scrope issued a writ for the investigation of William Curtis, a servant of both the Mortimer earls and the crown (as constable of Denbigh and Chester castles), on suspicion of his having aided his old associate, and fellow veteran in Arundel service, Sir Thomas Mortimer, in his flight to Scotland.[74] (Thomas Mortimer had been sentenced to forfeiture, in absentia, in the September 1397 Parliament, for his part in the death of Sir Thomas Molineux, at the battle of Radcot Bridge, ten years previously.[75]) Although Robert Parys may claim the credit for the profits extracted from the Arundel estates, his success may have owed much to the quiescent political climate fostered by the coercive forces at Scrope's disposal. Whereas Parys was essentially a civil servant, Scrope was too closely implicated in the political excesses of Richard II's final years to survive the collapse of his rule. By the summer of 1399, he had become the unacceptable face of Ricardian kingship, and was executed by Henry's forces at Bristol on 29 July.[76]

The greatest contrast to the oppression on the Arundel marcher estates can be found on the inherited lands of Eleanor Bohun, in the months following her husband's arrest and death. As has been noted already, Richard II's officials were ruthlessly efficient in laying hands on the duke's cash and chattels, and swept up all those lands which he had held by grant of his father, Edward III. However, once these men had completed their work, Duchess Eleanor enjoyed a strong measure of control over those lands which she had inherited from her father, Humphrey, the last Bohun Earl of Hereford. At Pleshey Castle, the seignorial bureaucracy remained intact, under the supervision of her veteran household treasurer, John Upton, and Paul Kirketon, master of the college of priests which she and her husband had founded in 1394.[77] In spite of the despoliation inflicted by the royal officials in the autumn of 1397, John

[71] In 1388, Scrope had donated a jewel worth £600 to Durham Priory as compensation for his invasion of the liberties of the palatinate, *Extracts from the Account Rolls of Durham Priory*, ii, ed. J. T. Fowler, Surtees Society, c (1899), pp. 444–5, 451.

[72] D. B. Johnston, 'The Interim Years: Richard II and Ireland, 1395–99', *England and Ireland in the Later Middle Ages: Essays in Honour of Jocelyn Otway-Ruthven*, ed. J. F. Lydon (Irish Academic Press, 1981), pp. 176–80.

[73] PRO SC 6/774/10 mm.1d–4d (chamberlain of Chester, 1398–9); PRO CHES 2/71 m.10; Oxford, Bodleian Library, MS Dodsworth 31 f. 74r.

[74] PRO CHES 24/19, box ii, bundle 1398 (Chester Gaol Files and Writs). It would seem that no further action was taken, and Curtis survived to serve as constable of Denbigh for Hotspur and Prince Henry (PRO SC 6/1184/23; /1185/4, 10–12, accounts of Denbigh lordship, 1397–1409).

[75] For the full context of the relationship between Arundel, Thomas Mortimer and William Curtis, see J. L. Gillespie, 'Thomas Mortimer and Thomas Molineux: Radcot Bridge and the Appeal of 1397', *Albion*, vii (1975), pp. 161–73.

[76] For the comments of his fiercest detractors, see Walsingham, *Annales*, pp. 223–4, 240, 246–7; *Chronicle of Adam Usk*, ed. C. Given-Wilson (Oxford, 1997), pp. 52–3. Walsingham called him 'the worst of men . . . truly hated by the community of the realm' whilst Usk characterised him as one of 'the king's most evil counsellors and chief fosterers of his malice'.

[77] Goodman, *Loyal Conspiracy*, pp. 82–3.

Lightfoot, the long-serving steward, succeeded in collecting over £150 of rents and other receipts.[78]

A similar pattern of continuity was apparent at Duchess Eleanor's Monmouth estates, which were centred on Caldicot Castle. Other than a single visit by an unnamed royal escheator, the administration run by Eleanor's household clerk, John Aston, continued as before. Life changed little for Duchess Eleanor's tenants in Monmouth, who were still subjected to the rigours of Bohun marcher lordship. (At Easter 1398, her cottagers still made their gifts of hens and eggs, and her manor court contributed nearly 30 per cent of the total receipts from the lordship.) Caldicot Castle, in spite of Richard II's apparently obsessive concern for the security of the Welsh marches, remained under the control of the late duke's squire, John Clopton, and his deputies, Roger Hay and Thomas ap Ivor. In the middle of August 1398, Eleanor's stewards (John Lightfoot and Ralph Chamberlain) went on a lengthy progress through Monmouth from Caldicot to Huntington castles, collecting revenues and auditing accounts.[79] Far from retiring into widowhood, Duchess Eleanor threw herself into estate management with all the vigour of her Bohun ancestors. In the summer of 1398, her travels took her from her Essex home to her marcher estates. Stopping off at Bristol on 10 April 1398, she granted her constable of Pleshey Castle, and travelling companion, Thomas Heveningham, a £10 life annuity – perhaps as a reward for staying in her service at this difficult time.[80] On 21 July – perhaps on her return leg from the marches to Essex – she appeared before the king at Northampton, where she was granted a 1,000 mark exchequer annuity.[81]

The reality of Eleanor Bohun's unbroken tenure of many of her ancestral lands in Essex and the Welsh marches, until her death in October 1399, permits some modification of Charles Ross's view that the forfeitures of 1397 were intended to 'strike at the dependants' of the principal victims.[82] Similarly, Philippa Mortimer, widow of the executed Earl of Arundel, enjoyed a substantial dower, until her death in 1401.[83] We should also note that when Richard II took the heirs of his enemies to Ireland, as hostages, in the summer of 1399, he gave them allowances appropriate to their rank, and even knighted the future Henry V.[84]

Although there were strong incentives for established officials to cooperate with the new masters of forfeited and confiscated estates, there were also important instances of dissent and subversion. At Warwick Castle, the new master, Thomas Holand, now Duke of Surrey, was an absentee from the time of his appointment.[85] Holand had relied very heavily on the continuing services of Beauchamp officials, and it appears that he trusted them sufficiently to leave Warwick castle in their hands while he was in Ireland. Although the Beauchamp servants had cooperated with Holand, it would seem that their enduring

[78] PRO DL 29/42/815 mm.4–5 (reeve of Pleshey, 1397–8).
[79] PRO DL 29/680/11012 mm.1–2 (reeve of Caldicot, 1397–8).
[80] PRO DL 29/42/815 m.4; Goodman, *Loyal Conspiracy*, p. 97.
[81] PRO E 404/14/96/412.
[82] C. D. Ross, 'Forfeiture for Treason in the Reign of Richard II', *EHR*, lxxi (1956), p. 574.
[83] *CIPM 1399–1405*, pp. 144–50, nos. 447–70.
[84] PRO E 403/562 m.7 (2 May 1399), Henry of Monmouth, £148 15s. 9d.; Humphrey of Gloucester, £100; Thomas Mowbray, £30 10s. 4d.; Saul, *Richard II*, p. 404.
[85] *CCR 1396–1399*, p. 325.

loyalty was to their imprisoned former master. Before the Lancastrian invasion of 1399, John Daniel, the Beauchamp chamberlain, and the esquire, John Monkington, were in contact with the imprisoned Earl of Warwick on the Isle of Man. By early July 1399, Warwick castle was being held in the name of the Beauchamp earl, by a group of his servants.[86] The speed and apparent ease with which Beauchamp personnel asserted their control at Warwick in the summer of 1399 also calls into question the degree and nature of the authority that Richard II's allies enjoyed over forfeited estates. In the case of Thomas Holand at Warwick, it would seem that he had lacked the resources, or political will, or inclination to assert his lordship more forcefully.

An even more widespread and destabilising insurrection erupted on the Lancastrian estates in the summer of 1399. In the aftermath of Bolingbroke's invasion, a large number of Lancastrian officials claimed, and received, rewards for serving their lord during the revolution. In his account of the 1399 Revolution, Somerville is inclined to accept, at face value, the descriptions of resistance that are contained in the duchy records.[87] Although it is certainly the case that many of Henry's supporters did uphold the Lancastrian cause in July 1399, we may also suspect that others dramatised and exaggerated their own roles.

The more credible claims of resistance by Lancastrian officials are those which are corroborated by chroniclers, or by the central Lancastrian records. Robert Waterton, the steward of Knaresborough, brought two hundred foresters to serve Henry, when news spread of his landing at Ravenspur.[88] Similarly, Sir Thomas Wennesley, the steward of High Peak, also rushed to join his master.[89] Another case of resistance was that of Roger Smart, who claimed to have held Kenilworth castle since 2 June 1399, one day after Richard II's landing in Ireland. During his parliamentary trial in the autumn of 1399, Sir William Bagot claimed to have passed information to Henry, while in exile, and to have used Roger Smart as his messenger. Henry seems to have appreciated Smart's loyalty, as he was granted a 20 mark life annuity, in November 1399. He was later trusted with the imprisonment of the Earl of Northumberland at Baginton castle, the Warwickshire seat of Sir William Bagot (in his Lancastrian political reincarnation), in 1403.[90]

The most colourful accounts of resistance by Lancastrian officials relate to south Wales. Henry's esquires John ap Harry and Thomas Toty claimed to have held Brecon castle 'to resist the malice of King Richard, returning from Ireland through these parts', and to have dispatched a body of men to secure the castles of Carreg Cennen and Kidwelly.[91] The porter of Kidwelly is recorded as having made 'emergency purchases of 'oil and stones' for the better defence of the castle against the malice of King Richard'.[92]

[86] Warks RO CR/1886/Bloom 481, mm.1d, 3d; R. A. K. Mott, 'Richard II and the Crisis of 1397', *Church and Chronicle in the Middle Ages: Essays Presented to John Taylor*, ed. I. Wood and G. A. Loud (London, 1991), p. 176.

[87] Somerville, *Duchy of Lancaster*, i, pp. 136–7.

[88] *Chronicle of Adam Usk*, pp. 52–3.

[89] PRO DL 29/728/11988 m.9.

[90] PRO DL 42/15 f. 66v; *Great Chronicle of London*, ed. A. H. Thomas and I. D. Thornley (London, 1938), pp. 75–81; *CPR 1399–1401*, p. 72; *POPC*, i, p. 217.

[91] PRO SC 6/1157/4 m.3 (keeper of Brecon, 1398–9).

[92] PRO DL 29/584/9240 m.2 (receiver of Kidwelly, Ogmore and Ebboth lordships, 3 Feb. 1399 to 28 Sep. 1400).

However, these accounts were written up some time after the events which they purport to describe, and the time-lag may have enabled officials both to distort financial irregularities, and emphasise their own achievements in the hope of staking a claim to the avalanche of cash flowing from the duchy coffers.[93] In those duchy of Lancaster accounts examined, over £6,800 were disbursed between 1399 and 1401 to officials and retainers who had served Henry during the revolution.[94] We shall never know how many of these claims were truthful and how many were opportunistic bids designed to cash in on royal goodwill. The extent to which the well-established auditing processes were able to screen such a deluge of claims at a time of major political upheaval is, perhaps, a matter for conjecture.

What conclusions can be drawn about the control of forfeited and confiscated estates in this period? Undoubtedly, the acquisition of great estates did represent the nominal extension of royal influence into areas of the realm which may have been dominated by a hostile or uncooperative power. However, the only truly systematic effort to exploit estates for the benefit of the crown, during this period, occurred on the forfeited Arundel lordships, following their annexation to the principality of Chester. Ultimately, the oppressiveness of Richard II's rule in this region proved to be entirely counterproductive, as the principality of Chester offered negligible resistance to Henry's usurpation in July 1399.

A number of reasons can be offered for both Richard II and Henry IV's failures to exploit estates more effectively. Richard II's fragmentation of forfeited estates benefited many of his allies, but diminished the potential for their direct exploitation. As we have seen, Henry IV fared little better than Richard II, in these endeavours. Many of the most valuable estates which he controlled, especially those of the Mowbrays and Mortimers, suffered devastation during the revolt of Owain Glyn Dŵr.[95] In spite of Henry's initial commitment to retain estates for his own profit, he could hardly have foreseen the magnitude of the rebellions which he would face, and the political debts that he would incur in their suppression. Overall, the efforts of Richard II and Henry IV to exploit their control of magnate estates had a piecemeal and ad hoc character. The claims of widows and heirs, and the demands for reward by royal retainers, soon frittered away estates which had come into crown hands. It was not until the later years of Edward IV's reign that the strengthening of the financial machinery of the royal household, and the relatively unchallenged domination of the localities by the royal affinity, enabled the crown to impose effective and systematic rule over the magnate estates which it had absorbed.[96]

Throughout this period, seignorial officials exhibited a remarkable pragmatism in adapting to changed political realities. Typical of this trend were the Beauchamp and Lancastrian servants, who were able to reconcile the political necessity of bending to a change of administration, whilst covertly upholding

[93] For corruption by seignorial officials, see R. R. Davies, 'Baronial Accounts, Incomes and Arrears in the Later Middle Ages', *EcHR*, 2nd series, xxi (1968), pp. 220–6; McFarlane, *Nobility*, pp. 219–20.

[94] PRO DL 29/728/11987–90.

[95] D. Walker, *Medieval Wales* (Oxford, 1990), p. 181; Davies, *Owain Glyn Dŵr*, pp. 278–9.

[96] Ross, *Edward IV*, pp. 373–5; C. Carpenter, *The Wars of the Roses: Politics and the Constitution in England, c.1437–1509* (Cambridge, 1997), p. 200.

the interests of their absent lords. However, the case of the Lancastrian officials clamouring for reward in 1399 should make us cautious about accepting all tales of dissent and resistance. Although Ricardian loyalists such as William Scrope, John Bussy and Henry Green were prepared to give their lives for his cause, others like Simon Felbrigg, the royal standard-bearer, maintained a discreet and low profile anti-Lancastrian recusancy.[97] Still more reconciled themselves to the service of new lords, although few quite as blatantly as William Bagot, whose effigial slab sports a Lancastrian collar, with the zeal characteristic of a very recent convert.[98]

In the difficult tasks of quantifying the effects of forfeiture and other abrupt tenurial changes, of calculating funds and tracking their movements, and of judging the conduct of officials whose accounts are often our only sources for their actions, we may be sure that the bare details of tenurial change belie a more blurred and equivocal reality at ground level.

[97] A. Rogers, 'Henry IV and the Revolt of the Earls', *History Today*, 16 (1968), pp. 280–3; J. D. Milner, 'Sir Simon Felbrigg, KG: The Lancastrian Revolution and Personal Fortune', *Norfolk Archaeology*, xxxvii (1978), pp. 84–91; *Chronicles of the Revolution*, ed. C. Given-Wilson (Manchester, 1993), pp. 236–7.

[98] For an illustration, see Saul, *Richard II*, pp. 242–3.

The Knightly Household of Richard II and the Peace Commissions[1]

Shelagh Mitchell

The peace commissions of Richard II's reign are already the subject of scholarly interest. For example, it is stated that the peace commissions of 1397 were 'particularly royalist'; that 'king's supporters were appointed as Justices of the Peace in the 1390's'; or that the composition of the 1397 Norfolk commission was 'clearly intended to help establish the authority of the court'.[2] All these conclusions concern the later peace commissions. The aim of this paper therefore is to try to redress the balance and to deal with peace commissions from the inception of the reign. More specifically it is to investigate the incidence of knightly household nominations to the peace commissions and the quorum.[3] Thus research has centred on the commissions enrolled on the dorse of the patent rolls since they provide information on quorum membership which is entirely lacking from the printed calendars. In order to discover the involvement of Richard's knightly household it is necessary first to establish who they were and, in doing so, to take cognisance of the current debate concerning Ricardian household knights and the so-called 'king's knights'.

Previous scholarship places only the steward, chamberlain and chamber knights within the king's household. It also claims a sudden demise for the term 'knight of the king's household' after 1360.[4] Yet the terms *militis de hospicio nostro*, *milites de hospicio Regis* and *chivaler de nostre houstiel* were still in use in chancery and exchequer documents of 1377–99 and even later. Sometimes these documents indicate a group of household knights far in excess of the few

[1] I am grateful for all the help received from Jim Bolton, Paul Brand, John Gillingham and Philip Mitchell.

[2] A. B. Steel, *Richard II* (Cambridge, 1941) p. 234; J. R. Lander, *English Justices of the Peace 1461–1509* (Gloucester, 1989) p. 109; R. Virgoe, 'The Crown and Local Government: East Anglia under Richard II', *Reign of Richard II*, p. 238. Also Saul, *Richard II*, pp. 263–265 for the July 1389 peace commissions.

[3] Nomination was investigated since this procedure can be charted for the whole reign whereas, for example, procedures for the payment of working justices did not become effective until 1392, *Proceedings before the Justices of the Peace*, ed. B. H. Putnam (London,1938), pp. xc, xci, 129, 236, 466–7; also, ibid. p. 242. For details of the peace commissions 1377–99 and documentary references, see Shelagh Mitchell, 'Some Aspects of the Knightly Household of Richard II' (unpub. London Univ. PhD thesis, 1998), chs 7, 8 (henceforth Mitchell).

[4] Given-Wilson, *Royal Household*, p. 209; Saul, *Richard II*, pp. 332, 266. A printed use of this term can be found in *CPR 1385–1389*, pp. 62, 99, but such a designation has been disregarded, for which see Given-Wilson, *Royal Household*, pp. 209, 310, n. 29. For the argument concerning previous scholarship see Mitchell, pp. 1–8.

recorded in the wardrobe books. The existence of a larger group of Ricardian household knights must therefore be accepted.[5] Identification of this group has been a very long process and it is set out in detail elsewhere.[6] Suffice it here to say that throughout his reign, on grant-giving occasions, Richard separated a group of knights from the generality of knights through the use of a style specially reserved for them. In brief, the style contained the key words *militi nostro, nostre . . . chivaler* (our . . . knight). Such a means of identification is not unknown. For example, King John's household knights were differentiated through special terminology that included the words *milites nostri.*[7] A comparison of the documentary evidence of the Ricardian wardrobe, great wardrobe and king's remembrancer made it apparent that Richard's separated group received robes and that they were referred to collectively either as 'knights of our household' or 'our . . . knights'.[8] Moreover, these recipients numbered many more than those recorded in the wardrobe books and significantly included the steward, chamberlain and chamber knights together with other knights. Such a circumstance reveals the two components of the knightly household: the officers who were recorded in, and financed by, the wardrobe and the ordinary household knights financed principally by the exchequer. Both components however were styled with the same style: *militi nostro / nostre . . . chivaler*'; words that the printed calendars render as 'the king's knight'. It is the nomination of this whole separated household group which has been investigated here.[9]

1. July 1377 to May 1381

Richard II's first peace commissions of 2–20 July 1377 were extensive, covering twenty-nine counties[10] with further issues and 'associations' made between August 1377 and June 1378.[11] During this whole period seven household knights were named to seven counties and one liberty. None were named to the quorum.[12]

[5] For details, see Mitchell, Appendix Ic, pp. 298–9.

[6] Mitchell, pp. 1–69; 233–7; Appendix I, pp. 239–92. For the disparity of numbers recorded in the wardrobe and great wardrobe, see ibid. pp. 52–4.

[7] S. Church, 'The Knights of the Household of King John: A Question of Numbers', *Thirteenth Century England*, iv (Woodbridge, 1992), p. 152, n. 10.

[8] For example 'vyngt et quatre noz chivalers', PRO E 159/156, brevia, Trin. 3 Ric. II, rot. xxvii; 60 pieces of red and black velvet for the household knights: 'pur le iour de lan a chivalers de nostre houstel', E 159/158, brevia, Trin. 5 Ric. II rot.vid. I am grateful to David Grummitt for drawing my attention to this source. See also Mitchell, p. 303.

[9] Numbers varied from year to year, see ibid. ch. 4, Appendix I. I am grateful to Philip Mitchell for his considerable help on the problem of numbers.

[10] To twenty-six counties and York, 2 July; to Bucks and Middx, 6 July; to Northumberland, 20 July, PRO C 66/297 mm.19d, 20d. Reissues were to Kingston-upon-Hull (Aug.), Coventry (Sep.), Ripon, Holland (Lincs), Berks, Norf., Wilts, West Riding, Dorset, Hunts, Corn. and Shrewsbury (Dec.), C 66/297 mm.19d, 18d, 3d. 'Associations' were made to Herts (Oct.), Dors. and Wilts (Dec.), C 66/297 m.5d; C 66/298 m.6d.

[11] Further issues in Jan., Feb., Mar., May and June 1378 to Rut., Berks, Corn., Som., Middx, Northants., North Riding, PRO C 66/297 m.18d; C 66/298 m.6d; and to Here. and Cambs, C 66/301 m.16d. Rut. and North Riding each had two commissions. Associations' were made to the North Riding, Derby. and Oxon Feb., April and May 1378, C 66/298 m.6d; C 66/299 m.7d; C 66/301 m.28d.

[12] This first peace commission further reveals nine future household knights amongst whom were

In the second year, two of the justices named on the continuing commissions for Staffordshire and Devonshire were given membership of the knightly household. Also in this year new commissions of the peace were issued to five counties between 28 June 1378 and January 1379, but the nomination of a household knight can only be found in Cornwall.[13] Thus in the first two regnal years, the nomination of household knights to the peace commissions was scarce and household knights were never named to the quorum. New peace commissions were issued to thirty-one counties on 26 May 1380; these included separate issues to the three divisions of Lincolnshire and Yorkshire. At that time eleven household knights were named to ten counties and one city.[14] In August 1380 and the months following, new peace commissions were issued to fifteen counties and 'associations' were made right up till 28 May 1381, the 'eve' of the Peasants' Revolt. Four knightly household members were nominated to four counties and one was added by association.[15]

2. The immediate aftermath of the Peasants' Revolt

Immediately following the Peasants' Revolt special commissions to keep the peace and deal with the rebels as well as to forbid unlawful assemblies were issued from June 1381 to December 1382.[16] A total of forty, or 56 per cent of the knightly household, were nominated to nearly all the counties which received a commission between June 1381 and March 1382.[17] In October 1382 a further peace commission concerning the Kentish rebels was issued to eight southern and eastern counties. Three justices only were named, one of whom was John Montagu specifically identified as the steward of the king's household and, as such, named to the quorum for the hearing and determining of cases in all the counties issued with a commission. That this was an exceptional role for the steward was recognised since the enabling clause stated that nothing from this commission was to accrue to the office of steward of the household.[18] The commissions of array with power to punish the rebels issued in July 1382 also named a household knight to the quorum: John Roches in Hampshire/ Wiltshire. Nomination to the quorum on all the other commissions immediately

four future sheriffs: John Beauchamp, John Beaumont, Ralph Ferrers, John Kentwode, Walter atte Lee, John Montagu, James Pickering, Robert Turk and John atte Wood. The future sheriffs were Pickering, Turk, atte Lee, and atte Wood, ibid. chs.6, 7, 8.

13 To Oxon (June), East Riding and Suff. (July), Corn. and Isle of Wight (Aug.). In Jan. 1379 John Kentwode was added to the Cornish peace commission by the Treasurer, PRO C 66/303 m.43d; see details, Mitchell, p. 141.

14 PRO C 66/307 mm.11d, 12d, 13d; C 66/308 mm.31d, 32d, 33d. Future household knights named in May and Aug. 1380 were John Beauchamp, Edward Dalyngridge, William Elys, Henry Green, John Montagu, Robert Straunge, Robert Turk, Robert Whitteneye and John atte Wood.

15 Mitchell, p. 142, n. 48.

16 Magnates as well as prelates and abbots were now nominated to the leadership; mayors and bailiffs of towns were included, PRO C 66/311 m.4d; C 66/312 mm.20d, 21d, 22d. These commissions had powers not only of keeping the peace but also of arrest, imprisonment, suppressing meetings and of determining.

17 Except Surr./Suss., Cambs/Hunts, Cambs/Herts/Essex which did not have a household knight nominated.

18 PRO C 66/311 m.20d.

following the Peasants' Revolt presents a problem since the quorum was stated numerically and not by name.[19] Nevertheless, in the immediate aftermath of the Peasants' Revolt there was a fourfold increase in the number of household knights nominated to the special peace commissions and for the first time quorum membership was assigned to two household knights.

3. 1382: 20 December (normal) and 21 December (extraordinary) peace commissions

Peace commissions were next issued on two consecutive days in 1382: 20 and 21 December. The former were normal peace commissions while the latter can be seen as an extraordinary issue. Both however gave justices their usual powers, including that of determining felonies, and both issues have already been dealt with in previous scholarship.[20] Comparisons reveal that while many of the names were common to these two issues, the extraordinary commissions of 21 December named twice as many household knights: thirty-eight were nominated to twenty-five counties and twenty-four were on the quorum of seventeen counties. In contrast, figures for the normal peace commissions of 20 December show the nomination of only nineteen household knights to eighteen counties with nine on the quorum of eleven counties. The extraordinary commissions thus nominated household knights in seven additional counties and had two and a half times the number of household knights on the quorum. However, this was to be the last extraordinary issue after the Peasants' Revolt and thereafter only normal or general peace commissions were issued.

4. Peace commissions from March 1383 until December 1387

Three months later, in March 1383, peace commissions were reissued to three counties and to the North Riding and three household knights were named.[21] Also, four 'associations' were made in March and April 1383 when a household knight was added to the Kesteven commission.[22] From July 1383 to June 1384 peace commissions were again issued, this time to eleven counties, and associations were made to ten counties. Eleven household knights were at that time named in seven counties but none were added by 'association'. At that time too, five counties each named a household knight to the quorum and significantly this number included Montagu and Burley, the steward and the sub-chamberlain.[23] Overall, knightly household nominations were not as high

[19] Stated as any 17, 16, etc. down to 3. A justice of one of the benches was required to be on the quorum, e.g. Robert Belknap in Kent, PRO C 66/312 mm.20d, 21d, 22d.

[20] For details, see J. B. Post, 'The Peace Commissions of 1382', *EHR*, xci (1976), pp. 98–101. Post uses the terms 'general' and 'extraordinary' whereas the present work uses 'normal' and 'extraordinary' for the Dec. 1382 commissions. Prof. Saul kindly supplied this reference.

[21] Cumb., Leics, Northants and North Riding. No household knight was named to the Leics commission.

[22] This was Ankatel Mallore, see Mitchell, pp. 155, 202, 203.

[23] Abberbury, Montagu, Gilbert Talbot, atte Lee and Simon Burley; Abberbury demonstrates

as those on the special commissions following the Peasants' Revolt, but they were higher than those of July 1377 and household knights were now also named to the quorum. New peace commissions were then issued to twelve counties between September 1384 and May 1385. This new issue named nine household knights in six counties.[24] It also named five household knights to the quorum of four counties and, again, amongst these were Montagu and Burley, the steward and sub-chamberlain.[25] Moreover, Kent received an additional household knight on its quorum, the future steward John Devereux. At this time also, the role of the household was strengthened in Cornwall, which received three commissions. Kentwode was nominated on the first; a week later there was a second issue when he was named to the quorum. Two months later there was yet another issue to Cornwall which still named Kentwode to the quorum. These commissions also reveal the nomination of six future household knights, including John Bussy and Edward Dalyngridge, both at some time Appellant supporters.[26]

In the next regnal year seventeen counties, one city and the county of Bristol received peace commissions between 26 June 1385 and 26 May 1386. Seventeen household knights were nominated to ten of these counties and seven counties had a household knight on the quorum.[27] All these commissions, except for one, were issued after the Scottish expedition with its crop of new household knights when John Beauchamp, Kennard de la Bere, John Cifrewas and Arnald Savage were given knightly household membership. All four were usual nominees to the peace commissions and now they appeared on these new issues for their normal counties, Worcestershire, Herefordshire, Berkshire and Kent respectively. However, because all these counties already had household knights nominated to them, there was no net increase in the household representation.[28] The most noticeable difference on this issue however was the presence of John Lovell on the Wiltshire commission in addition to the ones for Oxfordshire and Berkshire. One household knight was thus being named in a diversity of counties. During the next year new commissions were issued to seven counties and associations made to two between 28 June 1386 and 28 April 1387.[29] Otherwise existing issues remained in force. Household knights were only nominated to Kent, Suffolk and Leicestershire. Such nominations were not unusual in the first two counties, but they were unusual in Leicestershire, where John Beaumont was now named.[30] This was the first occasion

someone named to two counties but to the quorum of only one. Talbot was later removed from the Hereford quorum.

[24] Counted amongst this number is Hugh Despenser, for whose status see Mitchell, p. 149, n. 76.

[25] Another household officer, Thomas Morreux, master of the king's horse, was named to Beds. Both Burley and Morreux were at that time in receipt of fees and robes as chamber knights, PRO E101/401/2 f. 42, 30 Sep. 1384 to 30 Sep. 1385.

[26] The others were William Lisle, James Pickering, Arnald Savage and John Wadham, a lawyer who was possibly a special case. Pickering was also an experienced local administrator having served on the shrievalty, Mitchell, pp. 197–8, ch. 6 *passim*.

[27] Abberbury was on the quorum of two counties, Berks and Oxon.

[28] Ibid. ch. 7, tables 4b, 6.

[29] However, the cities of Coventry and York, as well as the liberties of the bishopric of Durham received peace commissions, PRO C 66/322 mm.46d, 47d.

[30] He received robes in year two and later, as warden of the West March, was paid within the chamber. For the July peace commissions to Leics, cf. PRO C 81/1352/17 and C 66/322 m.47; also

when a household knight was named to the normal peace commissions of Leicestershire, which was not only within the Lancastrian sphere of influence, but also within the joint shrievalty of Leicestershire/Warwickshire, where Thomas Beauchamp, Earl of Warwick and future Appellant, was sheriff for life. Beaumont however was no ordinary household knight but also a member of the peerage with local landed interests.[31] On this issue, one household knight was named to the quorum.

In the following regnal year, six counties received peace commissions between 8 July and 6 December 1387.[32] A household knight was named in each of four counties and two were on the quorum. By this time, 1387, Richard's knightly household had doubled from an initial thirty-nine to seventy-eight.[33] He was in control of patronage and dispensed many grants to his knights, even making John Salisbury sheriff of Wiltshire for life.[34] He also made extraordinary grants of office and title to Robert de Vere.[35] These activities manifested Richard's 'ascendancy', but they also brought about the November 1386 commission to investigate the household. Yet even at the time of his ascendancy, Richard's household knights were not nominated to the peace commissions of Derbyshire, Gloucestershire, Shropshire, Staffordshire, Surrey, Sussex, Warwickshire and Yorkshire.[36] In 1387 therefore, on the eve of the battle of Radcot Bridge, Richard's sphere of influence did not extend to the Fitzalan territories or to the Lancastrian or the Beauchamp areas.[37] His influence in Woodstock territory was marginal, exercised sporadically through the household knight Aubrey de Vere, one time vice-chamberlain, who was sometimes on the quorum of Essex and sometimes not. Neither did Richard's influence extend to those parts of Mowbray's Sussex lands which abutted Fitzalan territory.[38] The new commissions issued between July and December 1387 did not change this situation. This was a limited issue but unusually there was one for Middlesex, its first since 20 December 1382.[39] On the new issue Baldwin Raddington, the controller of the household, was named. Raddington

Mitchell, p. 105, n. 106; S. K. Walker, 'Yorkshire Justices of the Peace', *EHR*, cviii (1993), pp. 281–311.

[31] *CIPM 1377–1399*, xvii, pp. 284–91. For his household designation, see Mitchell, Appendix Ia.

[32] PRO C 66/324 m.32d.

[33] Mitchell, p. 77.

[34] Notably to John Golofre (II), Thomas Clifford, William Neville, James Berners, John Beauchamp of Holt and Simon Burley, see Mitchell, Appendix I, years 9, 10. Salisbury's office was granted by signet, ibid., Appendix I, n. 117.

[35] For which, see S. Mitchell, 'Kingship and the Cult of Saints', *The Regal Image of Richard II and the Wilton Diptych*, ed. D. Gordon, L. Monnas, C. Elam (London, 1998), pp. 117–18.

[36] Although John Worth had been nominated to Derby. and Donald Haselrigg to Yorks on 20 Dec. 1382.

[37] For the isolated case of Leics, see Mitchell, ch. 7 table 9. For this purpose, Henry Bolingbroke's sphere of influence is considered within the wider Lancastrian sphere; the Fitzalan territories encompass Suss./Surr. and also Salop.

[38] Like Bramber (Suss.), which takes on an added significance since Mowbray was married to Fitzalan's daughter. His other lands were scattered and his grandmother, Margaret, still enjoyed dower rights. See *Westminster Chronicle*, p. 89 and n. 2 with references therein; A. Goodman, *The Loyal Conspiracy* (London, 1971), p. 159.

[39] Chief Justice of the Common Bench Robert Belknap headed this commission, PRO C 66/324 m.32d. He was one of the judges who replied to Richard's questions concerning the validity of the 1386 commission.

was responsible for the military side of the household.[40] Significantly, before the battle of Radcot Bridge in December 1387, the Appellant forces mustered and set forth from Haringey in Middlesex.[41]

5. The Appellants' regime

It is very noticeable that widespread peace commissions were not issued at the inception of the Appellants' rule. Nor were they issued in the spring of 1388, prior to Burley's execution, when a Kentish uprising was rumoured.[42] Instead, in July 1388, the Appellants issued commissions to just five counties, Bedfordshire, Cornwall, Norfolk, Northamptonshire and Shropshire. As a consequence, thirty-five separate peace commissions covering thirty-one counties remained in force.[43] Of the new Appellant issues, the one for Cornwall removed John Kentwode from the quorum, but not from the commission. In Norfolk, Stephen Hales continued on the commission and in Northamptonshire, William Thorp not only remained, but was also named to the quorum. In Bedfordshire, in contrast to the previous commission of April 1385, there was no household knight named probably due to the absence of Thomas Morreux, first through membership of John of Gaunt's Spanish expedition and then through death. The Appellant Lords did not issue new commissions or 'associations' to Kent after Simon Burley's execution and, surprisingly, the June 1386 commission remained in force, even though Burley had both headed this and been on the quorum. The commissions which remained in force named twenty-one household knights including Baldwin Raddington, the king's controller. Indeed if the new and continuing commissions are taken together, the names of twenty-four household knights can be found. These include Richard Abberbury, Robert Bardolf, John Beaumont, John Lovell, Aubrey de Vere and John Worth all of whom the Appellants ordered to abjure the court.

Conclusions: 1377–99

From this summary it becomes obvious that following the Peasants' Revolt nomination of household knights rose substantially. The years 1389–99 have also been investigated but they are not here given in detail, only in table form. However, the research for the second half of the reign was carried out in the same detail and from the same documents as the early reign.[44] Both halves of the reign have therefore been subjected to the same type of analysis. Central to

[40] 'Already in 1386 Raddington had begun that development of the military side of the household which gives to his controllership a special place in administrative history', T. F. Tout, *Chapters in the Administrative History of Medieval England*, 6 vols. (Manchester, 1928–37), iv, p. 198.
[41] *Westminster Chronicle*, pp. 210–11, 222–3, n. 3.
[42] Tuck, *Richard II*, p. 126.
[43] Although the Earl of Arundel held a commission of trailbaston in Wales in Feb. 1389, *Westminster Chronicle*, p. 383; *Rot. Parl.*, iii, pp. 286, 302 for the Commons' 1391 petition that no further inquiries of trailbaston or general eyres be held. Also, Tuck, *Richard II*, pp. 150, 151, n. 1.
[44] Mitchell, pp. 136–69, ch. 8.

this analysis are two types of calculation. These calculations are meant to answer specific questions; they do not duplicate the figures or analysis given in the sections above. The first calculation deals with the question of the percentage of knightly household justices relative to non-household justices on *new* issues of the peace commissions. This is done for July 1377 to June 1389 (Table 2), and for July 1389 to 1399 (Table 3). The critical factor in this calculation has been to discover the knightly household nominations in each and every county. If a man was named to more than one county he has been counted amongst the personnel of *all* those counties.[45] The number of household knights on these new commissions has then been calculated as a percentage of all the named justices. The second type of calculation deals with the question of the number of knightly household justices expressed as a percentage of the total knightly household.[46] Again, this is done for July 1377 to June 1389 (Table 4), and for July 1389 to 1399 (Table 5). The object of this particular calculation is to discover what proportion of the knightly household was named on *new and continuing* peace commissions, year by year throughout the reign. Thus individual household knights have only been counted once no matter how many counties they were named to. The aim of both types of calculation is to try to determine any patterns and how these changed over the reign.

Table 2 shows that in 1377 knightly household nomination to the peace commissions was 3 per cent of total nominations on all *new* commissions, but that it more than doubled to 8 per cent in the special commissions issued just after the Peasants' Revolt – June 1381 to March 1382. In December 1382 there were two peace commissions issued and the extraordinary commission of 21 December shows a higher figure, 7 per cent, as compared with 5 per cent for the normal commission of 20 December. Yet the normal peace commissions now show a higher figure than at any time before the Peasants' Revolt. In fact, July 1377 to May 1381 shows a constant 3 per cent, while the figure for June 1381 to the end of the Appellants' regime is doubled to an average 6 per cent. Yet Table 2 goes on to show that the period June 1381 to March 1382 witnessed a massive leap in the number of all justices nominated to new peace commissions – 185 to 1,203. Such a quantitative leap in numbers only serves to highlight the significance of the increase in the proportion of knightly household nominations to these commissions during this same period: 3 per cent to 8 per cent. Table 2 further shows that in the period from 1382 to the end of the Appellants' regime, the percentage never again fell to the low levels of 1377–81. Table 3 shows that at Richard's reassertion in 1389 household knights were 5 per cent of all the named justices on new peace commissions; that this continued in 1390, the only occasion in the reign when the justices were named in Parliament and not by the Council; that this rose to 11 per cent in the penultimate year of the reign; and that this increased to 16 per cent in the last year, 1399. Thus again the percentage of knightly household justices to all other justices on new commissions continued, with the one exception of 1394/5, to exceed the low figures of 1377–81.

The second calculation again splits the reign and this time seeks to discover

[45] The word 'county' comprehends the ridings of Yorks and parts of Lincs.
[46] Mitchell, fig. 2a, p. 77.

Table 2. Knightly household (KH) justices (JPs) as a percentage of all justices named on new peace commissions, 1377–89*

Regnal year	*Date of commission*	*KH JPs*	*All JPs*	%
1.	July 1377–June 1378	14	513	3
2.	June 1378–Jan 1379	2	63	3
3.	May–June 1380	11	411	3
4.	Aug 1380–May 1381	5	185	3
5.	June 1381–Mar 1382	99	1203	8
6.	21 Dec 1382 (extraordinary)	47	646	7
6.	20 Dec 1382 (normal)	23	470	5
7.	July 1383–June 1384	14	231	6
8.	Sept 1384–May 1385	11	179	6
9.	June 1385–May 1386	21	297	7
10.	June 1386–April 1387	4	103	4
11.	July–Dec 1387	4	65	6
12.	July 1388: The Appellants	3	56	5

* Including 'associations'. Dec. 1382 (year six) saw two commissions issued: a normal peace commission of 20 Dec. and an extraordinary one of 21 Dec.; see n. 20 above.

Table 3. Knightly household (KH) justices (JPs) as a percentage of all justices named on new peace commissions, 1389–99

Regnal year	*Date of commission*	*KH JPs*	*All JPs*	%
13.	July; Dec 1389	30	598	5
14.	June; Dec 1390	31	680	5
15.	Nov 1391–May 1392	10	145	7
16.	Sept 1392–May 1393	7	89	8
17.	Oct 1393–June 1394	19	384	5
18.	July 1394–May 1395	1	64	2
19.	July 1395–June 1396	5	70	7
20.	June 1396–June 1397	12	180	7
21.	July 1397–June 1398	72	650	11
22.	Aug 1398–June 1399	27	169	16

two things: the proportion of the knightly household nominated to new and continuing peace commissions and the number of counties in which they were nominated. This is shown on Tables 4 and 5. An initial involvement of 18 per cent of the knightly household can be seen from Table 4. It also shows that this figure dips only to rise dramatically in the crisis period following the Peasants' Revolt when 56 per cent of the knightly household were named on the new and continuing peace commissions. In the following year, 1382, when there were both normal and extraordinary peace commissions, 52 per cent of the knightly household were nominated to the extraordinary commissions whereas 26 per cent were nominated to the normal commissions. From Table 4 it is also clear that the proportion of the knightly household nominated to normal commissions in the period December 1382 to June 1389 never fell below 26 per cent. In contrast, Table 5 makes it abundantly clear that in the second half of the reign, July 1389 to 1399, such a proportion never reached 26 per cent until the period

Table 4. Proportion of the knightly household (KH) named on new and continuing peace commissions, July 1377–June 1389: number of counties to which household knights were named†

Regnal year	*No. in KH*	*KH on comms.*	%	*(no. of counties)*
1.	39	7	18	(7)
2.	63	9	14	(8)
3.	78	11	14	(10)
4.	69	11	16	(10)
5.	71	40	56	(28)
6.	73	38	52	(25) *
6.		19	26	(18) +
7.	73	25	34	(21)
8.	71	27	38	(22)
9.	84	24	29	(18)
10.	78	23	29	(19)
11.	79	24	30	(20)
12.	73	24	33	(19)

* denotes extraordinary commissions
+ denotes normal commissions
† Year six features the 'extraordinary' commission of 21 Dec. and the 'normal' of 20 Dec. 1382; see n. 20 above.

Table 5. Proportion of the knightly household (KH) named to new and continuing peace commissions, July 1389–1399; number of counties to which household knights were named

Regnal year	*No. in KH*	*KH on comms.*	%	*(no. of counties)*
13.	72	15	21	(15)
14.	75	19	25	(16)
15.	82	19	23	(16)
16.	77	16	21	(15)
17.	82	12	15	(12)
18.	87	13	15	(13)
19.	83	15	18	(14)
20.	81	17	21	(16)
21.	87	26	30	(33)
22.	85	25	29	(31)
23.	83	25	30	(31)

June 1397 to 1399. Even more striking is the fact that following the Peasants' Revolt, more than 50 per cent of the knightly household was nominated to the special peace commissions. Further, for the years 1382 to 1399 the average proportion of the knightly household nominated to the new and continuing peace commissions remained almost double the average for the years 1377–81.

Tables 4 and 5 also highlight the geographic spread of knightly household nominations to the peace commissions. Table 3 shows that at the inception of the reign they were named to seven counties and that this rose to ten by June 1380 and peaked at twenty-eight in the special peace commissions immediately following the Peasants' Revolt. Thus, after the Peasants' Revolt the number of counties with knightly household nominations more than doubled. By June 1389, household knights were named to an average of nineteen counties although they were not normally named to Appellant counties. Table 5 shows the situation for the second half of the reign, July 1389 to 1399. This period began with nomination to the lesser number of fifteen counties and this rate continued on average until June 1397 when it more than doubled to thirty-three and then fell to thirty-one for the remainder of the reign. Therefore, Table 5 also suggests that nomination to an increased number of counties could not be achieved until the senior Appellants had been crushed and their lands redistributed.

The analysis undertaken in this paper strongly points to the Peasants' Revolt as being the initial determining factor in increasing knightly household nominations to the peace commissions. Yet it might be argued that such an increase was the normal governmental response to a situation of social unrest.[47] This is very possibly true and it could account for the fact that the proportion of the knightly household named to new and continuing commissions in the aftermath of the Peasants' Revolt jumped by a massive 250 per cent. It could also explain why, on new commissions, the proportion of knightly household justices compared to all other justices rose by 167 per cent. Yet it cannot account for what happened in 1382 and the years following when the proportion of knightly household nominations continued at a significantly higher level than at any time before the Peasants' Revolt. This is true for the whole of the rest of the reign with the exception of 1394/5, the time of Richard's first Irish expedition. Thus it would seem that an initiative taken in 1381, at a time of grave social unrest, was largely continued for the remainder of the reign, 1382–99.

What should now be stressed is that Tables 4 and 5 show, unequivocally, that 1389–99 was not the period when the greatest proportion of household knights was nominated to the normal peace commissions; nor indeed was it 1397–9. Instead the greatest proportion of household knights nominated to the peace commissions had occurred during the period June 1381 to June 1389 while year eight, 1384/5, showed the zenith of their nomination to the normal peace commissions. When median percentages are considered, the first half of the reign similarly shows a greater proportion of the knightly household nominated to the peace commissions: 29 per cent as opposed to 21 per cent for the later part of the reign. Also, October 1382 to June 1389 was the only period in the reign when household knights were named to the quorum. Thus, 1397–9 must not be seen as the period that instigated a strategy for control of the localities through the peace commissions; that had already been put into practice immediately following the Peasants' Revolt. From all the data presented it is possible to suggest that the strategy to nominate an increasing number of household knights to the peace commissions received its impetus from the Peasants' Revolt and that this lesson, once learnt, was not forgotten. That Richard had such a strategy is indicated by the accumulation of evidence from nominations to new and continuing peace commissions; from the intake into

[47] I am grateful to Professor N. Saul for this point.

the knightly household of experienced local administrators;[48] from nominations of household knights to the shrievalty, a pivotal office of local government;[49] from their simultaneous nominations to the shrievalty and the peace commissions; and from their eventual geographical spread into Appellant territories. Not all circumstances have been dealt with in this paper but all indicate the growing intensity of Richard's strategy for control of the localities.[50]

This paper commenced with certain well-accepted statements which singled out the years 1397–9 as the time when 'king's supporters' were nominated to the peace commissions. However, it has now been demonstrated that this process was even more marked in the earlier reign. Moreover, it has been shown that these 'supporters' were none other than members of the knightly household.[51] This is true for the 1390s and it is true for the early reign. In this respect, therefore, Richard was doing nothing new in the peace commissions of the 1390s. Instead, he was continuing a practice begun in the early reign and significantly strengthened after the Peasants' Revolt. Furthermore, members of the knightly household only had quorum membership from October 1382 to June1389 and on this count also the early reign should be singled out. The nomination of the same small group of the knightly household in an increasing number of counties is well known from previous studies of the 1397–9 peace commissions. What is possibly not so well known is that such an action set aside the precedence accorded to the usual noble justices. This must be seen as an overtly political act designed to interfere with, to control or to manipulate local politics and loyalties.[52] Actions such as these were amongst the novelties of the later peace commissions – not the knightly household nominations which were well established by 1397. Indeed, such an established practice provided an acceptable framework within which Richard could develop any further strategies for the localities. Thus, in the matter of knightly household nominations to the peace commissions, the two halves of Richard's reign have a certain unity that has previously been overlooked.

[48] For example after the Scots campaign, John Cifrewas and Arnald Savage; 1390, James Pickering a northern sheriff and justice; 1391, Edward Dalyngridge regularly named to the Suss. peace commissions; 1392, John Bussy, an experienced sheriff and justice from Lincs. 1393, Robert Whitteneye, a former sheriff of Here. 1396, Henry Green and William Bagot named to the peace commissions of Northants and Warks respectively and Robert Legh, then sheriff of Ches.; Mitchell, chs.7, 8, 9, and pp. 168, 199, 218–19.

[49] First initiated in Richard II's reign in 1382, Mitchell, ch. 6.

[50] Neither has this paper dealt with the nomination of household esquires, a subject that demands a separate investigation. Professor Tuck has already remarked upon Richard's supervision of local government through the peace commissions, Tuck, *Richard II*, p. 201.

[51] There was no concentration solely on the chamber.

[52] Mitchell, chs. 9, 10 *passim*.

The Earl of Warwick and the Royal Affinity in the Politics of the West Midlands, 1389–1399[1]

Alison Gundy

In May 1389, Richard II reasserted his right to the executive power which had been stripped from him in the political crisis of 1386–8.[2] Recent interpretations of the politics of the 1390s have tended to focus on Richard's novel formation of a royal affinity and its role in bolstering his coercive capabilities. Given-Wilson in 1986 and Saul in 1998 have argued that Richard's policy was a direct reaction to his inability in 1387–8 either to raise an armed force or to enforce the royal will, which left him at the mercy of the magnates. Following the suggestion first made by Tuck, they have interpreted the establishment of a magnate-style royal affinity from 1389 to 1397 as a successful attempt to counter the problem of asserting the king's rule in the localities. By tapping the growing power of the gentry, they have argued, Richard could communicate his policies more effectively and, if necessary, raise an armed force with which to defend himself.[3] Although it is generally agreed that the narrowing of Richard's retaining policy to the Cheshiremen in 1397–9 caused widespread alienation and contributed to his downfall, the inevitability of Richard's deposition has been questioned by Given-Wilson who has argued that, had Richard been in England in 1399 to lead his affinity in person, Bolingbroke would have faced much sterner resistance. In 1990, Barron even suggested that Richard was not a tyrant at all, and that his deposition was the result of a combination of bad luck and political naivety.[4]

The current interpretation of Richard's rule rests on dual assumptions. First, that a royal affinity could operate in exactly the same manner as a magnate's. Second, that Richard was in such a position of weakness in relation to his subjects that he could not rely automatically on their support and obedience, but had to buy it with retaining fees, offices and grants of land. Both these assumptions have come under scrutiny in other contexts. Castor has shown that the Lancastrian kings struggled to be both a private lord of men and the public king of all. Once the king had his own affinity, he had to consider the interests of his retainers, but at the same time he had to be the supreme arbiter

[1] I would like to thank Dr Christine Carpenter for her advice on this paper.

[2] T. Walsingham, *Historia Anglicana*, ii, ed. H. T. Riley, Rolls Series (1863), p. 181; *Historia Vitae et Regni Ricardi Secundi*, ed. G. B. Stow (Pennsylvania, 1977), pp. 121–2; *Foedera*, iii, pp. 37–8.

[3] Tuck, *Richard II*, pp. 149, 180–1; Given-Wilson, *Royal Household*, pp. 212–17; Saul, *Richard II*, pp. 261–9.

[4] Given-Wilson, *Royal Household*, pp. 222–6, 251; Saul, *Richard II*, pp. 393–4; C. M. Barron, 'The Deposition of Richard II', *Politics and Crisis in Fourteenth Century England*, ed. J. Taylor and W. Childs (Stroud, 1990), pp. 136–8, 145.

for all his subjects. As a result, his two roles were often irreconcilable, and the result was local instability.[5] It seems that the situation under the early Lancastrians could also be applicable to the 1390s. In Richard's case, the favouritism he showed to his retainers was intentional, though the adverse effects were the same.

The second assumption, often implied rather than stated, that Richard was in a position of weakness compared to his subjects, also needs reassessment. By concentrating on the king's dispersal of patronage as a key element of his success or failure, late medieval historians have begun to assume that the loyalty of the king's subjects needed to be bought. This approach stems from the notion that the late medieval monarchy was inherently weak, and that a royal affinity was the best solution to this weakness, since it was able to transmit royal power to the localities more effectively. This policy, it is argued, culminated in the success stories of Edward IV and the Tudor monarchs.[6] But the polity of the late fifteenth century was rather different from that of the 1390s. Should it be assumed therefore that what worked for the Yorkist and Tudor monarchs could be as effective for Richard II?[7] Moreover, were medieval kings always helpless in the face of their subjects' recalcitrance, and was a royal affinity a logical necessity? With these questions in mind, it is necessary to consider briefly the historiography of the localities.

There has been considerable debate concerning the relative power of nobility and gentry in the localities.[8] Whilst some historians have emphasised the independence of the gentry, others have shown the importance of noble rule in the localities.[9] These conflicting interpretations are highly relevant to an

[5] H. R. Castor, 'The Duchy of Lancaster in the Lancastrian Polity, 1399–1461' (unpub. Cambridge Univ. Ph.D. thesis, 1993), pp. 2–24, 203–28, 324–6; E. Powell, *Kingship, Law and Society: Criminal Justice in the Reign of Henry V* (Oxford, 1989), pp. 168–77, 189–94, 208–28.

[6] The modern emphasis on patronage stems from some aspects of the work of McFarlane, for example in McFarlane, *Nobility*, p. 119. The apotheosis of the use of patronage as an interpretative tool remains A. Tuck, 'Richard II's System of Patronage', *Reign of Richard II*, pp. 1–20. Given-Wilson, *Royal Household*, pp. 213–15, assumes that Richard was powerless in 1387–8 because he did not have an affinity on which to call. D. Starkey, 'The Age of the Household: Politics, Society and the Arts, *c.*1350–*c.*1550', *Context of English Literature*, ed. S. Medcalf, pp. 268–71, 273–4; Ross, *Edward IV*, pp. 312–13, 322–3; Saul, *Richard II*, pp. 440–1.

[7] Carpenter, *Locality and Polity*, pp. 597–614, who argues that civil war led to a decrease in noble influence locally, and increasing royal control; Watts, *Henry VI*, pp. 39–57.

[8] For recent critiques of patronage see: E. Powell, 'After "After McFarlane": The Poverty of Patronage and the Case for Constitutional History', *Trade, Devotion and Governance: Papers in Later Medieval History*, ed. D. J. Clayton, R. G. Davies and P. McNiven (Stroud, 1994), pp. 4–6 M. C. Carpenter, 'Political and Constitutional History: Before and After McFarlane', *The McFarlane Legacy*, ed. R. H. Britnell and A. J. Pollard (Stroud, 1995), pp. 186–93; Watts, *Henry VI*, pp. 1–11.

[9] For the argument that the gentry were more or less independent from the nobility: G. G. Astill, 'The Medieval Gentry: A Study in Leicestershire Society, 1350–99' (unpub. Birmingham Univ. Ph.D. thesis, 1977), pp. 207–30; N. Saul, *Knights and Esquires: The Gloucestershire Gentry in the Fourteenth Century* (Oxford, 1981), pp. 101–2; S. M. Wright, *The Derbyshire Gentry in the Fifteenth Century* (Derbyshire Record Society, viii, 1983), pp. 62–6, 143–4; S. Payling, *Political Society in Lancastrian England: The Greater Gentry of Nottinghamshire* (Oxford, 1991), pp. 1–18, 99–100, 104–8. For the alternative point of view: M. Cherry, 'The Courtenay Earls of Devon: The Formation and Disintegration of a Late-Medieval Aristocratic Affinity', *Southern History*, i (1979), pp. 71–89; S. K. Walker, *Lancastrian Affinity 1361–99* (Oxford, 1990), pp. 235–61 (with reservations); Carpenter, *Locality and Polity*, pp. 281–91; 'Gentry and Community in Medieval England', *Journal of British Studies*, xxxiii (1994), pp. 340–80.

understanding of Richard II's policy in the 1390s. Whilst Tuck emphasised the importance of the relationship between king and nobility, Given-Wilson and Saul have moved towards an interpretation which stresses the power of the gentry. By arguing that Richard needed to exploit the local influence of the gentry to create his own power base as a counter to the magnates, they imply that the nobility were not the natural supporters of the king.[10] A close examination of Richard's own attitude towards his magnates reveals a rather different picture. Far from attempting to base his rule solely on gentry support, Richard was well aware of the power his magnates possessed, and, in the 1390s attempted to harness it in novel ways. The king recognised that whilst the gentry had considerable landed power between them, the nobles were still vital to local government because their lands were concentrated in particular localities. What he failed to appreciate was that his subjects' loyalty and obedience was normally given freely: it did not need to be extracted or bought. Under normal circumstances the king was an integral part of the polity as the ultimate source of good order and sound government.[11] The unusual events of 1386–8 had created an equally unusual relationship between Richard and his subjects. Armed rebellion was not the norm in fourteenth-century politics, but Richard forfeited the support of his subjects through his actions in 1386–8 and forced many of them into taking sides.[12] The rising of the Appellants against Richard unfortunately broke the bond of trust and cooperation which bound king and nobles together. The politics of the 1390s were informed by the events of 1386–8, as Richard sought the security he had lost.

If Richard's actions in 1386–8 demonstrated his incomprehension of the polity, his policies in the 1390s show that his experiences had only exacerbated his lack of understanding. On the one hand, he attempted to build up support through his affinity. On the other hand, he was also intent on undermining and destroying the local power and influence of those outside his affinity, as the case of the Appellant Earl of Warwick will show. He did this using a wide range of resources; resort to judicial procedures outside the common law; rhetoric; bolstering alternative sources of lordship in a locality through grants of land and office; and through partiality to the members of his affinity. These policies, and Warwick's reactions to them, were conditioned by the differing geopolitical circumstances in the West Midlands, here defined as Warwickshire and Worcestershire. Throughout the 1390s Richard aimed at undermining Warwick's position, a policy in which he was temporarily successful, but which could never succeed on a permanent basis. The interventionist policy that Richard adopted towards the rule of the localities was not the result of existing local instabilities caused by Warwick's misrule. Rather, royal policy and the presence of the royal affinity in local politics were the root cause of growing tensions in the region. Instead of building a relationship of mutual cooperative trust with the political classes, Richard inculcated the opposite: distrust,

[10] Tuck, *Richard II*, pp. 1–2, 71–2; Given-Wilson, *English Nobility*, pp. 79–82; Given-Wilson, *Royal Household*, pp. 264–7; Saul, *Richard II*, pp. 265–9.

[11] This point was first made by McFarlane, *Nobility*, pp. 119–21, 189–94; Powell, *Kingship*, pp. 24–38, 125–34; Watts, *Henry VI*, pp. 16–31.

[12] K. B. McFarlane, *Lancastrian Kings and Lollard Knights* (Oxford, 1972), p. 27: 'The king's impetuousness gave a quarrel over policies and personalities the character of a constitutional crisis.'

alienation, violent feuding, and ultimately widespread support for his deposition. Thus, the deposition was neither the result of a good policy badly executed nor of bad luck. It was the logical reaction to a rule that was fundamentally misconceived.

Although the geopolitical structures of Warwickshire and Worcestershire were very different, it is necessary to give a brief description of the factors at work within the two counties in order to appreciate the advantages and difficulties faced by both Warwick and the king in their struggle for power. Worcestershire was a county dominated to an unusual extent by multiple franchises, the most important of which was the Beauchamp hereditary shrievalty. This gave Warwick an unrivalled opportunity to influence local politics: although a nominated deputy did most of the day-to-day work, the earl always retained the right to intervene when he wished. Warwick's influence was also enhanced by the fact that, apart from the Church, he was the only magnate with extensive estates in the county.[13] Such was Warwick's hold on Worcestershire that the king's attempts to undermine Warwick's authority through the royal retainer Sir John Russell were bound to lead to violent confrontation, simply because Warwick was in control of many of the judicial and representational bodies in the county.

Warwickshire, meanwhile, was subject to centrifugal political forces caused by a combination of geographical and landholding factors, as Carpenter has shown. Whilst the region of western and southern Warwickshire was dominated by Warwick, his lands in the north and east of the county were sparse. In addition, there were other substantial noble estates in the county, which meant that Warwick always found it much harder to dominate county politics. His position was made even more difficult by the fact that both the shrievalty and escheatorship of the county were held jointly with Leicestershire, where Warwick's landed influence was negligible.[14]

Warwick's position was further threatened, and the king's strengthened, by the transformation of the political landscape of Warwickshire from 1389. First of all, by 1389, Thomas Mowbray was officially of age and in possession of his father's inheritance in Warwickshire and Leicestershire. Mowbray's arrival in the county was marked by his employment of several men with Warwickshire-Leicestershire connections. These men were all to play increasingly prominent roles in Warwickshire politics as Richard appointed them to local office as an alternative to members of the Beauchamp affinity.[15] Secondly, the return of John of Gaunt in November 1389 and his new-found understanding with

[13] By the fourteenth century all five of the county hundreds were in private hands: R. H. Hilton, *A Medieval Society: The West Midlands at the End of the Thirteenth Century*, 2nd edn (Cambridge, 1983), pp. 25–33, 41–4, 232–3; *The Beauchamp Cartulary Charters, 1100–1268*, ed. E. Mason, Pipe Roll Society, n.s. xliii (1980), pp. xviii, xlviii–li; *HPT 1386–1421*, i, pp. 722–4; C. Dyer, *Lords and Peasants in a Changing Society: The Estates of the Bishop of Worcester, 680–1540* (Cambridge, 1980), pp. 7–9.

[14] *A List of Sheriffs for England and Wales*, PRO Lists and Indexes, ix, p. 145; *List of Escheators for England and Wales*, PRO Lists and Indexes, lxxii, pp. 168–9; Carpenter, *Locality and Polity*, pp. 17–34. The Beauchamps held just one manor in Leicestershire (Kibworth Beauchamp): Astill, 'Medieval Gentry', pp. 207–8.

[15] R. E. Archer, 'The Mowbrays, Earls of Nottingham and Dukes of Norfolk to 1432' (unpub. Oxford Univ. D.Phil. thesis, 1984), pp. 63–75. These men included Robert Goushill: ibid. p. 20; Hugh Dalby, ibid. pp. 116–17; William Ilshawe, *HPT 1386–1421*, iii, pp. 474–5.

Richard paved the way for the duke to play an active part in Warwickshire politics. Lancaster's influence both at the centre and locally grew rapidly in the early 1390s, aided by the power vacuum caused by the series of minorities suffered by the Earls of Stafford. Walker has shown how Gaunt, with the Stafford interest in abeyance, was able to extend his influence in Staffordshire, and this seems to have been the case in Warwickshire too.[16]

My analysis of West Midlands political society has focused largely on the nobility because as the leading land lords in the region they and their affinities were crucial to Richard's plan to oust Warwick from his position of political predominance. That Richard realised the potential value of the regional magnates as rivals to Warwick is apparent in his inclusion of them in his affinity. For example, as early as 1382, Thomas Mowbray, Earl of Nottingham and later Duke of Norfolk, had been retained for life.[17] He was followed into the royal affinity in 1394 by Roger Mortimer, Earl of March. Richard also attempted to attach the Earls of Stafford more closely to him when he retained Thomas Stafford in November 1389, though this plan was thwarted when the earl died shortly afterwards.[18] John of Gaunt was perhaps too powerful to become a retainer of the king, and to some it seemed as if the king was in fact the retainer of the duke, as Arundel complained in 1394.[19] But although Richard's symbolic wearing of his uncle's livery signalled the nature of the close cooperation between the two, it is clear that it was Richard who was using Lancaster. As Walker has shown, by 1395, when the king felt himself to be more secure, his relationship with Gaunt had cooled, and even the duke began to find himself threatened by Richard's aggressive retaining policy.[20]

For a king to retain members of his nobility was certainly unusual. The very fact that Richard felt this need to secure his nobles' loyalty so specifically suggests a deep-seated insecurity in the king. Normally, they would have been the king's men without the need for such measures. It is also clear that by retaining nobles, he hoped to retain by extension the services of their affinities, a royal affinity by proxy. This was necessary as he could not hope to influence local politics on a national scale simply through his own retainers, however many he had. In the light of Richard's policy of retaining his magnates, the definition of the royal affinity should be expanded to include not only gentry, but the nobility as well.

By favouring the members of the royal affinity over their non-retained counterparts, Richard created local tensions which soon boiled over into serious disputes, especially in the normally peaceful Worcestershire. By taking his own men's parts in these disputes, Richard sought both to humiliate Warwick in public, and, by skilful use of rhetoric, to justify his mandate for undermining the earl's influence in the region. Warwick, however, did not accept the king's attacks on his position tamely, but fought back using the local authority vested in him through the offices of sheriff and JP. The best demonstration of Richard's policies and Warwick's reactions is through the

[16] Walsingham, *Historia Anglicana*, ii, pp. 193–5; *Historia Vitae*, pp. 128–30; *Westminster Chronicle*, p. 407; Walker, *Lancastrian Affinity*, pp. 222–7.

[17] Given-Wilson, *Royal Household*, p. 285.

[18] *CPR 1391–1396*, p. 375; *1388–1392*, p. 160.

[19] *Rot. Parl.*, iii, pp. 313–14.

[20] Walsingham, *Annales*, pp. 187–8; Walker, *Lancastrian Affinity*, pp. 174–9.

careers of two of Richard's most prominent knights, Sir John Russell of Strensham and Sir William Bagot of Baginton.

Sir John Russell was retained by the king in September 1387, to Warwick's anger. The reasons for Russell's original defection are obscure, but Goodman's suggestion that he was in dispute with the earl over land seems to be correct. During the period of Appellant rule, Russell and the earl seem to have reached a *modus vivendi*, but this soon broke down after Richard's reclamation of power.[21] By June 1392, tensions between Russell and the Warwick affinity had become literally murderous. In the parliament of January 1393 Russell claimed that his steward had been murdered by a group of Warwick's tenants, and that Sir Nicholas Lyllyng, Warwick's chief steward and a JP, had known who the culprits were, but did nothing. Feeling between Russell and Lyllyng appears to have run high, since Russell also alleged that Lyllyng, with five hundred armed men, had prevented Russell from reaching his home. Finally, Russell claimed that John Blount, who was acting in Russell's support, had seized three bondmen belonging to Warwick and carried them off to Tutbury castle. In retaliation, Lyllyng had abducted Blount's son and priest, and imprisoned them in Wales.[22]

Although no records survive of such a procedure in the rolls of parliament, it appears that Lyllyng, who was present as MP for Worcestershire, was impeached and imprisoned in Windsor Castle.[23] Significantly, Russell was not an MP, yet with royal backing he was able to accomplish this unusual and experimental action against his opponent, an action over which Warwick had no control. Lyllyng was then brought before the council, where he gave surety for his future good behaviour; he was pardoned two months later.[24] Meanwhile, proceedings against the men accused of murder were begun in king's bench by appeal. It seems that Richard was determined to negate any vestigial influence Warwick might have had on the case, since an order was given that it was not to be determined by *nisi prius*, which meant it could not be returned to the local assizes to be heard there.[25] As a final measure, the removal of three verderers from Feckenham forest was ordered 'for causes moving the king and council'. Undoubtedly, they had been elected by Warwick in his capacity as sheriff, and were considered to be too closely connected to him.[26]

The proceedings against Lyllyng and the attempt to disgrace Warwick by association bear remarkable similarities to Richard's treatment of Edward Courtenay, Earl of Devon, in early 1392. Although, unlike Courtenay, Warwick himself was not hauled up before the council, both men were implicated in very similar charges of attempting to subvert the judicial

[21] *CPR 1385–1389*, p. 372; Goodman, *Loyal Conspiracy*, pp. 150–1. In March 1388 Russell enfeoffed his three manors of Strensham, Peopleton and Dormston to a group of Warwick's men, possibly as a surety for his good behaviour. It is unlikely that Russell would have made such a transaction unwillingly: *CCR 1392–1396*, pp. 504–5.

[22] *CPR 1391–1396*, p. 269. A more extended analysis of this dispute can be found in A. K. Gundy, 'The Rule of Thomas Beauchamp, Earl of Warwick, in the West Midlands, 1369–1401' (unpub. Cambridge Univ. Ph.D. thesis, 2000), ch. 4.

[23] *HPT 1386–1421*, iii, pp. 603–5; *CPR 1391–1396*, p. 269; *CCR 1392–1396*, pp. 43, 49.

[24] *CCR 1392–1396*, pp. 113–14; *CPR 1391–1396*, p. 269.

[25] PRO, KB 27/528 m.2; *CCR 1392–1396*, p. 50.

[26] *CCR 1392–1396*, p. 71. The men were: Alexander Besford, Thomas Hoddington and William Spernore.

system in favour of their own men.[27] It is clear from the similarities between the two cases that Richard was pursuing a deliberate policy. The context to this policy has its origins in the parliamentary Commons' complaints in 1388–9 concerning noble liveries and maintenance. Storey has argued that in these years Richard attempted to win the support of the Commons by treating their demands for reform sympathetically, notably by renewed experimentation with the composition of the peace commissions. In late 1390, however, it is argued that Richard abandoned this policy in favour of building up support through his own affinity.[28] The cases of Warwick and Courtenay demonstrate that in fact Richard was still exploiting the complaints about maintenance in 1392–3. Lyllyng's and Courtenay's very public disgraces allowed Richard to play to the gallery. Even more importantly for Richard's long-term policy, it also allowed him to justify the removal of both men from the peace commissions, and their replacement with men sympathetic to the king. In Worcestershire, Lyllyng was replaced by Sir Richard Stury, the king's knight and councillor.[29] At the same time, clever use of rhetoric allowed Richard neatly to sidestep the questionable activities of his own affinity. For example, we only know Russell's version of events. He claimed that Lyllyng was the aggressor, but it is hard to believe that Russell was entirely blameless.[30] Similarly, John Blount was not punished for the abduction of Warwick's bondmen. The explanation for his immunity lies in his connection to Gaunt. Blount's elder brother Sir Walter was one of Gaunt's most prominent retainers, and the fact that John took his captives to Tutbury, Gaunt's Staffordshire stronghold, suggests that Gaunt himself may have encouraged his actions. The involvement of the Lancastrian affinity in the affair is confirmed by mutual bonds between members of the Beauchamp and Lancastrian affinities, including Walter Blount himself, apparently to ensure they kept the peace.[31]

Once the king had succeeded in humiliating Warwick and his affinity, he was able to reshape the Worcestershire peace commission which was one of the few local judicial bodies not directly under the control of Warwick, although Warwick's dominance in the county meant that the majority of the JPs were his men.[32] Stury's appointment in 1393 was followed in 1394 by that of John Blount, who was connected to Gaunt, and was also a kinsman to Stury by marriage.[33] Although the king did not yet dare to remove the earl

[27] *Select Cases Before the King's Council, 1243–1482*, ed. I. S. Leadam and J. F. Baldwin, Selden Society, 35 (1918), pp. 77–81; Cherry, 'Courtenay Earls of Devon', pp. 89–92; C. J. Tyldesley, 'The Crown and Local Communities in Devon and Cornwall from 1377 to 1422' (unpub. Exeter Univ. Ph.D. thesis, 1978), pp. 159–70.

[28] R. L. Storey, 'Liveries and Commissions of the Peace, 1388–90', *Reign of Richard II*, pp. 131–52; Tuck, *Richard II*, pp. 145–51, 261–5.

[29] *CPR 1391–1396*, p. 292; Given-Wilson, *Royal Household*, pp. 148–9, 152–3, 184–5; Tyldesley, 'Crown and Local Communities', pp. 163–70.

[30] Goodman, *Loyal Conspiracy*, p. 151.

[31] Walker, *Lancastrian Affinity*, pp. 28, 223, 285; *HPT 1386–1421*, ii, p. 257; *CCR 1392–1396*, p. 113.

[32] For example the commission issued in December 1390 included Warwick himself and three members of his affinity, Robert Burgulon, Walter Cokesey and Nicholas Lyllyng: *CPR 1388–1392*, p. 344.

[33] *CPR 1391–1396*, p. 441; *VCH Worcs*, iii, pp. 153–4. Stury had married Alice, Blount's cousin, and held her manors of Thickenappletree and Hampton Lovett by courtesy.

himself, by 1394 the Warwick affinity was outnumbered by men with associations to either Russell, Lancaster, or the king. In response, Warwick began to act as sheriff in person for the first time. The first recorded instance of this was in late 1392, shortly after the murder of Russell's steward. This may have been an attempt by Warwick to stifle the case before it escalated.[34] The references to Warwick acting as sheriff at his tourn become more frequent after 1394, that is, from the time when he found himself squeezed out of the peace commission, and his situation became increasingly hard to maintain.[35]

If in Worcestershire the tensions between the royal and Beauchamp affinities soon became violent, in Warwickshire the effects of the accretions of power in the hands of Warwick's rivals were more subtle. In Warwickshire, there was no need for the king and his allies to bypass the judicial system, since it was not under Warwick's control to the same extent as in Worcestershire. The fragmented nature of the county and its links with Leicestershire also provided an opportunity for Richard to insert men favourable to him into local office. Increasingly, both the sheriffs and escheators were drawn from Leicestershire, where Warwick had little influence, but where Gaunt and Mowbray were prominent. By 1396, both escheatorship and shrievalty were in the hands of Mowbray men.[36] Because the situation in Warwickshire was so much more open to other influences, the peace commission did not loom very large in Richard's policy and it was not until after Warwick's fall that he packed it with his supporters.[37] This lapse gave Warwick a chance to use his power as a JP in Warwickshire, just as he used his power as hereditary sheriff in Worcestershire, to mount an attack on the chief representative of the king's policy in the county, Sir William Bagot.

For more than a decade, Bagot had exerted a fatal attraction over a succession of lords. Clearly, he had qualities that made him a much sought-after retainer. He served in turn or simultaneously Warwick, Lancaster, Bolingbroke and Mowbray. But the very qualities that made him so attractive also resulted in a series of unsavoury and violent incidents that meant lords also tended to be glad to be rid of his services.[38] Neither Bagot's support for the Appellants in 1388, nor his reputation as a troublemaker, prevented the king from employing him, even though he retained his links to Mowbray and Bolingbroke throughout the period.

Bagot's main seat was at Baginton, just south of Coventry. This was fortunate for the king, since, combined with the royal patrimony at Coventry and the Lancastrian holding of Kenilworth castle, there was already a potential centre of royal power centred on the Kenilworth–Coventry–Baginton axis which could rival Warwick's own *caput honoris* at Warwick castle.[39] As early as 1391, Richard had realised the significance of this power base. In

[34] *List of Sheriffs*, p. 157: Warwick seems to have accounted in person.

[35] Warwick was active as sheriff in April 1394: PRO, JUST 3/180, m.44; April 1395: ibid., m.48d; March 1396: *CIPM 1392–1399*, pp. 42–3; October 1396: JUST 3/180, m.48d.

[36] Astill, 'Medieval Gentry', pp. 150–4, 165–7, 210–20; *List of Sheriffs*, p. 145; *List of Escheators*, p. 169. The sheriff was Robert Goushill, the escheator, Hugh Dalby.

[37] *CPR 1396–1399*, p. 436.

[38] For Bagot's career, see *HPT 1386–1421*, ii, pp. 99–103.

[39] *VCH Warks*, vi, pp. 23, 134–8.

that year, he appointed Bagot steward of the royal park at Coventry.[40] Although Bagot did not always serve the king's interests in Coventry, the Coventry-Baginton region became Bagot's power base in the area. In the indictments brought against Bagot in 1396, Baginton is repeatedly mentioned as the scene of many crimes and a stronghold of felons maintained by Bagot.[41] In 1397, John Catesby, a Beauchamp retainer who was involved in a long-running feud with Bagot, noted that Bagot had contrived to empanel a jury in favour of Catesby's opponents at Baginton. The following year, it is likely that Richard II stayed at Baginton before the ill-fated joust at Coventry.[42]

Warwick soon recognised the dangerous build-up of royal power centred on Bagot, and used his position as JP to defend his own position and influence in the county. In 1391 and 1392 he was present at the indictments of a group of men accused of murder at Stretton on Dunsmore, just east of Baginton. The proximity of Stretton to Baginton suggests that these men may have been connected to and protected by Bagot.[43] In 1396, it appears that an attempt was made to bring Bagot himself to justice at the assizes, but he arrived at the sessions with armed men from his *familia*, one of whom assaulted a Beauchamp retainer, Robert Walden, in the presence of the justices. Bagot's behaviour led to his indictment before Warwick and other JP members of his affinity. The charges brought against him now linked him directly to the Stretton murder; Bagot was accused of receiving and maintaining the culprits.[44] Other accusations levelled against Bagot dated back to the time when he was sheriff, some fourteen years previously, and also included the murder of a Cheshireman, which was perhaps an attempt to appeal to Richard's well-known fondness for that region.[45]

In the same year, Bagot's activities came under further scrutiny. In September 1395, there had been disturbances in Coventry against the mayor; it seems that Bagot and other royal officers in the city had fallen out with the mayor and ruling oligarchy, and, with Bagot's help, had planned to besiege the city.[46] This led to a commission in May 1396, which named Bagot as the chief instigator of the troubles, and which was ordered to impose a peaceful settlement. Indictments made before the Coventry JPs also implicated Bagot, but he was not directly accused.[47] The presenting juries may have been afraid to accuse Bagot directly, but they had no such qualms about his associates. These included Adomar Taverner of Lichfield, alias Adomar Lichfeld, who had a long-standing connection with Bagot, and John

[40] *CPR 1391–1396*, p. 2.
[41] PRO, KB 27/541, rex, m.26.
[42] J. B. Post, 'Courts, Councils and Arbitrators in the Ladbroke Manor Dispute, 1382–1400', *Medieval Legal Records Edited in Memory of C. A. F. Meekings*, ed. R. H. Hunnisett and J. B. Post (London, 1978), p. 320; *HPT 1386–1421*, ii, pp. 101–2.
[43] PRO, KB 9/173/1, m.13.
[44] PRO, KB 27/541, rex, m.26.
[45] There were two sets of indictments before Warwick and the other JPs (John Catesby, Thomas Purfrey, William Purfrey): PRO, KB 9/176, mm.176, 13d.
[46] *Rolls of the Warwickshire and Coventry Sessions of the Peace, 1377–97*, ed. E. Kimball (Dugdale Soc., xvi, 1939), pp. 76–7; PRO, KB 27/546, rex, m.15. Bagot's co-conspirators included Thomas Quynton, a clerk at the king's manor and park of Cheylesmore: *CCR 1389–1392*, p. 112.
[47] *CPR 1391–1396*, p. 731.

Goldsmyth, who was a co-litigant of Bagot's in a separate dispute concerning Aston, in the north of the county.[48]

The fact that Bagot could summon support from the far north of the county suggests that by 1396 he was able to exert his influence on a county-wide basis. In 1394, Sir John Drayton, who had connections to the royal affinity, petitioned parliament concerning Aston, complaining that Bagot had by maintenance so terrorised Drayton and the sheriff that they had been too scared to enforce the king's writ.[49] The previous summer, Drayton had suffered a brief imprisonment in the Tower, and it is possible that his feud with Bagot may have been the cause.[50] By 1396 the dispute had both widened and escalated into actual bodily violence. In December 1396, two of Bagot's servants were murdered at Aston; a group of the most prominent gentry of the region were implicated. A year later, the dispute was still in progress, when Bagot and Drayton took out mutual bonds to keep the peace.[51] But like Russell and Blount, Bagot was able to escape punishment because he had the backing of the king. The indictments brought against him before the JPs were removed into king's bench, where a verdict of not guilty was reached, by a jury brought all the way from Warwickshire to Lincoln for the purpose.[52] Meanwhile, Bagot's involvement in the troubles at Coventry, whilst they were acknowledged in the governmental commission and stated by the jurors, was never pursued.

By mid-1396, therefore, the relations between Warwick and members of the royal affinity had deteriorated, and Warwick's position had been seriously weakened. This was Richard's cue to begin his final assault on the earl's remaining power base, his marcher lordships. In Michaelmas 1396 with the implicit backing of the king, Mowbray began proceedings in king's bench for the recovery of Warwick's lordship of Gower, which had been awarded arbitrarily to Warwick's father in 1354. This lordship, alone amongst the marcher territories, was vulnerable to royal intervention, which made it easy for Richard to target.[53] In addition, Richard may have remembered that much of the Appellants' military strength in 1387–8 had been drawn from this highly militarised region.[54] If Richard was already planning a pre-emptive strike, which seems likely, it was both a prudent action to negate his victim's potential power base and a test of the extent of Richard's power. In June 1397, judgement was made in favour of Mowbray, and a crippling settlement

[48] Lichfeld had been associated with Bagot since *c.*1382: PRO, CP 40/484, m.148. Goldsmyth, who came from Birmingham, had been involved in the Aston dispute since *c.*1382: PRO, JUST 1/1488, m.13d.

[49] *Rot. Parl.*, iii, p. 326; *HPT 1386–1421*, ii, pp. 794–7: Drayton was a brother of the king's knight, Sir William. Bagot became directly involved when his sister Margery enfeoffed the manor to him, Gaunt and others: *VCH Warks*, vii, p. 60; *CPR 1399–1401*, p. 9; PRO, JUST 1/1514, m.37d. For full details, see Gundy, 'Rule of Thomas Beauchamp', ch. 4.

[50] *CCR 1392–1396*, pp. 158, 163. It is also possible that his imprisonment may have been due to his activities in his native Oxfordshire: *HPT 1386–1421*, ii, pp. 794–7.

[51] PRO, JUST 3/188 mm.14d, 15; *CCR 1396–1399*, p. 128.

[52] PRO, KB 27/541, rex, m.26.

[53] R. R. Davies, *Lordship and Society in the March of Wales, 1287–1400* (Oxford, 1978), pp. 30–1, 51–2; Archer, 'Mowbrays', pp. 15–20; A. J. F. Sinclair, 'The Beauchamp Earls of Warwick in the Later Middle Ages' (unpub. London Univ. Ph.D. thesis, 1986), pp. 45–9.

[54] Davies, *Lordship*, pp. 43–58.

imposed. Warwick was forced to hand over the lordship, and to repay profits amounting to £5,333. In order to ensure his cooperation, he was made to enfeoff seventeen manors to Mowbray. If he defaulted on his payments or attempted to reclaim Gower, then these manors were to be settled on Mowbray permanently.[55]

On 10 July 1397, Richard began the final destruction of his former opponents. Warwick was imprisoned in the Tower, and those of his affinity closest to him had their goods seized.[56] In the parliament that followed, Warwick confessed to his part in the actions of 1387–8, and sentence of death was passed, which was then commuted to life imprisonment on the Isle of Man.[57] Meanwhile, as is well known, Richard showed himself fully aware of the geopolitical structure of the West Midlands in his division of the Beauchamp lands. They were apportioned in such a way as to break up the sociopolitical units long established under the Beauchamps.[58] Warwick castle and most of its surrounds were given to Thomas Holand, Duke of Surrey; Mowbray kept the lands he had received in June, but did not profit further in the region. The Beauchamp lands in southern and central Worcestershire were added to the Gloucestershire estates of Thomas Despenser, and the north and west Worcestershire estates went to the Earl of Salisbury, who was prominent in neighbouring Shropshire.[59]

It is generally accepted that Richard's policies in 1397–9 brought about his downfall; his retaining policy narrowed to the Cheshiremen; his use of blank charters and general pardons to those involved in the crisis of 1387–8 alienated and frightened the political classes; and his blatant disregard for custom and law regarding his subjects' property made every man fear for his own.[60] But recently the interpretations of Given-Wilson and Barron have attempted to play down the impact of the tyranny on political society. In particular, Given-Wilson has argued that the majority of the nobility supported Richard in 1399 or were at least neutral.[61] But was this the case in the West Midlands? Was it possible for Surrey and the other replacements for Warwick to win the support of the regional gentry in the two years following Warwick's fall? The evidence from the region suggests that they did not and possibly could not, because Richard's policy was fundamentally flawed.

An obvious problem for the new lords of the Midlands was that they had

[55] *CCR 1396–1399*, pp. 123–4, 128. The five manors in Warwickshire fitted perfectly with Mowbray's existing lands in the county: Given-Wilson, *English Nobility*, pp. 136–7.

[56] Walsingham, *Annales*, p. 199; Walsingham, *Historia Anglicana*, ii, p. 223; *Historia Vitae*, pp. 137–8; 'The Dieulacres Chronicle', ed. M. V. Clarke and V. H. Galbraith, *BJRL*, xiv (1930), p. 168; 'The Kirkstall Chronicle', ed. M. V. Clarke and N. Denholm-Young, *BJRL*, xv (1931), pp. 129–30; *CCR 1396–1396*, pp. 138–40. The men whose goods were seized were: John Catesby, Nicholas Lyllyng, William Spernore and Robert Walden: *CFR 1391–1399*, p. 227.

[57] *Rot. Parl.*, iii, pp. 347–51; Walsingham, *Annales*, p. 220; Walsingham, *Historia Anglicana*, ii, p. 226; *Historia Vitae*, p. 145; *Chronicon Adae de Usk*, ed. E. M. Thompson, Rolls Series (1904), pp. 161–2.

[58] Tuck, *Richard II*, pp. 191–2; Given-Wilson, *English Nobility*, pp. 136–7; Saul, *Richard II*, pp. 382–3.

[59] *CPR 1396–1399*, pp. 186, 200, 213–15, 219–20. The Earls of Salisbury held the castles and towns of Mold and Hawarden in Wales: *CIPM*, vi, pp. 313–24.

[60] C. M. Barron, 'The Tyranny of Richard II', *BIHR*, xli (1968), pp. 1–18.

[61] Given-Wilson, *Royal Household*, pp. 223–6, 267; Barron, 'Deposition', pp. 135–45.

wide-ranging and conflicting responsibilities. Although Richard showed himself to be aware of the geopolitical structure of the region in his grants to Despenser, Montague and Mowbray, the introduction of an outsider, Surrey, was almost certain to cause difficulties. Surrey's landed interests were widely scattered, and before 1397 he had possessed none in Warwickshire.[62] To impose himself on an entirely different region was a challenging task, and one that seems to have been beyond him, if only because he had so many responsibilities elsewhere. Saul has noted that Surrey seems rarely to have visited Warwickshire.[63] His duties at court, on his other estates, and, from mid-1398, in Ireland, kept him away.[64] Surrey's involvement in Warwickshire politics, apart from some inept and heavy-handed attempts to interfere in the Ladbroke dispute, seems to have been confined to symbolic actions. For example, he placed Richard's badge over the gate at Warwick Castle.[65] But symbols alone, whilst a potent adjunct to lordship, could not in themselves make a good lord. One prominent Beauchamp retainer, Guy Spyney, and several lesser officials transferred their loyalty to Surrey to the extent that they were never forgiven by the Beauchamps.[66] But in general the deed evidence for the period shows that the Beauchamp affinity remained a cohesive social and political force, its members relying on each other as feoffees, witnesses and mainpernors.[67]

Although necessity required the gentry to acknowledge the new political order – for example John Catesby petitioned Surrey's council for redress in the long-running dispute concerning his manor of Ladbroke – it seems that none of the new lords in the region was able to offer the type of lordship which would have drawn men into their service. In fact, their presence may have been resented. Surrey was forced to sue out a commission of oyer and terminer to deal with what appears to have been a series of guerrilla attacks throughout Warwickshire on the Beauchamp chases and parks he had acquired.[68] Similarly, in early 1398, an assize jury in a suit brought by Catesby to recover Ladbroke was unimpressed by the defendants' claim that they were jointly enfeoffed of the manor with the Dukes of Surrey and Exeter. The manor was awarded, with damages, to Catesby.[69] Finally, the Beauchamp administration, which was taken over wholesale by Warwick's replacements, seems to have become lax. This may have been the result of a combination of lack of supervision by the lords and a campaign of resistance by Warwick's officers.[70]

[62] R. A. K. Mott, 'Richard II's Relations with the Magnates, 1396–9' (unpub. Leeds Univ. Ph.D. thesis, 1971), pp. 46, 50.

[63] Saul, *Richard II*, p. 444, n. 30. Surrey's council was at Coventry in 1397, but he seems to have operated mainly from his house in London, and from Northampton: Post, 'Ladbroke Dispute', pp. 320–2.

[64] Mott, 'Relations with the Magnates', pp. 186–9; Saul, *Richard II*, pp. 287–8.

[65] Post, 'Ladbroke Dispute', p. 323.

[66] Spyney had become Surrey's receiver-general by 1398: BL Egerton Charters 8660, 8661; Post, 'Ladbroke Dispute', pp. 322, 338. He survived until at least 1412, but was never employed by Thomas or Richard Beauchamp or in local government again: Sinclair, 'Beauchamps', pp. 296–8.

[67] For example Ailred Trussell stood surety for Thomas Throckmorton and Thomas Hoddington: PRO, KB 27/546, rex, m.20. Groups of Warwick's men also took out pardons together, for example Robert Hugford and Thomas Knight: PRO, C 67/30, m.16.

[68] *CPR 1396–1399*, p. 434.

[69] Post, 'Ladbroke Dispute', p. 325.

[70] Compare for example the accounts produced for Beoley under Warwick and under Surrey: BL Egerton Chs. 8658 (1391–2), 8655 (1397–8).

Richard seems to have realised that Surrey was not asserting his authority in an effective manner, and attempted to insert John Russell into the political society of northern Warwickshire, through his marriage to the widow of John Clinton of Maxstoke, in late 1398. Elizabeth Clinton brought with her a sizeable dower, including most of the Clinton inheritance in Warwickshire, much to the chagrin of the heir, Sir William.[71] But Richard's plans were to no avail, because of the fundamental flaw at their heart. By acting as the head of a magnate-style affinity the king deliberately favoured his own men, at the expense of his subjects at large.

A further problem for the new lords of the West Midlands was the presence of the disinherited heir of Warwick, Richard Beauchamp. Beauchamp was born in 1382, and was thus in his late teens in the period 1397–9, old enough to become a focus for discontent.[72] Perhaps in an attempt to bind this potentially dangerous young man to him, the king retained Beauchamp's esquire, Walter Power, though this proved to be futile.[73] Beauchamp was put in the custody of Surrey, but he does not seem to have accompanied his guardian to Ireland in October 1398, or to have gone there with the king in June 1399.[74]

Finally, the king's tyranny must have had a profound effect on those who felt themselves to be the victims of it, which was most men of property. The sheer scale of Richard's operations is reflected in the hundreds of names of West Midlands gentry enrolled on the pardon rolls in these years. Some of them felt so insecure that they took out more than one pardon.[75] Added to this, the presence of king's bench in Coventry and Worcester in 1397–8 in its capacity as superior eyre, and accompanied by the king himself, surely deepened the atmosphere of unease in the region.[76] Some members of the Warwick affinity were also singled out for specific treatment. For example, Sir Giles Mallory and Sir John Trussell were summoned before the king's council in April 1398 'to declare what shall be laid before them'.[77] Richard's tyranny over West Midlands society was such that no one dared actively to oppose him, but judging by the speedy response to events by the Beauchamp affinity in July 1399, it seems that there may have been plans laid for action against the king, should an opportunity arise. To gain a true gauge of the destructive nature of Richard's policies it is necessary to look into the next reign, when often violent revenge was exacted. To give one example, the disgruntled heir of the Clinton estates took the opportunity offered by Richard's deposition to seize his inheritance from John Russell and his wife. A violent dispute ensued, during which Russell's servant was murdered, and it was only after Henry IV's intervention

[71] Most of the Clinton inheritance, including Maxstoke itself, had been settled on John and Elizabeth and their heirs in *c.*1389–90. This would have disinherited William Clinton if there had been issue: *Warwickshire Feet of Fines 1345–1509*, ed. L. Drucker, Dugdale Society, xviii (1943), p. 88; *CCR 1396–1399*, p. 412. Russell was immediately appointed to the Warwickshire peace commission in April 1399: *CPR 1396–1399*, p. 437.

[72] Sinclair, 'Earls of Warwick', pp. 81–4.

[73] Power had been retained for life by Warwick in 1383: *CPR 1381–1385*, pp. 277–8; he was retained by the king in October 1398: *CPR 1396–1399*, p. 418.

[74] *CPR 1396–1399*, p. 245. Unlike the heirs of Gloucester and Bolingbroke, there is no chronicle reference to Beauchamp being in Ireland.

[75] Nicholas Lyllyng took out pardons on 18 October 1397 and 16 June 1398: PRO, C 67/30, mm.3, 6.

[76] PRO, KB 27/ 546, /547.

[77] *CCR 1396–1399*, p. 277.

and a series of arbitrations that a settlement seems to have been reached in 1402.[78]

Throughout the 1390s and especially from 1397 to 1399, the Beauchamp affinity was under severe pressure, but it was not destroyed, and played an important part in Bolingbroke's successful coup. Given-Wilson's argument that in 1399 most of the available nobility supported Richard breaks down because he does not count the followers of the dispossessed lords as a political force. But as Tuck pointed out, Richard had attempted the largest redistribution of noble lands since the Conquest, which affected vast areas of the country and many men.[79] The fortunate survival of several accounts from 1399–1400 allows an unusual insight into the activities of the Warwick affinity after the arrival of Bolingbroke in July 1399. As soon as news of his landing at Ravenspur reached them, they sprang into action on behalf of their lord. Horses and men were dispatched to rescue Warwick from the Isle of Man. Members of the affinity were then sent around the country to seize Warwick's lands, whilst Richard Beauchamp, with Walter Power, rode to Cheshire to meet Bolingbroke.[80] Meanwhile, Bolingbroke himself had signalled his intentions towards Warwick and his attitude towards the settlement of 1397 by throwing down the badges placed on the gate of Warwick castle by Surrey.[81] Although some members of the Warwickshire gentry did attempt to raise troops for Richard, the groundswell of opinion, carried by the Warwick affinity, favoured Warwick and Bolingbroke.[82]

In conclusion, historians are right to attribute Richard's policies to his fundamental need for security.[83] But both Richard and the interpreters of his rule in the 1390s have misunderstood his need for such a policy. The medieval polity was not based on a weak king and powerful subjects, but on a powerful monarch who was supported willingly by all for the sake of good order. Richard's basic misconception of the fundamental workings of kingship is illustrated by his increasing emphasis on the obedience due to him from his subjects; he could not comprehend that such obedience was normally a given in the medieval polity.[84] Richard's misplaced search for security ultimately cost him his throne because his policies created the exact opposite of the security he sought. As a final thought, perhaps we should ask whether the royal policy of the 1390s was part of a consistent attempt by Richard to create a new, absolutist form of kingship?

[78] *CCR 1399–1402*, pp. 2–3, 134, 193–4, 197, 280, 286; PRO, KB 9/185/1, mm.43–4; KB 27/565, m.63; Carpenter, *Locality and Polity*, pp. 362–3.

[79] Given-Wilson, *Royal Household*, p. 267; McFarlane, *Lancastrian Kings*, pp. 62–76; Tuck, *Richard II*, p. 192.

[80] Warks RO, CR 1886/481; Birmingham RO, DV 1, 168245.

[81] Post, 'Ladbroke Dispute', p. 323.

[82] Thomas Clinton and William Astley raised a small force on Richard's behalf: *HPT 1386–1421*, ii, pp. 595–6.

[83] Given-Wilson, *Royal Household*, pp. 212–15, 223–4; Saul, *Richard II*, pp. 235–69.

[84] Saul, *Richard II*, pp. 384–8.

The Estates, Finances and Regal Aspirations of Richard Plantagenet (1411–1460), Duke of York

T. B. Pugh

Richard, Duke of York was the most powerful, but not the richest, of Henry VI's subjects. When he inherited the duchy of York on the death of his uncle, Duke Edward, in October 1415, Richard was four years old, and he did not obtain seisin of his paternal inheritance until 1433. The second Duke of York was the most distinguished of the English casualties at Agincourt and he left his nephew a heavily encumbered estate, burdened with debt and dowagers. Few English nobles in the later middle ages left their affairs and finances in a more ruinous state. Of the York lands the greater part was long in the possession of the late duke's feoffees and creditors. Duke Edward's accumulated debts probably exceeded the capital value of his estates and paying off these liabilities took a generation. Nearly half of the York lands were in the hands of two long-lived dowager duchesses; Duke Edward's consort, Philippa Mohun, lived until 1431, and Joan Holand, widow of Edmund of Langley, first Duke of York, survived until 1434. The Isle of Wight, held for life by Duke Edward, remained in the hands of his widow until her death, when it reverted to the crown. The lordship of Wark-in-Tynedale had been alienated to provide a dowry for Richard's sister, Isabel, on her first marriage with the young heir of Sir Thomas Gray of Heaton. Retainers receiving life annuities granted by Duke Edward were far too long an expensive burden on the duchy of York. The best paid of them, Sir Thomas Burton, of Tolethorpe Hall, in Little Casterton (Rutland), had three grants amounting to 200 marks a year. Two knights and seven esquires who had profited from the late duke's generosity were still alive in 1433, and in all these nine men were in receipt of annual payments totalling at least £240 (and probably more), at a time when the duchy lands were worth less than a thousand pounds a year.

After Duke Richard obtained seisin of his York heritage, he came to terms with his uncle's feoffees. He was required to assume responsibility for settling the residue of Duke Edward's debts within two years, besides meeting the cost of the life annuities and that of completing the York family mausoleum, Fotheringhay College, in Northamptonshire.[1] It was young Richard's great good fortune that in 1425 he had inherited the vast possessions of his maternal uncle Edmund Mortimer, Earl of March. The widowed Countess of March, Anne Stafford, did not long survive her childless husband, dying in 1432, and

[1] T. B. Pugh, 'Richard Plantagenet (1411–60), Duke of York, as the King's Lieutenant in France and Ireland', *Aspects of Late Medieval Government and Society: Essays presented to J. R. Lander*, ed. J. G. Rowe (Toronto, 1986) (hereafter Pugh, 'Richard Plantagenet'), pp. 107–41, esp. 110, 132–3.

leaving her dower share of the family estates to the young heir. For twenty years after 1415 the duchy of York was bankrupt. It was the lucrative Mortimer inheritance, probably the greatest private estate in England and Wales, that gave Richard, Duke of York, the material basis of his place in English politics.

The wealth of the earldom of March and the York *valor* of 1443

Duke Richard was in Normandy from June 1441 until his return to England in September 1445. In his absence, his estates were efficiently administered by capable officials. The *valor* for the year Michaelmas 1442 to Michaelmas 1443 records that after £945 12s. had been distributed in annuities, fees and wages and £370 6s. had been spent on repairs, his Mortimer heritage in Wales and the Marches was worth £2,879 13s. 10d. in clear value; that was the net sum that should have been realised from that year's issues and profits. Because of large amounts forthcoming in receipts from arrears, the duke's receiver-general in fact received considerably more. Cash paid to York's receiver-general, John Milewater, totalled £2,430 8s. 10d. at Michaelmas 1443, and on 6 February 1444 he made a payment of £1,000, a sum received since Michaelmas from the outstanding arrears, to the duke's attorney, John Wigmore. Furthermore 100 marks due from a fine imposed on two tenants of the lordship of Denbigh was paid to the duke by his estates steward, Sir William ap Thomas of Raglan, making a total of £3,497 2s. 2d. from the receipts of that year.

Duke Richard's Welsh lordships were producing more revenue than his English estates. The Mortimer heritage in the Marches was probably worth more in 1443 than it had been before 1400.[2] Casual revenues contributed a large proportion of seignorial income. In the late fourteenth century the fines of the Great Sessions (or sessions in eyre) had become as established a mainstay of the lord's income in the greater marcher lordships and huge sums were regularly paid to buy the lord's pardon for a wide range of criminal offences and other misdemeanours.[3] Large payments of *donum* and tallages were levied on many occasions: in 1442–3 *donum* worth £251 5s. 6d. was collected in Duke Richard's lordships of Builth, Clifford, Dinas, Ewias and Glasbury and those payments may have been made to buy off a visitation of the sessions in eyre. In 1924 William Rees ended his *South Wales and the March* with a depressing view of the state of Wales in the aftermath of the Glyn Dŵr rebellion. He believed that the consequences of that revolt and its failure were even worse than the effects of the Black Death. These familiar judgements have been reiterated by recent Welsh historians.[4] The prosperity of the Mortimer marcher lordships in the

[2] PRO SC 11/818. The lordships of Ceri and Cydewain are not included, so perhaps £800 should be added to the £3,494 2s. 2d. paid in cash for 1442–3. In 1398 the cash yield of the earldom of March totalled nearly £3,400, and £2,409 of that sum came from the Mortimer marcher lordships (R. R. Davies, *Lordship and Society in the March of Wales 1282–1400* (Oxford, 1978), p. 188). These figures, based on inquisitions post mortem, are probably underestimates, as they omit valuable casual revenues, such as the fines of the Great Sessions.

[3] Pugh, *MLSW*, pp. 145–9.

[4] W. Rees, *South Wales and the March 1284–1415* (Oxford, 1924), pp. 273–80; G. Williams, *History of Wales*, iii, *Recovery, Reorientation and Reformation: Wales c.1415–1642* (Oxford, 1987), pp. 14–24.

middle years of Henry VI's reign affords reasons for challenging these traditional verdicts. A panorama of gloom, ruin and decay has for too long obscured our view of fifteenth-century Wales before the Wars of the Roses and the advent of the Tudors.

The sale of charters to Ceri and Cydewain in 1447

When Duke Richard returned to Normandy in the summer of 1441, his reputation for great wealth impressed the French and he could afford to indulge his madly extravagant wife, Cecily Neville. In 1444, York's duchess spent nearly £608 in London. The most expensive purchase was a set of state robes, made of red velvet, lined with ermine and adorned with gold and pearls. What the duchess chose to buy from London merchants during that year amounted to more than an English baronial income. Few women in English history have been able to spend more than the Duchess Cecily did in the heyday of her husband's fortunes.[5]

During the following decade York saw his financial position deteriorate and after 1450 conspicuous affluence gave way to acute money problems. The period of high prosperity for the Welsh marcher lords did not last beyond the middle of the fifteenth century. The York *valor* of 1443 commemorates the success of a rigorous and exacting system of estate management, which had largely restored the lord's revenues and profits to what they had been before Glyn Dŵr's rebellion. This notable achievement marked the end of an era. At Michaelmas 1443, the total of unpaid arrears amounted to £3,692,[6] and probably a large proportion of that sum remained outstanding and was never paid. The pressure of seignorial exactions on a thinly populated land was too great to be maintained beyond the 1440s. Two charters granted by Duke Richard at Montgomery Castle on 31 August 1447 show an awareness that concessions had to be made.[7] In this grant of liberties to the people of Ceri, the duke reduced or remitted certain rents and fines, in return for the payment of the sum of 600 marks, at the rate of 100 marks a year for a term of six years. The main feature of York's charter to the inhabitants of Cydewain was the abolition of serfdom, which was bought by a cash payment of 1,000 marks. It is significant that these bondmen were already prosperous enough to be able to pay at once the whole sum due for enfranchisement, without delay or recourse to instalments. York's willingness to grant (or rather sell) these two charters shows his acute need to raise money, at the price of permanently reducing his income by losing and surrendering seignorial rights in perpetuity. He was to receive £1,066 13s. 4d. in all during the next six years. No other Welsh marcher lord is known ever to have granted a charter enfranchising all the bondmen of his marcher lordship.

The ending of York's term as lieutenant-general in France in 1445 had involved considerable financial loss. During his four years in Normandy he had

[5] Pugh, 'Richard Plantagenet', p. 112.
[6] PRO SC 11/818 m.17.
[7] *CPR 1494–1509*, pp. 523–4; PRO C 66/ 602 m.27 (7); see Appendix I.

been paid annually from Norman revenues the equivalent of £4,000 sterling for the maintenance of his vice-regal household.[8] Once back in England, he had to pay his own household bills, which were by far the heaviest charge on his resources. After 1450, the declining income from his Welsh estates suggests that he was no longer able to meet the cost. K. B. McFarlane denied that the political conduct of the English higher nobility during the Wars of the Roses was much influenced by financial considerations. He maintained that the leading protagonists in these civil wars were all richer than their fathers had been, but he adduced no evidence to support that assertion.[9] York was indisputably much richer than his father, Richard, Earl of Cambridge, who never possessed an acre of land in his own right, but after 1450 it looks as though he may not have been able to pay his way.

Duke Richard's financial problems

Duke Richard's taxable income in 1436 was declared to be £3,230, and that may have been an accurate and reliable statement of his net landed income in England, after all costs and charges had been met. This declaration did not include the revenues of his Welsh lands, which were outside the scope of parliamentary taxation.[10] The duchy of York, freed of dower interests, was perhaps bringing in about £1,000 a year. The yield of the Mortimer lands in England, including the honour of Clare, is difficult to estimate and at that date York's share of the Holand inheritance (not yet finally partitioned) can hardly have amounted to manors worth less than £450 a year. How much he was receiving from his hereditary annuities worth £761 is not clear (and they were apparently not included in his 1436 tax return). His total landed income in England and Wales in 1443 probably amounted to between £6,000 and £7,000 a year. He was by far the richest of the English nobles, almost as wealthy as John of Gaunt had been in his early years. Professor J. T. Rosenthal's miscalculations of York's landed income are best ignored. He thought that Wales was already incorporated in England before 1436 (that happened a century later), and he was unaware that the Duke of York's Welsh revenues were not taxable in 1436.[11]

The great affluence that Duke Richard enjoyed during these years did not last long, perhaps no more than a decade. While he was serving in France, York enjoyed an income of some £10,000 a year (including his Norman household subsidy), exclusive of his large salary of £20,000 as lieutenant-general. He was never so prosperous again. In 1445 he lost the lieutenant-generalship of France,

[8] *Letters and Papers Illustrative of the Wars of the English in France*, ed. J. Stevenson, Rolls Series (1864), ii.ii, pp. 587; P. A. Johnson, *Duke Richard of York 1411–60* (Oxford, 1988), p. 37.

[9] K. B. McFarlane, *England in the Fifteenth Century* (London, 1981), p. 240.

[10] For Duke Richard's income tax declaration delivered to Lord Cromwell on 29 June 1436, see PRO E 163/7/31 Part i, no. 3; York was then at Rouen. For the scope of the income tax of 1436, see *Rot. Parl.*, iv, p. 436. For York's Holand lands, see Pugh, 'Richard Plantagenet', n. 10, pp. 133–4. For his annuities, see H. L. Gray, 'Incomes from land in England in 1436', *EHR*, xlix (1934), p. 614.

[11] J. T. Rosenthal, 'Fifteenth-Century Baronial Incomes and Richard Duke of York', *BIHR*, xxxvii (1964), pp. 233–9, and 'The Estates and Finances of Richard, Duke of York (1411–60)', *Studies in Medieval and Renaissance History*, ii (Nebraska, 1965), pp. 115–204.

the most valuable office of profit in the crown's gift, so that it could be conferred on his great rival Edmund Beaufort, soon to be created Duke of Somerset. The lord-lieutenancy of Ireland, to which York was appointed in 1447, was no adequate compensation for what he had lost. His wages were not regularly paid, and his service in Ireland probably cost him dear. Shortly before his return to England in 1450, he was owed 4,700 marks by the exchequer. In 1450 he lost the lucrative Norman lordships granted to him and his second son Edmund, Earl of Rutland, by Henry VI.[12] We have been assured that 'poverty was not the spur that drove Richard of York into opposition and rebellion'.[13] Duke Richard was never reduced to poverty, but he had to adjust his vice-regal lifestyle as a consequence of a considerable loss of landed income. It is difficult to believe that York's growing financial problems did not influence the part he played in English politics after his abrupt return from Ireland in September 1450. If English rule in Normandy had been prolonged for another ten years and York had remained in command in Rouen, he would have caused no trouble to Henry VI or his ministers.

The York *valor* of 1453

The York *valor* of 1452–3 is a neglected document, overlooked by generations of researchers because it was wrongly classified long ago in the Public Record Office.[14] These *valors* of 1443 and 1453 appear to be the sole survivors of what was an annual series of records of the Duke of York's Welsh lands. The bulk of Duke Richard's muniments were probably destroyed by the victorious Lancastrians during the sack of Ludlow Castle in October 1459. The *valor* of 1443 already had enough scarcity value for it to be enrolled among the exchequer records by the lord treasurer's command in 1494.[15]

This *valor* of 1453 is unfortunately damaged and mutilated and only seven membranes survive; the previous *valor* of 1443 consists of seventeen membranes. The top of the roll and at least the first two membranes dealing with the lordships of Denbigh and Montgomery are missing. Little is left of the Shropshire membrane which followed. Work on this *valor* was never completed and it ends with a statement of clear value for the year 1452–3. There is no information about the accumulated arrears, which probably amounted to considerable sums in the last decade of Duke Richard' s life. Although this *valor* is incomplete, it can be dated from internal evidence. Edmund Cornwall of Berrington (Shropshire) died on 3 December 1452, leaving as his heir his son Thomas, aged eight years, and the wardship of this minor was claimed by the Duke of York.[16] Expenses totalling 31s. 1d. were paid to the receiver of

[12] Johnson, *Duke Richard*, pp. 67, 69, Pugh, 'Richard Plantagenet', p. 122.

[13] Rosenthal, 'Estates', p. 151.

[14] PRO SC 11/918, *valor* of lands of Richard, Duke of York in Wales and Marches 31–2 Henry VI (1452–3), wrongly listed as a *valor* of lands of the archbishopric of York.

[15] For the enrolment of the *valor* of 1442–3 in 1494, see PRO E 368/ 267 LTR memoranda roll 9 Henry VII m.1.

[16] For the Cornwall family, see Lord Liverpool and Revd Compton Reade, *The House of Cornwall* (Hereford, 1908). York's claim to the wardship and marriage of the Cornwall heir, Thomas (1444–1500), was unsuccessful, see *CFR 1452–1461*, pp. 2, 30, 32–3, 37.

Clifford, Glasbury and Dinas and others of the lord's council for work at Hereford and Bromyard after the issuing of the writ *diem clausit extremum* for the late Edmund Cornwall on 11 December 1453. The *valor* sheds some light on Duke Richard's movements during his period of political eclipse. He was at Fotheringhay in March and May and the receiver went to Stamford (Lincolnshire) twice in June to take money to the Duke, while in October York was at his manor of Fasterne, in Wiltshire. Little is known of the Duke's activities for over two years after the failure of his first rebellion early in 1452 and during that period he appears to have been confined to his estates.

The collapse of the Duke of York's Welsh revenues

The clear value of York's Welsh lordships for the year ending Michaelmas 1453 was £1,958 18s. 6½d. That was the sum total of the cash that the Duke should have received after the cost of repairs, fees and annuities had been deducted. No doubt what was paid was a great deal less than the clear value declared. Probably the Duke received less than half the profits that had accrued from these lordships ten years earlier. His cash receipts were not much reduced by payments of annuities to officials and retainers, which amounted to only £171 13s. 4d., including a fee of £20 a year paid to the Duke's chief steward, Sir Walter Devereux. Duke Richard's retinue in his Welsh lordships was not large nor distinguished. Ten years earlier, in 1443, annuities had cost £354 18s., but that sum had included the huge fee of £200 a year paid to John, Lord Talbot (afterwards Earl of Shrewsbury), which had probably already ceased before his death in the last battle of the Hundred Years War in July 1453.[17] The main reason for this drastic decline in seignorial income was the absence of fines and *donum* in most of the Duke's Welsh lordships in 1452–3. Fines of the Great Sessions and the render of *donum* had produced £860 16s. 8d. in 1442–3. Ten years later all that was due for payment was £200 in *donum* in the lordships of Caerleon and Usk and £33 6s.8d. in Builth lordship. The failure to hold the Great Sessions may indicate a waning of seignorial authority. Probably the sessions were not held in 1452–3 because the fines imposed in previous years remained unpaid. The situation revealed in 1453 cannot be dismissed as exceptional or regarded as merely the consequence of an isolated bad year. The income that the Duke was receiving from his English lordships and manors was not affected.

There is nothing to suggest that this collapse in Welsh seignorial revenue was caused by prolonged bad weather. In the middle years of the fifteenth century, York's kinsman (and nearest rival among the English higher nobility) Humphrey Stafford, Duke of Buckingham, was experiencing similar difficulties in his marcher lordships of Brecon, Hay and Huntington. Little of the fine of 2,000 marks granted for redeeming the sessions in those lordships in 1450 was paid during the next four years and a respite from holding the sessions followed. Although these lordships were reckoned to be worth £1,014 in clear value in 1448, all the cash that Buckingham received in the two years

[17] This total (£171 13s. 4d.) may be incomplete, as part of this *valor* is missing. For annuities paid in 1442–3, see PRO SC 11/818.

between 1453 and 1455 amounted to only £515.[18] The crisis in seignorial revenues in the Welsh marches that began in the middle of the fifteenth century was permanent and catastrophic, and it is a phenomenon in which Welsh historians have so far shown little interest. Perhaps the presence of a resident marcher lord could have arrested the trend. Between 1465 and 1468 William Lord Herbert, as keeper, was able to take £488 on average in profit from the lordships of Newport, Wentloog and Machen in his charge, considerably more than the marcher lord, the late Duke of Buckingham, had been able to do.[19]

The decline in marcher revenues is most clearly seen in the lordship of Denbigh, once the most valuable part of the Mortimer estates and the most lucrative lordship that Duke Richard possessed. In the late fourteenth century, Denbigh had been worth well over £1,000 a year and its clear value was still £904 in 1443. By 1468–9 its clear value had dwindled to £277 15s. 7d. and by the close of the fifteenth century grants of life annuities by Henry VII had reduced its net value to less than £52 a year.[20] The collapse of the revenues of the marcher lordships marked the ending of the middle ages in Wales.

Duke Richard's unpaid debts

Although York left a valid will, he died intestate because his executors refused to act.[21] Probably the assets at their disposal were insignificant compared with the mountain of accumulated debts. Prominent among these were the arrears of the unpaid dowries of the Duke's elder daughters, Anne and Elizabeth. When Duke Richard's eldest daughter, Anne, aged six, married the Duke of Exeter's heir, Henry Holand, aged seventeen, in 1445, her dowry was £3,000, but only one-third of that sum had been paid when Exeter died two years afterwards, and it unlikely that his executors were ever able to recover the balance of 3,000 marks mentioned as outstanding in Duke John Holand's will. York's second daughter, Elizabeth, was contracted in marriage in 1458 to the young John de la Pole, second Duke of Suffolk, and her dowry was fixed at 4,000 marks (£2,666 13s. 4d.). Only 1,200 marks had been paid by 1472, when Edward IV settled this debt by granting Alice Chaucer, Dowager-Duchess of Suffolk, the lordship and manor of Leighton Buzzard (Bedfordshire), but the de la Poles did not hold that estate for very long. After the death of the dowager-duchess in 1475, her son John, Duke of Suffolk, was coerced by his brother-in-law, Edward IV, into granting Leighton Buzzard as an endowment to St George's Chapel, Windsor.[22]

[18] Pugh, *MLSW*, pp. 175–8.

[19] Ibid. pp. 179–80.

[20] *Glamorgan County History*, iii, *The Middle Ages*, ed. T. B. Pugh (Cardiff, 1971), p. 683, n. 96. For the revenues of the lordship in the later middle ages, see D. H. Owen, 'The Lordship of Denbigh 1282–1425' (unpub. Wales Univ. Ph.D. thesis, 1967), pp. 328, 347. The receiver of Denbigh paid £1,331 to the receiver-general in 1366 and £1,123 was paid in 1370.

[21] For Duke Richard's intestacy, see *Registrum Thome Bourgchier Archiepiscopi, 1454–1486*, ed. F. R. H. Du Boulay, Canterbury and York Society, 54 (1956), p. 200 (commission to Thomas Colt, 15 Dec. 1461).

[22] *The Wills of the Kings and Queens of England*, ed. J. Nichols (London, 1780), pp. 283, 289; *Descriptive Catalogue of Ancient Deeds*, iv, nos. A.6337–A.6343; *Letters and Papers of the Reigns of Richard III and Henry VII*, ed. J. Gairdner, Rolls Series (1857), i, p. 281.

Suffolk gained little materially from his marriage to the king's sister Elizabeth, which in Tudor England led to the ruin and destruction of his house.

In the theology of the late medieval Church, those who died with their debts unpaid on earth could not go to heaven, saving always the infinite mercy of God. York, in company with many other royal and noble souls, probably did not make it. The failure to pay much of his daughters' dowries suggests that the grand total of his indebtedness amounted to considerably more than the sum of about £6,000, as his recent biographer has conjectured.[23] If York had no scruples about bilking his social equals among the English higher nobility, it is unlikely that his creditors of lesser rank fared better. The piety of York's widow, Cecily Neville, has been commended, but although she had ample resources, she did nothing to help pay off her late husband's debts and so to ensure his soul's transit to heaven. The Duchess Cecily prudently took the whole of her huge jointure of 5,000 marks a year from York's lands and annuities in England and she left the Welsh marcher lordships, with their declining revenues, to her eldest son, Edward IV. In 1462 the king assigned to Thomas Colt, one of York's servants, the late duke's lands in Yorkshire, Dorset and Essex, together with £700 a year from the customs, to establish a fund to pay off Duke Richard's debts. Nothing came of this arrangement, which should have made available cash amounting to over £1,000 annually. Colt died in 1467 and eventually, in 1480, when £681 was still owing, York's surviving creditors had to settle for what they could get.[24] Probably most of the late duke's debts were never paid. When Edward IV died in 1483, he too did not leave enough to pay for the cost of his funeral and once again intestacy ensued.

York's dealings with Sir John Fastolf

The collapse of York's first rebellion in February 1452 exhausted his resources. Hiring troops was expensive: the rate of pay was 6d. a day and the campaign lasted several weeks. York's household was as costly as that of John of Gaunt; a fragmentary household account for the period between October 1450 and the end of January 1451 indicates that household expenditure was running at the rate of over £5,000 a year.[25] The drastic fall in the receipts of his Welsh lands suggests that he was no longer able to meet costs on such a scale. He was obliged to borrow £3,000 from Cardinal Beaufort's executors. Sir John Fastolf, York's long-time associate and one of his former councillors in France, stood as a surety for the repayment of this loan. On 18 December 1452 York raised

[23] Johnson, *Duke Richard*, p. 221.

[24] *CPR 1461–1467*, pp. 107, 132–3; *1467–1477*, p. 362. C. A. J. Armstrong, 'The Piety of Cicely, Duchess of York', *For Hilaire Belloc*, ed. D. Woodruff (London, 1942), pp. 73–94; J. M. W. Bean, 'The Financial Position of Richard, Duke of York', *War and Government in the Middle Ages: Essays in Honour of John Prestwich*, ed. J. C. Holt and J. Gillingham (Woodbridge, 1984), pp. 182–97, esp. p. 197. Payment of £396 13s. 4d. of the late duke's debts was ordered on 27 April 1480.

[25] Fragmentary York household account, 1 Oct. 1450 to 31 Jan. 1451, lists expenses totalling £1,842 8s. 5d, i.e. over £5,000 a year, Hampshire RO, Marker Mill MS 57; V. J. Gorman, 'The Public Career of Richard, Duke of York: A Case Study of the Nobility of the Fifteenth Century' (unpub. Catholic Univ. of America Ph.D. thesis, 1981), p. 108, n. 659. For wages of war, see *Rot. Parl.*, v, pp. 230–1 and J. H. Ramsay, *Lancaster and York* (Oxford, 1892), ii, pp. 162, 169.

more cash by borrowing from Fastolf, but on very hard terms: he obtained a loan of 700 marks, and for reasons not specified, he was also indebted to Fastolf for a further sum of 400 marks (£266 13s. 4d.), possibly the interest on this loan. In return for these moneys, York pawned to Fastolf the most valuable jewels he possessed, namely 'a very rich brooch called in English "a White Rose"', ornamented with a great pointed diamond, together with 'a nowche [brooch] of gold in the facion of a ragged staf, with 2 ymages of a man and a woman garnysshed with a ruby, a diamande and a greet perle' worth 500 marks, and 'a floure of gold' worth £40. The White Rose ornament is said to have cost 4,000 marks when it was purchased, probably in the late fourteenth century. It is the most expensive jewel known to have been in private hands in medieval England and it was no doubt a cherished family heirloom of the House of March. York had been obliged to pledge jewels worth some 4,560 marks to secure a loan of 700 marks and furthermore these valuable treasures were to become Fastolf's property if Duke Richard failed to redeem them by paying £437 by 24 June of the following year. York could not find the necessary cash and consequently these jewels were still in Fastolf's possession when he died in 1459. K. B. McFarlane misunderstood this singular transaction. He believed that the White Rose was a jewelled collar (not a brooch) and he was pleased to think of Fastolf wearing around his neck on some splendid occasion a magnificent ornament that had cost as much as his nine Suffolk manors. More importantly, McFarlane was persuaded that these costly jewels were a gift from York to Fastolf for services rendered. He imagined that York was rich enough to give away jewellery worth thousands of pounds at a time when Duke Richard was in desperate financial straits.[26] After Fastolf's death, his executors chose to pretend that the White Rose and the other jewels had been given to their late master as a free gift and they were therefore entitled to keep them as part of his estate. Early in his reign, although he had great financial problems, Edward IV took prompt action to recover the lost family jewels. Shortly after his coronation, on 27 July 1461, he undertook to pay 700 marks (£466 13s. 4d.) to redeem them, and also an obligation for 100 marks on which Duke Richard had stood bound to Fastolf.[27] Few of York's creditors were fortunate enough to secure such early repayment.

York's sales of land

In parliament in February 1454, Duke Richard declared that because of the government's failure to pay him the wages for his terms of service in France and Ireland, he had been forced to 'celle a grete substance of my lyvelood, to leye in plege all my greete Jowellys, and the most partie of my Plate not yit requited'.[28] York exaggerated his misfortunes. His financial problems were made acute by his own folly in launching his ill-considered rebellion. He was owed large sums

[26] *The Paston Letters 1422–1509*, ed. J. Gairdner, 6 vols. (London, 1904), ii, pp. 280–1; iv, p. 233. K. B. McFarlane, 'The Investment of Sir John Fastolf's Profits of War', *TRHS*, 5th series, 7 (1957), pp. 91–116, esp. pp. 108–9; McFarlane, *Nobility*, p. 98.

[27] *CPR 1461–1467*, p. 96.

[28] *Rot. Parl.*, v, p. 255.

of money by the Lancastrian government and like the rest of Henry VI's creditors he had to wait for payment, but he did not do too badly. Most of what was due to him as wages for his years as lieutenant-general in France were eventually paid, but he was less successful in recovering his salary as the king's representative in Ireland and, later on, as Lord Protector of England. Signs of financial stringency appeared in 1449, when sales of wood in seven English counties produced over £107.[29] Probably York was having difficulty in raising the funds he needed to pay for his Irish expedition. Between 1448 and 1452, he sold or alienated sixteen manors and other lands, and he mortgaged two Welsh lordships.

Duke Richard could afford to lose a few manors, because he had inherited (or acquired) more lands than his uncles Edward, Duke of York and Edmund Mortimer, Earl of March had ever held. After the death of Humphrey, Duke of Gloucester, in February 1447, York gained valuable properties formerly held by his late kinsman.[30] As grandson of Eleanor Holand (d. 1405), Countess of March, he was heir to a one-fifth share of the estates of the earldom of Kent, which were partitioned in 1408 among the five coheirs of the last Holand earl, Edmund. Most of the lands of the Kent earldom were at that time in the hands of the four dowager-countesses. The inheritance originated in Edward I's undertaking to Philip IV in 1306 to settle lands worth 7,000 marks (£4,666 13s. 4d.) a year on his youngest son, Edmund. In 1353 the dower of Countess Elizabeth of Juliers (d. 1411) was assessed a £1,025. Early in the fifteenth century, the Kent lands were valued at £2,958 6s. 1d. in inquisitions post mortem, which excluded property worth around £64 *p.a.* held by Countess Joan Stafford. As the Holand lands of Joan, Duchess of York, were worth at least £456 in 1434, York's share after 1442 cannot have amounted to lands worth less than £500 a year.[31]

Those who profited when York was obliged to dispose of some of his property included men prominent in the duke's service, including the lawyers, William Burley and Thomas Young, and York's chamberlain, chief councillor (and evil genius) Sir William Oldhall. As early as 1441, Oldhall had acquired a life-interest in four of York's manors in the counties of Buckingham, Oxford and Kent, and subsequently by 1449 he had obtained a grant for life of lands belonging to the duke in Gloucestershire. Oldhall's most spectacular acquisition was the manor of Hunsdon (Hertfordshire), which York sold or granted him. Sir William built at Hunsdon one of the finest houses in fifteenth-century England, at a cost of 7,000 marks. If York was short of money, it is significant that his chief henchman was not. J. S. Roskell regarded Oldhall as the leader of the 'disappointed, sour and unforgiving men' who had arrived on the scene too late to make their fortunes from the Hundred Years War and who were determined out of revenge to bring down the House of Lancaster, which had

[29] BL Egerton Roll 8785.

[30] See below, Appendix II. After Gloucester's death in 1447, York came into possession of Great Wratting manor (Suff.) and was granted Hadleigh manor (Essex), *CPR 1446–1452*, pp. 43, 79. He later recovered the Isle of Wight, which was granted to him for life (Wolffe, *Royal Demesne*, p. 258).

[31] For the Holand estates, see Pugh, 'Richard Plantagenet', p. 134, McFarlane, *Nobility*, p. 26; *CCR 1349–1354*, p. 530; M. M. H. Stansfield, 'The Hollands, Dukes of Exeter, Earls of Kent and Huntingdon, 1352–1475' (unpub. Oxford Univ. D.Phil. thesis, 1987), pp. 154, 166; *CFR 1430–1437*, pp. 208–9.

failed them. It is clear that Oldhall did well enough out of his service to Richard, Duke of York. He had started life as a Norfolk esquire with property worth about £30 a year. In 1436 he declared his taxable income in England to be worth £216 a year, and probably much was gained by his profitable marriage with Lord Willoughby's sister Margaret, the well-jointured widow of Sir Thomas Skipwith. By 1449 Oldhall's fortunes had greatly improved and he admitted to having a taxable income of £369 a year.[32] In lands and wealth he now ranked with the lesser baronage, and if he had not died late in 1460, he would probably have been one of the newly-created peers summoned to Edward IV's first parliament. Oldhall's conspicuous wealth has been overlooked. He was doubtless well aware of the possibilities of greater enrichment if his master became king of England. Like Henry VI, Duke Richard was in the hands of men who put their own interests first.

York's claim to the crown

Duke Richard's re-entry into English politics in the autumn of 1460 shattered the governmental stability established after the battle of Northampton, fought on 10 July. When parliament began its proceedings at Westminster on 7 October, York was not present. He arrived three days late, having allowed time for the repeal of his attainder at the Coventry parliament of 1459. During the last stage of his march to London, York had assumed royal state when he reached Abingdon. When he strode into the parliament house on 10 October, he expected to be enthroned after acclamation by the assembled peers and that did not happen. Instead Archbishop Bourchier asked him if he wished to see the king. The Lords as a body were still loyal to Henry VI. This episode shows once again York's lack of political sense. He had not expected to have to argue his case.

His claim to the throne, submitted on 16 October, was a genealogical table. York contended that he was the rightful king of England by virtue of his descent from his great-grandmother, Edward III's granddaughter, Philippa (1355–81), Countess of March. York's claim was unconvincing and preposterous. The sovereign's daughters could not take precedence over his sons and there was no reason why the descendants of Edward III's granddaughter should disinherit the line established by Henry IV, who had a good claim to be regarded as Richard II's lawful heir. York's claim was plausible only if the kingdom of England was regarded as being no different in kind from a tenancy-in-chief or a piece of real estate in land, liable to partition among female coheiresses. As Fortescue later observed, if York's premises were valid, he had proved that the rightful king of England was neither Henry VI nor Duke Richard, but the child king of the Scots, James III. York was maintaining that there had been no lawful government in England since the deposition of Richard II in 1399. When King Richard was overthrown, no one had suggested

[32] For Oldhall's career, see J. S. Roskell, 'Sir William Oldhall, Speaker in the Parliament of 1450–1', *Nottingham Medieval Studies*, v (1961), pp. 87–112; *The Commons and their Speakers in English Parliaments 1376–1523* (Manchester, 1965), p. 242. For Oldhall's tax returns, see PRO E 163/7/31 pt 2 (1436); E 359/29 m.24 (1450).

disinheriting the English royal house in order to transfer the crown to the child Edmund Mortimer, a descendant of Edward II's alleged murderer. The English nobility as a class had gained much from the reigns of the three Lancastrian kings and the lords had a strong vested interest in keeping Henry VI on the throne. Their reaction to York's claim to the throne was, for most of them, to absent themselves from parliament.[33] Some of the peers met in conference at Blackfriars and their deliberations produced proposals for a compromise.

The *Accord* of 1460

The *Accord* designed to resolve this constitutional crisis was announced in parliament on 25 October; Henry VI was to remain king for life, unless he chose to abdicate, but York was to succeed him. The task of dealing with this unprecedented problem was left to the Lords. The Commons were not consulted and no one seems to have thought of asking their opinion. When the Lords came before the king on 17 October, he had asked them to formulate objections on his behalf to York's claim to the crown. They did not make a good job of it. The defence of Henry VI's title that was devised was feeble; it looks like an argument put up so that it could easily be knocked down. The Lords at first sought to refer this assignment to the judges; perhaps with memories of 1388, the latter replied that the matter was beyond their learning. The law officers of the crown followed the example set by the judges and likewise evaded responsibility. The *Accord*, which apparently took over a week to emerge, may have owed much to the influence of the chancellor, Bishop George Neville of Exeter, and later the papal legate, Francesco Coppini, claimed that he had played an important role.

What was being settled in October was the succession to the English throne. As York was ten years older than Henry, there could be no certainty that he would live long enough to succeed the last Lancastrian king. The Lords seem to have been attached to their sovereign by ties of loyalty, but they had no difficulty in disinheriting his son, Edward, Prince of Wales. Probably hostility to Henry VI's French queen, Margaret of Anjou, enabled them to reach that decision. If Prince Edward had succeeded his father, Queen Margaret would have become ruler of England.

Although the king assented readily to these proposals when they were put before him, on 25 October, York did not want the *Accord*. It was not until 31 October that Duke Richard, accompanied by his elder sons, Edward and Edmund, came into parliament to declare their acceptance of the agreement. The bait that at last secured York's reluctant acquiescence was financial. He appears to have been short of money in the last months of his life. He was promised an endowment of 10,000 marks (£6,666 13s. 4d.) a year, which

[33] *Registrum Abbathiae Johannis Whetehamstede*, ed. H. T. Riley, Rolls Series (1872–3), i, 377. Whetehamstede did not attend parliament in 1460–1 and thus did not witness the exchanges between Archbishop Bourchier and York: J. Fortescue, *The Governance of England*, ed. C. Plummer (Oxford, 1926), p. 353. For the absence of peers from parliament in Oct. 1460, see 'William Worcester, Annales', in Stevenson, ii.ii, p. 774. For the conference at Blackfriars, see Johnson, *Duke Richard*, p. 214.

included 3,600 marks (£2,400) annually for his heir Edward, Earl of March, and £1,000 (£666 13s. 4d.) a year for his second son Edmund, Earl of Rutland. It looked like a solution to York's financial problems, as it would have more than doubled his landed income, but how this generous settlement was to be realised was far from clear. The new heir to the throne and two of his sons were to be provided for out of the revenues of the dispossessed Lancastrian Prince of Wales, but in the previous year his possessions (including the principality of Wales, duchy of Cornwall and earldom of Chester) had been rated as worth no more than £876 annually.[34] The impoverished Lancastrian dynasty could not find 10,000 marks a year to endow the rival House of York.

Duke Richard had no intention of allowing the *Accord* to remain in force for so long. The agreement twice referred to the possibility that Henry VI might prefer to abdicate, and, after York had given his assent to it, the king was removed from the palace of Westminster and taken to reside at the bishop of London's house. Duke Richard had been left in an unprecedented position. He had been recognised as the rightful king of England, but he could not have the crown that he had coveted for so long. The *Accord* cobbled together in October 1460 solved no problems and it made inevitable the outbreak of civil war. The inanity of Henry VI has been identified as one of the main causes of the Wars of the Roses, but York's ruthless ambition was more decisive in reducing England to civil war, an outcome which the nobility as a class did not desire.

Duke Richard's place in English history

Duke Richard's greatest achievement was to deprive the House of Lancaster of its right and title to the crown of England. By assenting to the *Accord* of October 1460, Henry VI conceded the whole justice of the Yorkist case. York had avenged the death of his father Richard, Earl of Cambridge, executed for treason in 1415, and he reduced the Lancastrian kings, who had ruled England not unsuccessfully for three generations, to the status of usurpers. York's claim was accepted by a parliament from which all active Lancastrians among the Lords had already been excluded. The *Accord* of 1460 never became a parliamentary statute because the parliament of 1460–1 was dissolved by the deposition of Henry VI on 4 March 1461, but henceforth possession of the crown of England was regarded as legally vested in the House of York. Duke Richard contended that the English crown belonged in perpetuity to his family and he maintained that no power on earth could deprive the true heir of his just title and undoubted right to the kingdom. York's doctrine of pure legitimism was to become the foundation of the divine right of kings. The Lords agreed in 1460 that parliament could not alter the succession to the crown by statute and that doctrine prevailed until the end of the seventeenth century. The Act of Settlement of 1701 abolished hereditary right as a title to the crown of Great

[34] *Rot. Parl.*, v, pp. 373–8, 380–1. For the value of the lands of Edward, Prince of Wales, in 1459, see *CPR 1452–1461*, p. 515. To finance his last campaign in Dec. 1460, York borrowed £671 from twenty-five Londoners, including £345 loaned by Alderman Christopher Wartler; see Gorman, 'Richard, Duke of York', p. 321.

Britain and substituted instead parliamentary statute as the sole source of right to the British throne.

Towards the end of his reign, Edward III appears to have intended to settle the succession of the crown on his male heirs, to the exclusion of his female descendants. His aim was to make his favourite son, John of Gaunt, heir to the throne, after the accession of the king's young grandson, Richard. Edward III's reign ended before his death and that purpose was never accomplished.

No woman ever ruled as queen in medieval England. Henry I's daughter Matilda failed to make good her claim to become her father's heir. In 1290 Edward I settled the succession to the crown on his five daughters, in order of seniority, if the last of his sons by Eleanor of Castile predeceased him, but that royal ordinance never took effect and it had been long forgotten before 1460.[35] The kingdom of England had existed for five hundred years and it had never had a female sovereign. England had in effect an unwritten Salic law before Richard Plantagenet (the surname he assumed in 1460) changed the law of succession to the crown. He established the right of a woman to transmit a valid title to the English throne, and that fundamental change in the law governing the succession made possible the accession of his descendants Queens Jane, Mary I and Elizabeth I, in Tudor England. Seldom has a mediocre man had more influence on the course of English history.

Appendix I

Henry VII's confirmation on 2 July 1507 of charters granted to the tenants of the lordships of Ceri and Cydewain on 31 August 1447 by Richard (1411–60), Duke of York.[36] [PRO C 66/602 m.27 (7)]

For the residents of the lordship of Kery and Kedewen.

[1] The king to all to whom, etc. We have inspected two charters of Kery and Kedewen granted by our dear cousin Richard, late Duke of York, to the tenants, inhabitants and residents of our lordship of Kery and Kedewen, of which charters the tenor of the charter of Kery follows in these words.

[2] Richard, Duke of York, Earl of March and Ulster, lord of Wigmore, Clare and Kery. Know that we by the present letters have granted to all our tenants and residents of our lordship of Kery that they and their heirs shall in future be quit and discharged of all fines and amercements which should belong to us and our heirs by occasion of any summons called *comanva* [cymanfa = assembly] made there hereafter between courts by our ringild[37] of the aforesaid

[35] *Rot. Parl.*, v, pp. 380–1. The text of Edward I's ordinance of 1290 has not survived; for the oath taken by Gilbert de Clare (d. 1295), Earl of Gloucester, concerning the succession to the crown, see Rymer, *Foedera* (1727), ii, p. 747; F. M. Powicke, *Henry III and the Lord Edward* (Oxford, 1947), pp. 733, 788. For Edward III's unsuccessful attempt to entail the crown in the male line, see M. Bennett, 'Edward III's Entail and the Succession to the Crown, 1376–1471', *EHR*, cxiii (1998), 580–609.

[36] Numerals and words inserted by the editor are in square brackets. Place names have not been modernised. Modern forms of Welsh words have been inserted in brackets. The editor is obliged to Professor R. R. Davies for his assistance.

[37] Beadle: a subordinate officer of the commote who collected rents and issued summonses.

lordship on his own behalf. Provided always that they obey every summons by the lord or his council, steward, receiver or lieutenant.

[3] And that where for cutting down or lopping any trees or branches in a certain wood called in Welsh *Ewayter*, the tenants and residents of the aforesaid lordship before this time were bound by the law of the country to pay three pounds in silver for such a trespass whenever they trespassed, we have also granted to them and their heirs that they should be quit and discharged of such fine of three pounds, but that they should be bound to pay five shillings for every trespass made in future to our injury in the lord's wood.

[4] And where formerly, according to the law and custom of our aforesaid lordship, the usage was that if any woman had brought before the aforesaid officers any appeal of rape, that the defendant for that deed should pay us a fine of three pounds, we will and grant by these present letters that all defendants in such cases shall hereafter be quit and discharged of such fines of three pounds.

[5] We have also granted to them and their heirs that wherever they or their beasts or cattle are taken within our forest of Herethowell,[38] that they shall pay for that cause five shillings and not more.

[6] We have by the present letters remitted and released to the same tenants and residents and their heirs all our right and claim which we have in a certain rent called in Welsh *Kyllch goyle* [Cylchgwyl][39] and *Nerthhave* [nerth haf][40] which used to amount to the annual sum of four pounds and ten shillings.

[7] We have also pardoned and released to Ieuan ap Howell ap John, Maddoc ap Howell and Gryffith ap Dykos and their heirs a certain service which our ringild of the aforesaid lordship before this time used to compel them and their ancestors to make, namely to drive and bring distraints to the lord's pound there for the lord's rent, amercements and fines.

[8] We have also granted that no ringild in the aforesaid lordship shall in future take from the aforesaid tenants and residents and their heirs any fine exceeding four pence, except in the case when the lord should take the fine of seven pounds, and in such a case the ringild should take a fine as of old time they used to take, according to the law and custom of the country.

[9] We have approved, ratified and confirmed by the present letters all privileges, liberties, laws and customs before this time lawfully and legitimately had, used and enjoyed by the said tenants and residents and their ancestors. For which gifts, grants, remissions, pardons and releases, the said tenants and residents have granted us six hundred marks, to be paid in six terms of the year[s] next coming, to wit the first payments beginning at the feast of All Saints [1 November] and the apostles Philip and James [1 May] next coming, and so from year to year equally at the aforesaid feasts until the aforesaid sum of six hundred marks shall be fully paid.

[10] In witness whereof we have put our seal to the present letters. Given at our castle of Montgomery, the last day of August in the twenty-fifth year of the reign of Henry the Sixth after the Conquest [1447].

[38] Probably Hirhowell, a district to the east of Llandinam, co. Montgomery, *Montgomeryshire Collections*, xxv (1891), p. 30.

[39] This was the circuit due, amounting to £3, formerly payable for the progress of the king's household at Christmas; see Rees, *South Wales* p. 228.

[40] *Nerth hav* was the summer subsidy, worth 30s. a year.

[11] Another charter of Kedewen follows in these words;

[12] Richard, Duke of York, Earl of March and Ulster, lord of Wigmore, Clare and Kedewen, to all to whom our present letters shall come, greeting in the Lord.

[13] Know that we the aforesaid duke, for a thousand mark of lawful money of England which all our bondmen belonging and pertaining to the aforesaid lordship of Kedewen have with their assent fully paid to us by hand, have manumitted them and made free each of them, of whatever sex or condition, and all his descendants and each of them, both born and to be born, and have freed them from all yoke of servitude and servile condition. So that neither we the aforesaid duke nor our heirs nor any other by us or in our name shall in future demand, claim or lay claim to any right or claim in our aforesaid bondmen or any of them, or in the descendants of them or any of them born or to be born, or in their goods and chattels, in whatever parts of the world they resort or happen to resort, but what we shall be wholly excluded in future from all action of right and claim concerning them in perpetuity.

[14] And know moreover that we by these presents have remitted released and quitclaimed for us and our heirs forever to all and each of our said bondmen and to all their descendants all right, title and claim which we have had, have or in any way in future can have in a certain rents and servile custom called in Welsh *ardreth* [rent] otherwise called *mergynyaethe*,[41] which our aforesaid bondmen are bound and are accustomed to render annually at the feasts of Christmas and the Nativity of St John the Baptist [24 June], both in money and in the price of hens, which rent and custom amount annually to the sum of £7 17s. 11¾d., whereof the ringild of Egville[42] is charged in his office yearly at 26s. 6½d., and the ringild of Treganon[43] in his office in 57s. 11¼d., and the ringild of Llanlloghaidron[44] annually in his office with 73s. 6d., as more fully appears in their rolls of account of their offices under the title of custom.

[15] And where all our said bondmen of old are bound and accustomed to pay to us the aforesaid duke and our ancestors every year a certain rent called in Welsh *guerth gwenith* [the value of wheat], to wit when a measure of corn is priced at twelve pence, then they ought to pay that sum, and when a measure is priced higher, they ought to pay more and when less, less, according to how much it is valued in the market of Newtown.[45] Because the aforesaid rent is uncertain and changeable, we have given and granted to our said bondmen and their descendants, born and to be born, that in future they should pay to us and our heirs annually for each measure of corn 6d., and for each measure by name of *gullyn* 6d., and that they should not have regard to the price of the measure in the aforesaid market, provided that the said bondmen and their heirs pay the aforesaid rent annually at the accustomed terms.

[16] We also give and grant to our aforesaid bondmen and all their descendants that they and each of them shall in future be free and excused of a certain rent called in Welsh *keyrch march stuart* [the oats of the steward's

41 Probably *maeroniaeth*, the payment due for the upkeep of the *maer* (steward or local official).

42 Eginlle, the southern part of the lordship of Cydewain; see W. Rees, *An Historical Atlas of Wales* (Cardiff, 1951), plate 28.

43 Tregynon, a parish in the commote of Cydewain, five miles north of Newtown, co. Montgomery.

44 Llanllwchaern, a parish in the commote of Cydewain, adjoining Newton on the north-east.

45 Newtown, co. Montgomery.

stallion][46] and that they be discharged and quit of the bringing forward and pursuit of distraints taken in the lordship aforesaid for our rent or that of our heirs.

[17] And moreover we have granted to our aforesaid bondmen by these present for us and our heirs for ever that if hereafter it befall that any tenant or resident of the aforesaid lordship or any other, a stranger, shall kill any of our said bondmen or those of our heirs, that then the person responsible for the killing shall pay four score and ten pounds [£90] for the death of the person killed, whereof a third part ought to belong to us and to our heirs, whoever they may be at that time, for every person killed, as often as that case shall happen to occur.

[18] And moreover we will and grant by these present letters patent that our said bondmen and all their descendants, and all lands and tenements which they now hold from us or shall hold from our heirs within our aforesaid lordship, shall in future be quit, free and discharged for ever from all servitude and servile conditions and customs whatsoever, so that in every way they enjoy the liberties which our free tenants have and enjoy throughout our aforesaid lordship.

[19] And for perpetual affirmation of this our aforesaid grant we have caused our present letters to be confirmed with our seal of arms. Given at our castle of Montgomery, the last day of August in the twenty-fifth year of the reign of King Henry the Sixth after the Conquest [1447].

[20] Know that we, for certain causes and considerations moving us, have ratified, approved, granted and confirmed all and singular grants, customs and liberties contained and specified in the aforesaid charters of our aforesaid cousin and by these presents ratify, approve, grant and confirm them to our aforesaid tenants, inhabitants and residents of Kery and Kedwen, their heirs and successors, provided namely that neither we, nor our heirs and successors shall or ought in future be able to demand, claim or lay claim to any right, title, demand or interest of or in the aforesaid grants, customs or liberties, nor in any parcel thereof in future, but that we shall be wholly excluded from them for ever.

[21] And moreover know that we of our more abundant grace have remitted, released and quitclaimed for us and our heirs and successors for ever to all and singular our aforesaid tenants, inhabitants and residents of our lordship Kery and Kedewen and to their heirs and successors, all our right, title, and claim which we have ever had, have or in any way whatsoever shall have in future of and in a certain custom called in Welsh *amobrythiaeth*, otherwise called amobrships,[47] provided namely that neither we nor our heirs and successors shall be able nor ought in future to demand, claim or lay claim to or in any right, title or claim concerning or in the aforesaid custom from henceforth, but that we shall be wholly excluded from them for ever.

[22] In witness whereof etc. Witnessed by the king at Westminster, the second day of July. By writ of privy seal and of date etc. For forty shillings paid in the hanaper.

[End of the enrolment]

[46] Probably *ceirch* (oats), not *cylch* (circuit); see Rees, *South Wales*, pp. 54, n. 3, 226–7, n. 7, 228.

[47] *Amobr*, i.e. amobrage, the marriage fine payable to a lord.

Appendix II

Lands alienated by Richard, Duke of York

Date	Property	Purchaser
1443	Grays-in-Cavendish manor (Suffolk)	Edmund Mulso[48]
1448–9	Cressage manor (Shropshire), Arley manor (Staffordshire)	William Burley[49] and his wife
*c.*1448	Hunsdon manor (Hertfordshire)	Sir William Oldhall[50]
	10 manors in Kent, Surrey and Sussex	Thomas Browne, undertreasurer of the exchequer[51]
1449	Castle and lordship of Traen March, parcel of St Clears Lordship, co. Carmarthen	Gruffydd ap Nicholas[52]
1449	Castle and lordship of Narberth, co. Pembroke	Gruffydd ap Nicholas[53]
1451	Easton-in-Gordano (Somerset)	Thomas Young[54]
1452	Hambleton (Rutland)	Ralph Lord Cromwell[55]
n.d.	Lands in Oxfordshire	William Lord Lovel (d. 1455)[56]

48 *CCR 1461–1468*, p. 114.
49 Ibid. *1468–1476*, p. 165.
50 *CPR 1446–1452*, pp. 77, 233.
51 Bean, 'York', pp. 194–5; Johnson, *Duke Richard*, pp. 60–1. This transaction was probably intended to facilitate payment at the exchequer of sums due to Richard, Duke of York.
52 *L&P, Henry VIII*, ii(i), no. 557.
53 *CPR 1446–1452*, pp. 234–5; *1452–1461*, p. 41.
54 Bean, 'York', p. 192; Johnson, *Duke Richard*, pp. 63, 241.
55 *CPR 1446–1452*, p. 218; Bean, 'York', p. 104, n. 64.
56 *CCR 1476–1485*, nos. 255, 284.

Middlesex in the Fifteenth Century: Community or Communities?

Jessica Freeman

The question in my title is intended to pull together, albeit briefly, my thoughts on the existence – or otherwise – of a late medieval county community in Middlesex.[1] That is, did the gentry elite, the knights and esquires who were the county's leaders, see themselves as defined by a corporate shire identity based on their greater landholdings and monopoly of important offices within Middlesex? Or did the county consist of a number of diverse communities, bound only by overlapping ties of kinship, trade, neighbourhood or allegiance to a great magnate? Did those living within the shire, led by the gentry elite, consider themselves 'men of Middlesex', who expressed a sense of county community through their participation in parliamentary elections as well as through their shared involvement in the administration of the shire, or were elections simply a temporary coming together in response to a specific summons?

There have been several studies of fifteenth-century gentry based on their county structure, although none is directly comparable. Simon Payling, in his research into thirteen greater gentry families in Nottinghamshire, in the first half of the fifteenth century, thought that it was difficult to discern any corporate county identity amongst them, although he did conclude that there was a 'sense of community of shared interests'. Susan Wright, in a larger study of some fifty Derbyshire gentry families (*c.*1430–1500), considered that their interests were largely confined to the neighbourhood of their estates and within kinship networks. However, she did note that the gentry were bearing an increasingly large proportion of the burden of county administration. Eric Acheson's examination of 176 Leicestershire gentry (*c.*1422–*c.*1485) suggested that there was both a social community of the county, shown by an inclination to use men of their own shire as witnesses or feoffees, as well as a political community of gentry from whom the administrators of the county were selected, and who provided a cohesive force within the shire. Christine Carpenter, on the other hand, in her study of Warwickshire landed society (1401–99), considered that it was the Earl of Warwick and his household who provided the county's dominant unifying force.[2]

[1] I am grateful to Professor Caroline Barron for her advice and assistance in the preparation of this article.

[2] S. J. Payling, *Political Society in Lancastrian England: The Greater Gentry of Notttinghamshire* (Oxford, 1991), pp. 216–18; S. M. Wright, *The Derbyshire Gentry in the Fifteenth Century*, Derbyshire Record Society, viii (1983), pp. 11, 58–9, 143, 146; E. Acheson, *A Gentry Community: Leicestershire in the Fifteenth Century c.1422–c.1485* (Cambridge, 1992), pp. 39, 41–2, 92, 134, 201–3; Carpenter, *Locality and Polity*, pp. 288, 618, 638.

My approach has been along political lines, by which is meant a study of the forty Middlesex men elected as shire-knights between 1399 and 1491, who invariably came from the ranks of the gentry, together with the several hundred men who made up the fifteenth-century parliamentary attestors, and who cover the social spectrum from knight to yeoman. Parliament in 1406 had laid down new electoral procedures, so that, after an election had been held, an indenture was to be drawn up on which were recorded not only the names of the knights-elect but also the names and seals of all those present, that is the electors, who would attest to the validity of the election. In 1429 another parliamentary statute restricted the electorate to the forty-shilling freeholder, a qualification which remained in place until the nineteenth century.[3] This franchise was, however, sufficiently wide to make parliamentary elections the concern of more than simply the gentry, which in turn suggests that the more prosperous yeoman and artisan was considered to have a legitimate interest in who represented them in the House of Commons.

In Middlesex there survive thirty-one parliamentary indentures out of a total of forty-three parliaments between 1407 and 1478: the numbers in each indenture range from fourteen to sixty-seven, giving 1,007 readable names, or about 480 individuals. However, although the 1406 statute required everyone attending to attest to the election's validity, this is unlikely to have taken place; each indenture simply gives a sample of those present.[4] Elections took place at the Middlesex county court, the assembly of the freemen of the shire; from the end of the thirteenth century this met not at one fixed point, but on a regular circuit of Brentford, Ossulston (at or just south of present-day Marble Arch) and Stone Cross (in the Strand). This county court was still active in the mid-fifteenth century, for in 1469 two men were outlawed because although the sheriff of Middlesex had ordered them to appear at five consecutive county courts, held in rotation at these three places, they had failed to do so.[5]

The right of Middlesex to elect two knights of the shire was significant, for down to this present century the county has suffered from a lack of collective institutions (and now even the name itself has virtually disappeared, although there is at least a county cricket team!). Henry I had granted the citizens of London the right to appoint the sheriffs of both London and Middlesex, regarded for that purpose as one unit; from 1132 onwards the two sheriffs were always London citizens, and were not drawn from the Middlesex gentry.[6] Yet the picture may not have been quite as it appeared. John Carpenter's *Liber Albus*, his 1419 compilation of the customs of the city of London, states that 'the person . . . appointed by the sheriffs to be their lieutenant in the county of Middlesex . . . shall be sworn each year'; presumably by this he meant that one

[3] O. Ruffhead, *Statutes at Large*, 9 vols. (London, 1769), i, pp. 469–70, cap. xv, and pp. 544–5, cap. vii; *HPT 1386–1421*, i, p. 62.

[4] PRO C 219/10/4–/17/3; C 219/330/24; J. A. F. Thomson, *The Transformation of Medieval England, 1370–1529* (London, 1983), pp. 398–401; S. J. Payling, 'County Parliamentary Elections in Fifteenth-Century England', *Parliamentary History*, 18 (1999), pp. 237–59, particularly pp. 242–3, 248.

[5] J. R. Maddicott, 'The Making of Public Opinion in Fourteenth Century England', *TRHS*, 5th series, 28 (1978), pp. 27–43, at pp. 29–30; D. Sullivan, *The Westminster Corridor* (London, 1994), pp. 47–9; *CPR 1467–1477*, p. 178.

[6] *Liber Albus*, p. 114; B. B. Orridge, *Citizens of London and their Rulers* (London, 1867), pp. 218–25.

of the three undersheriffs bore responsibility for the shire, and was to be differentiated from his fellow undersheriffs responsible for London.[7]

Middlesex was the second smallest county in England during the medieval period, and also the second richest, no doubt because within the shire lay the town of Westminster as well as the overspill from several London parishes. The irregular northern boundary with Hertfordshire included wooded uplands as well as the hunting park of Enfield Chase, whilst on the south, east and west were natural borders formed by the rivers Thames, Lea and Colne respectively, waterways alive with ferries and fishing boats, set with willow-covered islands, and home to an abundance of swans. Corn and hay, wheat and barley flourished on the fertile southern and central farmlands, well watered by streams flowing down to join the Thames: the Crane, Brent, Tyburn and Fleet. Husbandry, the carriage of produce, and malting were the main occupations.[8]

The shire was named for those Anglo-Saxon invaders who, settling as farmers along the river Thames, were given an early identity as the 'Middle Saxons'. Yet although it emerged as a separate administrative unit, with London as its burgh, the shire was never an independent kingdom, falling under the successive overlordship of the kings of Essex, Kent, Mercia and Wessex. This was why the diocese of London seems to have followed the boundaries of the kingdom of Essex, and why Middlesex did not receive a bishop in its own right. There is, however, an intriguing paragraph, apparently stressing the county's identity, to be found in the *Liber Albus*. Annually, on the Tuesday after Pentecost the mayor and aldermen of London were preceded into St Paul's Cathedral, the mother church of the diocese, by a procession of the people of Middlesex; there was a similar procession the next day for the people of Essex.[9]

Looking at the late medieval population of Middlesex, the *Nomina Villarum* of 1316 lists forty-eight vills (plus two sokes).[10] By the early sixteenth century there were seventy-five parishes of considerable diversity, ranging from the large, populous and urbanised parishes adjoining the city of London, for instance St Leonard Shoreditch, to the many small rural villages, like Cranford. In between these extremes were parishes such as St Clement Danes, which filled in the fields between London and the town of Westminster, whilst spread over the rest of the county were many semi-rural villages, for example Chiswick.[11] About forty of these seventy-five parishes (53%) had fewer than two hundred

[7] *Liber Albus*, p. 406; N. L. Ramsay, 'The English Legal Profession, *c.*1340–*c.*1450' (unpub. Cambridge Univ. Ph.D. thesis, 1985), p. 135; M. Blatcher, *The Court of the King's Bench 1450–1550* (London, 1978), pp. 42–3. Although at the beginning of the fifteenth century undersheriffs were appointed on an annual basis, by the 1450s the same person could be in office for years; he was often one of the clerks of King's Bench, whose knowledge of legal processes could have been invaluable in executing writs.

[8] *VCH Middx*, ii, pp. 61, 87, 127, 209.

[9] Sullivan, *Westminster Corridor*, pp. 16–20; *Liber Albus*, pp. 26–7.

[10] *Feudal Aids 1284–1431*, 6 vols. (London, 1899–1920), iii, pp. 372–4. This survey lists the holders of manors.

[11] 'The City of London from Prehistoric Times to *c.*1520', ed. M. Lobel and W. Johns, *British Atlas of Historic Towns*, iii (Oxford, 1989), parish map *c.*1520; D. Keene and V. Harding, *A Survey of Documentary Sources for Property Holding in London before the Great Fire*, LRS, 22 (1985), pp. xvii–xix; C. Humphrey-Smith, *Atlas and Index of Parish Registers* (Chichester, 1984), map 22.

communicants according to the 1548 chantry certificate, and no doubt even fewer a century earlier.[12]

However, there was no county town and Norden, in his *Speculum Britanniae*, published in 1593, mentions only four market towns: Westminster, Brentford, Staines and Uxbridge, with Harrow 'formerly' one. Westminster, Staines and Uxbridge did have strong and flourishing gilds, but these, together with Brentford, Enfield and Edmonton, were the only places that could justifiably be called towns, although none was of great note. It seems that much of Middlesex, as the hinterland of the city with all highways radiating from London, remained essentially a rural county serving the needs of the capital.[13]

Middlesex did present several unusual characteristics. Firstly, there were no parliamentary boroughs in the county, for although in 1275 Staines and Uxbridge had returned burgess Members of Parliament, no Middlesex town was to do so again until modern times.[14] Thus those yeomen and artisans who could have taken part in borough elections attended instead the elections for the knights of the shire, and this may have been of importance in forming a sense of county identity.

Yet, the shire's foremost distinction was its position vis-à-vis London, which crouched ever-expanding on the county's southern boundary, drawing immigrants from all over England as well as Europe, and providing in return a stream of wealthy citizens and prosperous craftsmen to purchase land in the surrounding counties and to participate in their government and administration.

To take one example, amongst the two lawyers elected for Middlesex was the London official Alexander Anne, the younger son of a Yorkshire gentry family, who was appointed Justice of the Peace for both counties. A member of the Drapers' Company, Anne was undersheriff for London in 1423, escheator for Middlesex in 1432, and recorder of London by 1436. He attended the Middlesex hustings in 1429 and 1433, and was thrice elected to parliament for the shire. In 1436 Anne held lands worth £44 in Somerset, Yorkshire and at Hackney, Middlesex, in whose church he asked to be buried, whilst towards the end of his life he acquired a country estate at North Aston, Oxfordshire.[15]

These parishes include the three chapelries of St Lawrence, West Brentford, nominally in Hanwell, St Margaret, Uxbridge, in Hillingdon, and St Mary, Stratford-le-Bow, in Stepney, although not the chapel of St John, Pinner, in Harrow. Brentford and Stratford, but not Uxbridge, had the right of burial for their parishioners by the mid-fifteenth century. Also judged as lying in Middlesex were four parishes which were partly in the county and partly in London: St Andrew Holborn, St Giles without Cripplegate, St Dunstan in the West and St Sepulchre without Newgate.

[12] *London and Middlesex Chantry Certificate, 1548*, ed. C. J. Kitching, LRS, 16 (1980), p. xxxi. This division of the county on broadly based population grounds agrees with that based on charitable donations by W. K. Jordan, *The Charities of London 1480–1660* (London, 1960), pp. 42–6.

[13] BL Harl. MS 570 f. 16; *VCH Middx*, ii, pp. 85, 121, 205; *CPR 1436–1441*, p. 448; *1446–1452*, p. 186; *1452–1461*, p. 287.

[14] C. H. Jenkinson, 'The First Parliament of Edward I', *EHR*, xxv (1910), p. 234.

[15] *Readings and Moots at the Inns in the Fifteenth Century*, ed. S. E. Thorne, Selden Society, lxxi (1952), pp. l–li; *CPR 1429–1436*, pp. 620, 628; A. H. Johnson, *History of the Drapers' Company*, 3 vols. (Oxford, 1914), i, pp. 291, 296; *London Possessory Assizes*, ed. H. M. Chew, LRS, 1 (1965), no. 228n; *CFR 1430–1437*, p. 116; R. R. Sharpe, *Calendar of London Letter Book K* (London, 1911), p. 194; PRO C 219/14/1 and /4; S. Thrupp, *The Merchant Class of Medieval London* (Ann Arbor, 1948), p. 378; GL MS 9171/3 f. 514. The other lawyer was Thomas Luyt, who also sat for Shrewsbury.

Thirdly, and politically speaking perhaps even more significantly, Westminster lay within the shire, with its palace frequently home to the king, his household and his courtiers, and holding as well the royal courts of justice and parliament, with all the opportunities for advancement this implies. The esquire Thomas Holgyll of Chiswick, attestor in 1433 and escheator of Middlesex in 1434, may be identified as the same man serving in the Harfleur garrison in 1422, and in Henry VI's retinue in France in 1431; William Holgyll of Chiswick, in the retinue of the Duke of York in 1440–1, was probably his son.[16] Links amongst the lower ranks of royal officials are more difficult to discover, but in 1445, amongst the royal valets of the chamber who received their expenses for waiting on Queen Margaret in France, were John Scorier and John Merewether. Scorier later inherited lands at Church Acton and Ealing from his mother Alice, heir to her father John Holmes and to her brother Thomas, who took as a second husband Henry Fenyngley, attestor in 1427, 1429 and 1430. Her stepson Richard Fenyngley was an attestor in 1436. In 1458 Scorier appointed his one-time fellow servant, John Merewether, now Serjeant of the Scullery and elected member for Middlesex in 1459, as one feoffee of these lands.[17] Merewether's rise in status was undoubtedly linked to his marriage to Matilda, the widow of John Shordich, MP, who held the manors of Ickenham and Chelsea.[18]

To offset the sway of commerce, crown and law, there was no major influence from magnates since there were no great lay estates in the county. The subsidy of 1428 (levied on parishes and knights' fees) lists sixteen lay holders of knight's fees in Middlesex, of which only two were of baronial rank, Lord Strange and Sir John Arundell, whilst there were eight religious institutions holding a knight's fee in whole or part.[19] Due to generous gifts to the Church by successive Anglo-Saxon royal houses, over half the county was held by ecclesiastical institutions, with Westminster Abbey, St Paul's Cathedral, the bishopric of London and the archbishopric of Canterbury the major landowners. The holders of these offices were rich men: the Abbot of Westminster had an income of £546 in *c.*1400, and £664 by 1535.[20] As with other great landholders, they retained influential men: in 1478 Sir Thomas Frowyk, four times member for Middlesex, received 40s. a year from the Bishop of London for counsel and advice.[21]

That is not to deny lay magnates any influence, for many had lesser

[16] PRO C 219/14/4; *CFR 1430–7*, p. 222; *VCH Mdx.* vii, 82; J. H. Wylie, *The Reign of Henry the Fifth*, 3 vols. (Cambridge, 1914–29), ii, p. 90; Deputy Keeper of the Public Records, *48th Report* (London, 1887), p. 283; PRO E 101/53/33 m.1.

[17] PRO E 404/62/143; SC 2/188/77 f. 4; GL MS 9171/2 f. 167v; GL MS 11,765 f. 106; *CPR 1452–1461*, p. 486.

[18] G. Hennessy, *Novum Repertorium* (London, 1898), p. 227; *Feudal Aids*, vi, pp. 488–9; *HPT 1286–1421*, iv, pp. 369–71.

[19] *Feudal Aids*, iii, pp. 380–3. The eight religious houses mentioned in 1428 as holding knight's fees or parts thereof, the threshold being a quarter fee, in Middlesex were Hounslow, Westminster, Ankerwyke, St John of Jerusalem in England, St Bartholomew West Smithfield, Syon, Holy Trinity Aldgate and the London Charterhouse. Other religious houses of fifteenth-century Middlesex were the nunneries of Stratford at Bow, Kilburn, Haliwell and St Mary Clerkenwell and the leper hospitals of St James, Westminster and St Giles-in-the-Fields, *VCH Middx*, i, p. 153.

[20] B. F. Harvey, *Westminster Abbey and its Estates* (Oxford, 1977), p. 63.

[21] PRO SC 6/1140/27.

holdings in the shire. The Strange lords of Knockin in Shropshire held the manors of Edgeware, and Colham, Uxbridge, and produced one fifteenth-century Middlesex Member of Parliament, Sir Roger. The 1412 subsidy shows that the Earl of Oxford held the manor of Kensington, and Joan, widow of Humphrey, Earl of Hereford, the manor of Enfield. After her death in 1419 and the partition of the de Bohun estates, Enfield was assigned to Henry V and then in dower to his widow, Katherine, in 1422; subsequent queen-dowagers held the manor during much of the rest of the fifteenth century. John, Lord Tiptoft (d. 1443) who already held the manor of Shepperton, inherited the manor of Worcesters Elsing, Enfield, through his mother, Agnes Wroth, in 1413. These lands passed to his son John, Earl of Worcester, executed in 1470, and then eventually to Isabel Roos and her husband, Sir Thomas Lovell, MP for Middlesex and Speaker of the House of Commons.[22] Connections between Middlesex men and magnates existed, although they are difficult to substantiate. Andrew Danyell esquire, for example, a parliamentary elector in 1442, nephew and one heir of John Walden, a wealthy city merchant and Middlesex shire-knight, who held large estates in and around Tottenham, was awarded an annuity of £5 a year between 1442 and 1447 by Humphrey Stafford, Duke of Buckingham.[23]

Looking at the county community of Middlesex through an examination of the shire-knights and parliamentary attestors, these men can be divided into three broad groups, the elite or greater gentry (where a knight had an income of at least £40 a year and an esquire £20), the parish or lesser gentry (with a minimum annual income of £5, more probably £10–£20), and the freeholders or commoners.[24] The proportions of these groups varied slightly at each election, but I have chosen the parliamentary indenture of January 1449 as an example, partly because it comes from the middle of the century, and because most of the forty-two attestors listed can be identified.[25] This demonstrates that, at this election, held at Stone Cross, men from at least twenty-four out of seventy-five parishes, i.e. a third, from across the shire were represented on the parliamentary indenture, suggesting that the election was a unifying force within the county.

The names of the attestors on this indenture were headed by a knight, Thomas Haseley, royal official and Middlesex JP and landowner, followed by five men designated *armiger*: Thomas Charlton, Walter Green, Miles Windsor, William Wroth and Henry Boys (eldest son of Sir John Boys, late MP) together with Thomas Frowyk junior. Next were the lesser gentry, men with legal or clerical training, who were described as gentleman in other documents, Simon Elrington of Hackney, attorney of Common Pleas and filazer of that court for Norfolk and William Deynes of Edmonton, both Middlesex coroners, Edmund Plofield of the Middle Temple, and John Drayton, one-time clerk to John Walden of Tottenham, who was appointed Middlesex undersheriff in 1438 and

[22] *HPT 1386–1421*, iv, p. 503; *Feudal Aids*, vi, p. 486; *CFR 1405–1412*, p. 176; *1413–1422*, p. 43; *VCH Middx*, v, pp. 224–6; *HPT 1509–58*, iii, pp. 548–9.
[23] PRO C 219/15/2; *CCR 1435–1441*, pp. 44–5; C. Rawcliffe, *The Staffords, Earls of Stafford and Dukes of Buckingham, 1394–1521* (Cambridge, 1978), p. 236.
[24] D. A. L. Morgan, 'The Individual Style of the English Gentleman', *Gentry and Lesser Nobility in Late Medieval Europe*, ed. M. C. E. Jones (Gloucester, 1986), p. 16.
[25] PRO C 219/15/6 no. 53.

had previously been coroner.[26] John Derham was a London mercer who held land at East Bedfont, and Nicholas Yerde, yeoman of Cowley Peachley, was yet another coroner for Middlesex, elected that same year. Of the remaining attestors, eight were maltmen from Enfield and Edmonton, where this trade was concentrated, probably indicating the influence of William Wroth and Thomas Charlton, both important landholders in these two parishes. There was a barber and a tailor of Westminster, a baker from Stratford at Bow, a miller of Tottenham, an Uxbridge innkeeper and an Enfield tanner, whilst the remainder were yeomen or husbandmen from throughout the shire. This is roughly 15 per cent each for the elite and parish gentry, and 70 per cent for freeholders.[27] The fact that, unusually, the two shire-knights elected were both part of the strong representation of the royal Household in this Parliament, and had few links with Middlesex – Robert Tanfield was Queen Margaret's attorney-general, and John Lemanton a royal official whose career had commenced in the Northern Marches, although he held several tenements in the parish of St Giles without Cripplegate – implies a formal mechanism via the sheriffs or an informal agreement on the part of the Middlesex gentry elite to support royal policy.[28]

The gentry elite was by far the most important group in the county, both because of their substantial landholdings, and because of their control of the more notable local offices. These men were Members of Parliament, Justices of the Peace, sat on numerous royal commissions for the shire, and might play a role on the national scene: Sir Thomas Charlton of Edmonton was Speaker of the House of Commons in 1454.[29] The most important county appointment for the gentry elite was to the Middlesex commission of the peace, of which there were 112 members between 1399 and 1509, discounting three noblemen, seven royal princes or dukes, and assorted ecclesiastics such as the bishops of London. The justices were mainly drawn from the gentry elite and from lawyers who held land in Middlesex, together with the king's justices. Just over half (twenty-two) of the Middlesex shire-knights were appointed to the county bench and virtually all sat only for Middlesex. In addition, Members of Parliament and others of the gentry elite were amongst those appointed to commissions for specific duties: a Middlesex commission to collect for war in

[26] Thomas Haseley, *HPT 1386–1421*, iii, p. 307; Simon Elrington, *CPR 1476–1485*, p. 126; J. H. Baker, *A Catalogue of English Legal Manuals in Cambridge University Library* (Cambridge, 1996), pp. 161–3; PRO KB 9/999 m.25; William Deynes, PRO C 140/35/64; KB, 9/997 m.4; Edmund Plofield, *CPR 1436–1441*, p. 250; *CCR 1447–1454*, p. 332; John Drayton, PRO C 67/39 m.13; KB 9/211 m.26; D. Moss and I. Murray, 'A Fifteenth-Century Middlesex Terrier', *TLMAS*, xxv (1974), p. 286; *CCR 1435–1441*, p. 195.

[27] John Derham, *CCR 1476–1485*, no. 288; Nicholas Yerde, PRO C 67/51 m.24; KB 9/997 m.27; John Hunnesdon, Enfield, PRO C 115/25; John Selle, sr, John Selle, jr, William Cordell, Enfield, *CCR 1454–1461*, p. 34; John Barley, Enfield, *CPR 1452–1461*, p. 580; Richard Langford and Robert Saberne, Edmonton, *CCR 1454–1461*, pp. 365–6; *CPR 1467–77*, p. 3; John Faun, Westminster, and John Possemore, Stratford at Bow, *CCR 1447–1454*, pp. 129, 92; John Rowe, Tottenham, *CPR 1446–1452*, p. 454; Simon Godewyn, Uxbridge, PRO PROB 11/4 f. 152v; Thomas Hunnesdon, Enfield, *CCR 1468–1476*, no.299.

[28] J. S. Roskell, *The Commons and their Speakers in English Parliaments 1376–1523* (Manchester, 1965), p. 231; Griffiths, *Henry VI*, pp. 262, 368; unpublished biography of John Lemanton. I am grateful to the History of Parliament Trust, and to Dr Linda Clark for permission to draw on this research.

[29] Roskell, *Speakers*, pp. 71, 352.

January 1420, for example, consisted of Sir Robert Chalons, Henry Somer, Thomas Frowyk, Thomas Charlton, Walter Gautron, Simon Camp, Robert Warner, Walter Green and Robert Haxey, all, except the first and last, past or future Members of Parliament for Middlesex, and all Parliamentary attestors apart from Chalons.[30] Very few of the gentry elite were appointed to royal commissions other than for Middlesex.

For most of the gentry elite, their Middlesex estates were their main landholdings, although, as would be expected, several held lands in adjoining counties such as Hertfordshire and Essex, as well as in London. The Windsors and the Wroths were the only families with extensive lands elsewhere. The close-knit nature of Middlesex gentry in the fifteenth century can be illustrated through their marriages and by the numerous occasions when they acted as feoffees, witnesses or sureties for each other. There is not space to look at this in detail, but a glance at the pedigree will show the network of kinship links, at the centre of which were the Frowyks and Charltons.

Many prominent fifteenth-century Middlesex families, such as the Frowyks, Charltons and Wroths, had gained their wealth through London commerce during the previous century and then translated it into landed estates in the shire.[31] Knightly incomes often reflected London's influence: Sir Adam Fraunceys of Edmonton, son of a wealthy and eminent city merchant and mayor of London, had a minimum annual income, according to the 1412 subsidy, of £229, of which £67 came from Middlesex but £162 from London.[32] Other families advanced through administrative service: Robert Warner, citizen of London, who served the City for thirty-six years in various offices, including a lengthy period as undersheriff of Middlesex before being elected MP for the shire in 1425, settled in Hayes, whilst also holding a Stepney manor; his daughter and heir, Elizabeth, married as her third husband Walter Green, one-time servant of Philip Morgan, Bishop of Ely. Their son Robert, a member of the royal household, was knighted by Edward IV after the battle of Tewkesbury in 1471. The Shordich family rose on the back of the service of Sir John Shordich in the reign of Edward III, and the land dealings of his brother Nicholas and nephew John.[33]

The 1436 subsidy, which named thirty-eight taxpayers resident in the county who had a net annual income of £5 or more from lands, rents and annuities, included the prior of Hounslow, and Alice, Lady Butler. She was the widow of Sir Thomas Butler and of Sir John Dallingridge, governess to Henry VI, and the only one of baronial rank.[34] Lady Butler was the largest individual taxpayer, with an annual income of £233 from Warwickshire, Gloucestershire

[30] *CFR 1413–1422*, p. 316.

[31] Thrupp, *Merchant Class*, pp. 342–4; *VCH Middx*, iv, pp. 44, 72; Roskell, *Speakers*, p. 255; *HPT 1386–1421*, iv, pp. 908–10.

[32] *HPT 1386–1421*, ii, pp. 118–20; *A Calendar of the Cartularies of John Peyl and Adam Fraunceys*, ed. S. J. O'Connor, Camden 5th series, ii (1993), pp. 3–22; *Feudal Aids*, vi, p. 487; J. Stahlschmidt, 'Original Documents', *Archaeological Journal*, xliv (1887), p. 60. The 1412 subsidy was levied at 6s. 8d. per £20 worth of land.

[33] *CCR 1413–1419*, p. 347; Sharpe, *Letter Book K*, p. 114; Ramsay, 'English Legal Profession', app. 5, p. xxxiii; *HPT 1386–1421*, ii, pp. 231–2; *Paston Letters and Papers of the Fifteenth Century*, ed. N. Davis, 2 vols. (Oxford, 1971–6), ii, p. 594; *VCH Middx*, x, pp. 81–2; *CPR 1330–1334*, pp. 38, 398, 405, 534.

[34] PRO E 179/238 dorse (the proportion for Middlesex is not stated); *HPT 1386–1421*, ii, pp. 458, 742.

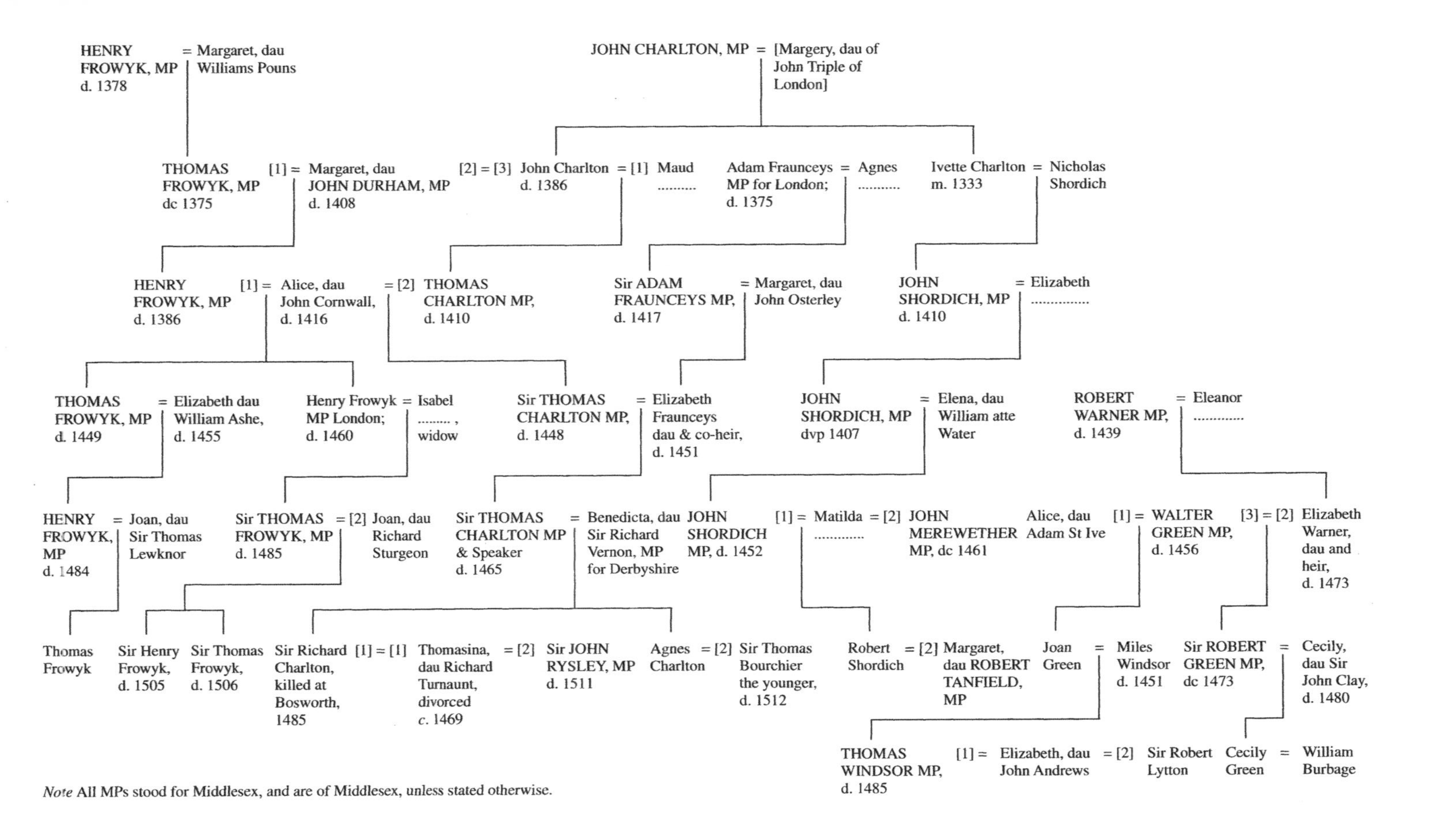

Note All MPs stood for Middlesex, and are of Middlesex, unless stated otherwise.

Simplified Chart of Knightly and Gentry Relationships in Fifteenth-Century Middlesex

and elsewhere, followed by Sir Thomas Haseley and Sir Thomas Charlton, both with annual incomes of £100 from land in Middlesex and elsewhere. (Charlton's son probably had triple this income since his wife was ultimately to inherit all the Frauncеys estates). Excluding the prior and Lady Butler, the combined tax paid by the remaining thirty-five men and one woman amounted to £1,064, so that the gentry were an important force within the county. Several Members of Parliament had the minimum wealth, that is an annual income of more than £40, to qualify for knighthood, and eleven of the gentry elite were distrained for knighthood, amongst them John Gedney and John Shordich in 1430, Thomas Frowyk in 1439 and 1458, and his son Henry in 1465, Walter Green and John Shordich (again) in 1439, and John Wroth the elder and younger in 1457–8 and 1465.[35]

One important factor for cohesion was that the Middlesex gentry elite was remarkably stable for much of the later fourteenth and fifteenth centuries. Exceptionally, the Windsor family had held their manor of Stanwell since at least Domesday Book, together with estates in Hampshire and other south-western counties; except that they were plagued by minorities during much of the fifteenth century, they were undoubtedly one of the most important families in the shire.[36] The 1323–4 return of knights lists four Middlesex knights, all of whose families were represented a century later. Richard de Windsor's six times great-grandson, Thomas Windsor, was elected Member of Parliament for Middlesex in 1478, and Thomas de Lewknor's descendants, although their main estates were in Sussex, still held land in South Mimms in 1500, and had intermarried with the Middlesex gentry families of Frowyk, Goodyer and Wroth. William de Harpeden was represented in the female line by the Lovells and Olivers of Harlington, whilst John de Enfield's descendant, another John, had alienated his estates to his step-father, John Wroth.[37]

It is difficult to estimate numbers of a social group over a period of time, since families rose and fell, or failed in the male line. A 1501–2 listing of the 'gentlemen of Middlesex', includes four knights and eighteen esquires – the gentry elite – and thirty gentlemen – the parish gentry. This is probably the median over the century. A few of the same names appear amongst the esquires in 1501–2 as were prominent sixty years earlier: Frowyk, Windsor and Wroth, whilst others were related to earlier gentry families.[38] Of course the proximity of London and Westminster did mean there was a constant influx of new families.

[35] PRO E 372/275 (February 1430); E 372/284 m.21 (March 1439); E 403/812 m.3 (October 1457; E 159/234 m.21 (1458), E 159/242 m.42 (1465); additional were William Yorke, 1458, Richard Turnaunt, 1465, John Pury, 1458, and William Chedworth, 1465.

[36] *VCH Middx*, i, pp. 114–15; iii, p. 37; A. Collins, *The Peerage of England*, 5th edn, 8 vols. (London, 1779), iv, pp. 62–77; *Parliamentary Writs*, ed. F. Palgrave, 2 vols. in 4 (London 1827–34), ii(ii), p. 657.

[37] J. S. Roskell, *The Commons in the Parliament of 1422* (Manchester, 1954), pp. 197–9; *CPR 1452–1461*, p. 280; J. Comber, *Sussex Genealogies, Lewes Centre* (Cambridge, 1933), p. 150; *VCH Middx*, iii, p. 262; PRO C 139/86/28/2; *CCR 1369–1374*, p. 546; J. Collinson, *History and Antiquities of Somerset*, 3 vols. (London, 1791), i, pp. 62–8.

[38] BL Harl MS 6166 ff. 112–13. Also an esquire was John, son of Simon Elrington of Hackney, attorney to Margaret of Anjou and related to the MP Sir John Elrington: D. A. L. Morgan, 'The King's Affinity in the Polity of Yorkist England', *TRHS*, 5th series, 23 (1973), pp. 14–15; GL MS 9171/71 f. 15v; Baker, *English Legal Manuals*, p. 163. The four knights in 1501–2 were Thomas Lovell and John Rysley, both Middlesex Members of Parliament, Robert Litton, who had married Thomas Windsor's widow, and John Fortescue.

Table 6. Members of Parliament from Middlesex gentry elite families

Family	No. of individuals	No. of times elected
Elite families containing more than one knight of the shire for Middlesex		
Charlton	2*	12
Frowyk	3*	11
Green	2	11
Wroth	3*	6
SUBTOTAL		40
Individuals from elite families elected for Middlesex		
Boys	1	1
Durham	1	1
Fraunceys	1*	1
Shordich	1*	1
Straunge	1	2
Windsor	1*	1
SUBTOTAL		7
TOTAL		47

* denotes that previous members of the family were knights of the shire for Middlesex in the fourteenth century.

Note There were 55 elections between 1399 and 1491, for 43 of which the names of Middlesex MPs are known.

The heralds' visitation of 1593 provides a snapshot of the then county gentry. Of the 181 families named just 24, or 18 per cent, can be proved to have fifteenth-century roots in Middlesex. On the other hand, the Wroths, Elringtons and the representative of the Greens, the Burbages, were still considerable landholders. The Charltons had lost their lands under attainder in 1485, although much of their Middlesex estates at Edmonton and Hillingdon were granted to Sir Thomas Bourchier the younger and his wife Agnes, sister of Sir Richard Charlton who was killed at Bosworth fighting for Richard III.[39] The two main Frowyk branches left only daughters, and the Shordiches had suffered financial reverses.[40]

It is clear then that for much of the fifteenth century several elite families had been resident in Middlesex for at the very least three generations, and provided a succession of Middlesex Members of Parliament. Table 6 shows those gentry elite families who dominated the county elections between 1399 and 1491, and reliance on a small pool of families surely fostered a sense of identification with the county. Six of the eight generations of the Wroths of Enfield were knights of the shire between 1350 and 1550, and four generations of both the Frowyks and Charltons between 1355 and 1465. The latter were also the successors to the

[39] *The Coronation of Richard III*, ed. A. F. Sutton and P. W. Hammond (Gloucester, 1983), pp. 315–16; *CPR 1485–1494*, p. 63.

[40] *Middlesex Pedigrees*, ed. G. J. Armytage, Harleian Society, lxv (1914), *passim*; *Rot. Parl.*, vi, p. 276; *VCH Middx*, x, p. 82; L. Blackmore and I. Schwab, 'From the Templars to Tenement: A Medieval and Post-medieval Site at 18 Shore Road, E9', *TLMAS*, xxxvii (1986), pp. 148–52. The Shordich pedigree on pp. 150–1 requires amendment.

Fraunceys family through the marriage of the heiress Elizabeth Fraunceys to Thomas Charlton. Three successive John Shordiches were members from 1380 to 1450, and Robert Warner, his son-in-law Walter Green, and the latter's son Sir Robert Green and grandson, Thomas Windsor, stood for Middlesex between 1414 and 1478. These men, of course, also frequently appeared heading the list of attestors on the parliamentary indentures.

The second category of Middlesex Members of Parliament and attestors was formed by the parish gentry, who were usually described as gentleman (but occasionally esquire). Also included in this group were an increasing number of lawyers, together with merchants, London citizens, royal officials and stewards. It thus encompasses a very broad band of men, with inevitably some overlap with the gentry elite on the one hand, and with the prosperous yeomen on the other. One difference which set such families apart from the gentry elite and from the freeholders of Middlesex was that, whereas they occasionally provided Members of Parliament, they were not usually appointed as Justices of the Peace nor did they sit on many – if any – royal commissions. What they did serve as was escheators, undersheriffs, coroners and, occasionally, as assessors or collectors of the taxes known as the tenth and fifteenth. However, although the offices of undersheriff and coroner were invariably filled by men who held land in Middlesex and also often had legal training, the escheatry was joined to that of Kent, and was usually executed by Kentish gentry.

William Brockhurst of Islington (d. 1444) provides a good illustration of the world of the parish gentry. His family had owned land in Haringey at least since 1382, whilst he himself engaged in brewing, with a varied property portfolio, including a house and eighty-eight acres, all of which was said to produce an annual income of £10 in 1436. Brokhurst was collector of the subsidy for the first time in 1428, and an attestor from 1429, being of sufficient status in 1434 to be one of the influential men of his county to swear not to maintain peace breakers. He served as constable of Islington in 1440, although in the same decade he was accused of assaulting the ploughman of a fellow parishioner.[41] Brokhurst also had close connections with London: his daughter and heir, Johanna, whose third husband was William Underhill, citizen and wax chandler, left, by her second husband John Oliver, a Westminster Abbey official of Charing Cross, one surviving daughter Cecily, who married a London grocer, Thomas Walker.[42]

Of a higher social status was Thomas Beaufitz, admitted to Lincoln's Inn by 1424, who held land in Warwickshire and elsewhere valued at £20 in 1436, but who was a Middlesex attestor in 1442 and 1450, and was appointed to several Middlesex commissions. Beaufitz chose to be buried at St Mary's, Stratford at Bow where he was commemorated by a monumental inscription stating that he was '*generosus*', Justice of the Peace for Middlesex and [Deputy] Coroner of the city of London.[43]

[41] *VCH Middx*, vi, p. 146; GL MS 9171/4 f. 137v; PRO E 179/238/90d; *Feudal Aids*, iii, p. 377; PRO C 219/14/1, /3, /4, 15/2; *CPR 1429–1436*, p. 408; PRO KB 9/233/47; C 1/1489/79.

[42] PRO C 1/17/266; *Catalogue of Ancient Deeds*, vi, no. C7117; G. Rosser, *Medieval Westminster* (Oxford, 1989), p. 393; GL MS 9171/7 f. 74. Nothing is known of Johanna's first husband, apart from his surname, Morys: GL MS 9171/6 f. 309.

[43] *Lincoln's Inn Admissions, 1420–1799*, i, (London, 1896), p. 5; Thrupp, *Merchant Class*, p. 378; GL MS 9171/5 f. 272v; PRO C 219/15/2 and 16/1; *Middlesex Pedigrees*, p. 134. Thomas perhaps

The last category of attestor was that of the freeholder of the county, both yeoman and craftsman. Many were from peasant families long resident in the county. In 1400 Richard Vincent of Northolt received a pardon as headborough, or constable; Roger Vincent of Northolt was an attestor in 1421 and 1422, and John Vincent in 1433 and 1460, whilst in 1521 William Vincent, yeoman, requested burial in Northolt churchyard near his father.[44]

The richer freeholder normally filled the offices of constable and churchwarden, and was frequently appointed a collector of taxes. John Boner of St Dunstan, Stepney, was an attestor in 1431 and 1432, a collector of taxes in 1431, and refers in his will of 1433 to 6s. 8d. owing to him from his 'time as a parishioner when I had governance of the goods of the same church'. Interestingly, some two-thirds of tax collectors, the majority of whom were of yeoman or artisan status, were also Parliamentary attestors. Most make an appearance as an attestor before being appointed a collector, indicating that they may have come to the sheriffs' attention by this route.[45] This service could also foster an awareness of acting for the whole county, and not simply for a parish.

Only occasionally can Middlesex be set in a wider context. The manor court rolls of Topsfield Hall, Crouch End, reveal that Nicholas Kingsden, who should have been admitted tenant in his father's place in September 1457, was with the army of Edward IV at the battle of Shirburn in Elmet (Towton), and was reported slain. Happily, the report of his death was exaggerated and he subsequently came forward to displace his sister Amy, wife of John Preston, claimant of the land.[46] Social activities strengthened a sense of being part of a county community; a rare example of such pursuits amongst the gentry can be found within the 1465 steward's accounts of the Charlton family, one entry of which reads: 'In expenses for my master Richard Charlton my master Frowyck and my master Richard Turnaunt and their men to hunt at Swalcliffe [near Uxbridge] in Christmas week.'[47]

It is clear that fifteenth-century Middlesex did contain a stable, long-serving group of gentry elite families, who controlled the major offices and held much of the non-ecclesiastical land. With sheriffs drawn from the ranks of the London citizens, and with no significant magnate presence, although always subject to a degree of royal influence, the Middlesex gentry elite enjoyed a certain independence as standard-bearers for their county. The fact that there were no large numbers of men listed on any Middlesex indenture, which elsewhere meant a contested election, suggests that the choice of member by the gentry elite and the crown was approved by the freeholders of the shire. The insistence of the Commons on the necessity of members being 'stakeholders' in the shire, and the 1445–6 statute laying down that members should be 'notable Knyghtes of the same Counties for the which they shall be chosen or otherwise

owed his post as coroner to Ralph Butler, Lord Sudeley, coroner of London from 1435, for whom John Beaufitz of Balsall (Warks), probably Thomas's brother, was feoffee: *CCR 1435–1441*, p. 147; *1468–76*, no. 1058; PRO PROB 11/8 f. 158.

[44] PRO C 67/32 m.23; C 219/12/5, 13/1, 14/4 and 16/6; GL MSS 9171/4 f. 235; 9171/9 f. 183v.

[45] PRO C 219/14/2, /3; *CFR 1430–1437*, p. 68; GL MS 9171/3 f. 426.

[46] W. M. Marcham, 'The Village of Crouch End, Hornsey, and Manor of Topsfield Hall', *TLMAS*, xiii (1937), pp. 396–7.

[47] WAM 5471 f. 13v.

notable Esquires Gentlemen of Birth of the same Counties' surely indicate that a county was seen as a readily identifiable unit, with its most prominent members charged with putting forward the best interests of all those living within its borders.[48]

Participation in elections by men of differing status implies that an attestor believed that he was acting for a common purpose and had a share in the administration of his county. And this was not the only occasion when the men of Middlesex acted together outside the parish or hundred. For the gentry elite there was the commission of the peace and other royal commissions, and for the lesser gentry and freeholders, appointment as a collector of the tenth and fifteenth for Middlesex. In June 1410, for instance, the six men named (of whom five were attestors) came from across the county:[49]

William Abbot of Bedfont	William Bury of Kingsbury
John Dernewell of Barnet	Richard Morden of Holborn
John Multon of Tottenham	John Standen of Uxbridge

Service as a juror may also have supported a perception of county identity, for the commoners of Middlesex were more heavily burdened in this service than other shires, since the king's courts sat in Middlesex during the four terms of the year at which times the freeholders were bound to attend as jurors. Indeed, from 1435 to 1436 the Justices of the Peace in Middlesex were permitted to hold two, instead of four, general sessions a year, because of this workload.[50] The session held at Brentford in July 1428, for example, lists thirteen jurors, who came from Uxbridge, Stanwell, Staines, Twickenham, Ealing, Heston, Feltham, Islington, Fulham, Kingsbury, Westminster, Edgware and South Mimms, most of whom were also parliamentary attestors.[51]

The same sense of county identity was also true for service on inquisitions post mortem. When, in March 1439, the inquisition of the Middlesex lands of Richard Windsor of Stanwell was held, it took place at Whitechapel, the opposite end of the county. Seven at least of the twelve jurors were from this eastern part of Middlesex, such as Roger Whitbarrow, a Hackney brewer, and not from the neighbourhood of Richard's principal manor. Three of the jurors are known to have been parliamentary attestors, like Simon Cock, a fishmonger of Aldgate, who was present at the 1435 elections held at Stone Cross.[52]

Yet it is also the case that for the majority of Middlesex men and women the parish was their focus, a point which comes out strongly in their wills. It is interesting that these show that of a sample of 940 wills of Middlesex testators, virtually no bequests were made to London hospitals, prisons or lazarhouses, although about 15 per cent made a bequest to the mother church of the diocese, St Paul's Cathedral. Wills can, however, reveal family networks as well as county links. Thomas Windsor, lord of Stanwell, and also a lawyer, an attestor

[48] Ruffhead, *Statutes*, i, p. 616, cap. xiv.

[49] *CFR 1405–1413*, p. 181. Dernewell's name does not appear on any surviving indenture.

[50] *Middlesex County Records*, i, *3 Edward VI–45 Elizabeth*, ed. J. C. Jeaffreson (London, 1886), pp. xx–xxii.

[51] PRO KB 9/224 m.223d.

[52] PRO C 139/92/36; GL MS 9171/5 f. 289v; John Burgh, attestor 1430 (PR0, C 219/14/2); William Spencer 1429, 1430 and 1435 (C 219/14/1, 2 and 5); Simon Cock, 1435 (C 219/14/5); C 1/192/66.

in 1467 and Member of Parliament in 1478, was one executor of his mother-in-law, Elizabeth, widow of John Andrews of Suffolk, and of her sister, Alice, wife Sir Hugh Wyche, alderman of London. In addition he also discharged this duty for his cousin William Yorke, variously designated as merchant, 'of the King's cellar', citizen and fishmonger, esquire and gentleman, whose country estate was at Twickenham, and for his fellow justice, the king's serjeant William Mulso, esquire, of Staines. Richard Lorde, vicar of Stanwell, appointed Windsor supervisor of his will, as did Nicholas Toller, citizen and skinner of London, who originally came from Stanwell.[53]

It has been argued that the county should be regarded as a community because of the corresponding division of administrative records. However, this can equally well apply in reverse: if taxes were collected on a county-wide basis, and Members of Parliament elected likewise, could this not have engendered a sense of county community amongst fifteenth-century taxpayers and electors? The whole county, for example, had to contribute to the wages of their Members of Parliament, as a directive from the crown of 1414–15 indicates:

> To the Constables of West Smithfield, Stoke Newington, Islington, Shoreditch and Finsbury through the Sheriffs of Middlesex . . . We command you that you cause to be raised jointly and severally from the aforesaid townships, 9s. 7½d. for the expenses of John Walden and Thomas Charletoun, knights of the aforesaid shire, coming to the Parliament . . . for the commonalty of the said county.[54]

The smaller parish community was no doubt of more importance for day-to-day affairs, but on a wider level, and particularly in response to the government's directives and proclamations, the county community was surely significant. It was important that the choice of shire-knight was seen to be openly and publicly affirmed in the county court, for he had to have power to bind his constituents to the decisions of parliament, especially with regard to taxation. Access to office holding at a county level allowed participation in the administration of their shire by men of varied social status, whilst the pre-eminence and political predominance of their gentry elite gave a sense of awareness and cohesion to the men of Middlesex, particularly in relation to London. The knights and esquires perhaps saw themselves not as the county community of Middlesex, but as the county leaders *for* Middlesex, the most effective way to ensure security and good government in the shire, and in this they were supported by the parish gentry and the freeholders of Middlesex.

[53] PRO C 219/17/1; Collins, *Peerage*, iv, pp. 70–2; PRO PROB 11/6 f. 188v; PROB 11/7 f. 88; M. Albertson, *London Merchants and their Landed Property during the Reign of the Yorkists* (Bryn Mawr College, 1932), pp. 12–13; *CCR 1461–1468*, p. 32; GL MS 9171/6 f. 96 and f. 169v.

[54] F. Consitt, *The London Weavers' Company*, 2 vols. (London, 1933), i, p. 234.

Regional Prosperity in Fifteenth-Century England: Some Evidence from Wessex

John Hare

Influences on rural society

It is an increasing commonplace that England is a land of regions: the difficulty comes when we try to define these. After the Norman Conquest, Wessex ceased to be a term of any political meaning. It provides, nevertheless, a useful name that may be used, with thanks to King Alfred and to Thomas Hardy, to describe an area of considerable importance in later medieval England. This Wessex comprises the historic counties of Wiltshire, Hampshire and Dorset, together with Berkshire and Somerset. It was an area of relative prosperity in the fifteenth century and two of its counties climbed dramatically in the rankings of county wealth in the later middle ages produced by Schofield: Somerset and Wiltshire rose sharply to second and fifth respectively, Berkshire rose slightly to sixth. In comparison, Hampshire and Dorset, which had been less wealthy, dropped a few places in the rankings.[1] Wessex is not proposed as a typical area, but rather one that needs to be given considerable importance in any discussion of what was happening to the late medieval economy. How far was this a period of general recession driven down by demographic decline, as M. M. Postan argued? 'An age of recession, arrested economic development and declining national income.' Sixty years after the publication of his classic article on the fifteenth century, it seems appropriate to reflect again on some of the issues that he raised, and with which we still need to wrestle.[2]

The rural society and economy of the period will be viewed as the product of an interaction between the forces of continuity linked to geography and land ownership, and the forces of change linked to population decline and the growth of commercial activity, particularly in the cloth industry. Wessex was to be a key region in the dramatic transformation of England into an exporter of manufactured products: cloth replaced wool as a key element in overseas trade.

Geographically, the area is dominated by the great bands of chalk downs that run from Dorset through Wiltshire to Berkshire and Hampshire. Around this lay other areas with very different rural economies: the clay vale and the Cotswolds and Mendips beyond to the west, the Hampshire basin with its claylands and heathland to the south and the London basin to the north.

[1] R. S. Schofield, 'The Geographical Distribution of Wealth in England, 1334–1649', *EcHR*, 2nd series, xviii (1965), pp. 483–510.
[2] M. M. Postan, 'The Fifteenth Century', *Essays*, pp. 41–8.

Compared with the chalklands these supported very different farming and settlement patterns, with a greater emphasis on pastoral farming.[3]

In the chalklands, settlement tended to concentrate along the river valleys that dissected it or along the chalk escarpments. Settlements were nucleated with the open fields around, usually with half the arable being cultivated at any one time. Estates, tithings and parishes tended to be long and thin, running back from the valley. Each settlement had its own portion of the available types of land: meadow, well-drained land at the spring line for settlement, heavier more fertile soils, thinner arable soils and the downland pastures. All were an integral part of the economy of the settlement. Thus sheep produced wool and meat, but they also generated and spread manure which helped to enhance the arable yields, and thus linked downland and arable. This may not have been so systematic as in later centuries, but people showed their awareness of its value by paying to rent the flock. In some cases extensive areas of clay with flints overlying the chalk had led to the survival of woodlands and later to their medieval colonisation.

These chalkland settlements were major producers of grain for the market, of wheat, barley and oats, although the balance varied according to the soil. They had their pigs and their cattle, but it was the large sheep flock that was such a distinctive feature of the rural economy. They were particularly large and capital-intensive. Many manors possessed over a thousand sheep belonging to the lord. Smaller estates possessed flocks of several thousand sheep. Thus Hyde Abbey had 4,869 in 1282–3, Bindon (Dorset) had 7,000 in 1329–33. They reached their peak in the late fourteenth century when the priory of St Swithun possessed 20,357 in 1390 within twenty different flocks. On the bishopric of Winchester estate, the flocks reached 35,000 in 1369 and averaged 33,000 between 1388 and 1397. These flocks were also highly organised, sheep being moved from one manor to another, both to replace particular short-term gaps, and because such movements were built into the whole structure of the management of the estate. Some manors did not have the full range of sheep – the breeding, juvenile and wether flocks – and so needed to purchase or import sheep to replace the elderly wether sheep.[4]

Outside the chalklands, settlements and demesnes were often smaller but still with open fields, here usually cultivating two-thirds of the arable. There were also more farmsteads, hamlets and enclosed fields. Here the taxation units tended to conceal separate settlements, whereas in the chalklands, the tithings tended to be taxed by themselves. Sheep flocks were found, as in the Cotswolds, but tended to be much smaller, non-existent or more transient. Thus on the Glastonbury estate it was only on the Wiltshire chalkland manors of Idmiston,

[3] J. N. Hare, 'Lord and Tenant in Wiltshire, *c.*1380–*c.*1520' (unpub. London Univ. Ph.D. thesis, 1976); 'Durrington: A Chalkland Manor in the Later Middle Ages', *Wiltshire Archaeological Magazine*, 74/5 (1979–80), pp. 137–47; 'Change and Continuity in Wiltshire Agriculture in the Later Middle Ages', *Agricultural Improvement: Medieval and Modern*, ed. W. Minchinton, Exeter Papers in Economic History (1981), pp. 1–18; 'Agriculture and Rural Settlement in the Chalklands of Wiltshire and Hampshire from *c.* 1200 to *c.* 1500', *The Medieval Landscape of Wessex*, ed. M. Aston and C. Lewis (Oxford, 1994), pp. 159–69; I. J. E. Keil, 'The Estates of Glastonbury Abbey in the later Middle Ages' (unpub. Univ. Bristol Ph.D. thesis, 1964), 74–146; *AHEW*, *passim.*

[4] Hare, 'Agriculture and Rural Settlement', pp. 160–1; C. Taylor, *Dorset* (London, 1970), p. 120; WCL stockbook; M. J. Stephenson, 'Wool Prices in the Medieval Economy', *EcHR*, 2nd series, xxxxi (1988), pp. 385–6.

Damerham and Monkton Deverill that large flocks were to be found.[5] As settlement expanded into the woodlands, with daughter settlements and farmsteads, parish populations might become particularly large. Some of the most densely populated and highly taxed parishes in Wiltshire were those in the west of the county, in the former forest lands. Colonisation had led to an increased amount of land being enclosed that had probably never been part of an open field system, whether in the form of small enclosed purpestures carried out by the peasantry or large-scale assarts carried out by the lord.[6]

These regional contrasts increased during the later Middle Ages. Further enclosure took place away from the chalk, as on the estates of Titchfield Abbey in south Hampshire, on the claylands of Wiltshire, or at Coleshill (Berkshire).[7] There were also signs of a growing emphasis on cattle-rearing away from the chalklands. Thus at Bitterne in south Hampshire, the bishopric of Winchester abandoned arable farming in *c.*1380, with the dairy stock being increased from twenty-four to fifty cows, and there were still forty-five cows together with younger stock there in 1409–10. Cattle stock were also considerable increased at Coleshill, where they trebled between the 1390s and the mid-fifteenth century.[8] Such regional contrasts with the chalklands were noticed by Leland in travelling round Hampshire in 1542, when he contrasted the open champion land between Winchester and Salisbury (the chalkland) with the wooded enclosed land south of Winchester and in the south-east, with their greater emphasis on cattle.[9] This contrast between chalk and cheese, so familiar to writers of later centuries, was also reflected in contrasting social structures. Already the chalkland was becoming much more obviously an area of large-scale farming, by contrast to the more family-dominated structure of the claylands.[10]

The chalklands were also dominated by large and above all ecclesiastical estates, many of which went back to large-scale grants from Anglo-Saxon kings. Thus in Wiltshire such grants included those to pre-Conquest Wiltshire foundations or their successors (Wilton, Malmesbury and the bishopric of Salisbury) and to others that lay outside the county, such as the Winchester houses (Hyde Abbey, St Mary's Abbey and the cathedral priory), the bishopric of Winchester, the nunneries of Romsey and Shaftesbury and Glastonbury Abbey, all of which retained extensive Wiltshire lands. But within this broad area there were also differences. The *Nomina Villarum* of 1316 suggests a contrast between the counties of Hampshire, Wiltshire and Berkshire and the counties further west (Dorset and Somerset). The former were much more dominated by ecclesiastical lands, with about 40 per cent of vills falling into this category. Royal and noble lands were much less important although still more so than in the counties to the west. The latter possessed a higher proportion of

[5] Keil, 'Glastonbury', table 22.

[6] Hare, 'Agriculture and Rural Settlement', pp. 162–3.

[7] *VCH Hants*, v, p. 421; H. L. Gray, *English Field Systems* (Harvard, 1913), pp. 101, 529; K. H. Rogers, 'Steeple Ashton' in *VCH Wilts*, viii; R. Faith, 'Berkshire', *The Peasant Land Market in Medieval England*, ed. P. D. A. Harvey (Oxford, 1984), pp. 169–70.

[8] *AHEW*, p. 298; *The Pipe Roll of the Bishopric of Winchester, 1409–10*, ed. M. Page, HRSer, 16 (1999), p. 206; Faith, 'Berkshire' p. 171.

[9] *John Leland's Itinerary*, ed. J. Chandler (Stroud, 1993), p. 202.

[10] Hare, 'Change and Continuity', *passim*; 'Agriculture and Rural Settlement', *passim*.

gentry estates and a smaller proportion of ecclesiastical vills.[11] Wiltshire and Hampshire (above all in the chalklands) were areas of large, long-established and ecclesiastical estates. This may have encouraged further the conservatism and continuity that may be seen in agriculture and economic policy during the fifteenth century.

The decline in population was one of the dominant themes, some argue the most important, of this period. The population was cut back by 40 per cent or more from the Black Death and it remained low thereafter. For Postan, it was this which marked out the period from what had happened before and what was to happen afterwards, and which was the driving force for change in this period. The lowness of population generated in this largely agrarian society the characteristics of the period: rising wages, falling rents and empty tenements, stagnant prices, and the decline of serfdom. A country that had fed perhaps six million people now had something over two million for a century and a half. The features that characterised the agrarian economy elsewhere were evident here, but demographic changes were not uniform. In some areas where fertile land or new jobs were to be found, people were sucked in from the areas around and this counterbalanced part of the demographic fall. This may be seen in the influx of the Irish and French into parts of Wiltshire, but others would have come from elsewhere in England. They were simply not recorded by the taxman. In other areas demographic decline was augmented by an outflow of population. The area, particularly in the chalklands, is scattered with the signs of former villages.[12] Some of these, such as Charlton (Dorset), Shaw (Wiltshire), or Lomer and Northington (Hampshire), were deserted during this period, but most others merely shrank and desertion had to await a later century.[13] There may have been a regional element as arable was replaced by pasture in areas where the population was already shrinking. Many of the deserted villages of Dorset that concentrate so clearly in the chalklands have been ascribed to this period.[14] When Leland travelled across Dorset, he recorded that the downlands north of the Frome had 'little arable and no woodland, but everywhere were large flocks of sheep, which are of great benefit to the soil locally'. Only the absence of corn comes as a surprise in a description of chalkland agriculture. It may suggest a shift from arable to pasture and depopulation occurring in lands that were poorer in quality or more distant from major markets.[15]

The second driving force for change was the growth of the cloth industry. This was the period when England shifted from being an exporter of raw material to one of a manufactured product, cloth, and this area was central to this process. On a national level the breakthrough had occurred by the 1390s. Exports had risen from an average of 6,413 cloths, in the 1350s, to 40,291 in the

[11] Thanks are due to Toby Purser for information on the *Nomina Villarum*.

[12] Hare, 'Agriculture and Rural Settlement', pp. 164–8; Taylor, *Dorset*, pp. 111–18; M. Aston, 'A Regional Study of Deserted Settlements in the West of England', *The Rural Settlements of Medieval England*, ed. M. Aston, D. Austin and C. Dyer (Oxford, 1989).

[13] J. N. Hare, 'Growth and Recession in the Fifteenth-Century Economy: The Wiltshire Textile Industry and the Countryside', *EcHR*, 2nd series, lii, (1999), pp. 15–16; 'Netley Abbey: Monastery, Mansion and Ruin', *PCFC*, xlix (1994), p. 216; Hare, 'Agriculture and Rural Settlement', pp. 166–7.

[14] Taylor, *Dorset*, pp. 113–25; J. H. Bettey, *Wessex from AD 1000* (Harlow, 1986), pp. 110–13.

[15] *Leland's Itinerary*, p. 134.

1390s.[16] Somerset and Wiltshire were by far the pre-eminent counties in this expansion. Somerset produced 12,000 cloths each year making it by far the most productive county, and Wiltshire with 7,000 was well ahead of any other rivals. Altogether the region, including Wiltshire, Somerset, Dorset, Hampshire and Bristol produced 54 per cent of England's cloth production in 1394–8.[17] At this time, the industry was predominantly urban, each county's production being generally dominated by a single centre. Salisbury produced 89 per cent of that of Wiltshire, Sherborne 87 per cent of that of Dorset and Winchester 77 per cent of Hampshire's, while the great cloth-producing city of Bristol was legally separate, but economically part, of this area. But in addition the industry was now developing in the countryside. Nowhere was this more apparent than in Somerset. Here the old towns of Bath, Wells, Frome and Taunton together produced only 45.5 per cent of the county's production. The most obvious example of such rural industry here was at Pensford. This was a settlement that had grown up at the ford at the edge of two adjoining parishes, and became a marketing and fulling centre for the area around. It was the most productive marketing centre in the county in 1394–5. Elsewhere rural communities were being transformed, as in parts of west Wiltshire. Thus at Christian Malford, the poll tax figures show that in 1379 there were eighteen weavers and two shearers out of twenty-six named occupations. In Heytesbury hundred in the chalklands, thirteen weavers and thirteen fullers were recorded among the 651 adults with occupational descriptions.[18]

But the process did not stop, and considerable further expansion took place in the early fifteenth century after an initial recession. Thus in Wiltshire the growth of the west Wiltshire industry was reflected in its responsibility for an increasing percentage of production: in 1394–5 it produced nearly 11 per cent of the county's production, in 1414–15 this was up to 26 per cent, and in 1467 to 77 per cent. Less dramatic changes could also be seen in Hampshire and Somerset. Finally, expansion resumed after the deep mid-century recession. It is important to emphasise that industrial expansion and its effects had not just occurred in one burst, but rather in a series of waves that took the industry to different locations.

Postan was cautious in his assessment of the impact of this industry, suggesting that it might have occupied 0.65 per cent of the population, at the most, to produce the cloths that were exported.[19] From our point of view, there were other factors that could not be included in his calculations. What was happening to production for the domestic market, at a time when in per capita terms people were better off and had more money to spend? Moreover, jobs created in this industry themselves generated other jobs: the clothiers and cloth workers produced demand for food, for food products, and for consumer goods. Thus in the well-documented manor of Castle Combe, butchers, bakers and fishmongers came in from neighbouring towns to sell their wares. Here two

[16] A. R. Bridbury, *Medieval English Clothmaking* (1982), p. 116.

[17] Calculated from H. L. Gray, 'The Production and Exportation of English Woollens in the Fourteenth Century', *EHR*, xxix (1924), Appendix ii. Berks is linked with Oxon in Gray's figures and has therefore been excluded.

[18] Hare, 'Growth and Recession', pp. 5, 9; *VCH Wilts*, iv, pp. 122–3.

[19] Postan, 'The Fifteenth Century', *Essays*, p. 45; 'Some Agrarian Evidence of a Declining Population in the Later Middle Ages', *Essays*, p. 198, where the calculations are provided.

inventories provide an indication of the wide range of goods that were being bought with the profits of the cloth trade, the one showing the sale of the dead rector's possessions to others in the village, and the other of the possessions of a bailiff of the manor.[20] Moreover, the cloth workers were not thinly spread throughout the country, but were concentrated in certain counties and certain areas, and nowhere more so than in parts of Wessex. Such concentration increased the economic impact of the industry here. On a regional level, the counties being studied produced 54 per cent of the country's cloth production in the 1390s, but a few years before, in 1377, they had been occupied by only 14 per cent of the population.[21] Even within these counties there was considerable local variation.

This growing industry also produced demands for new housing. At Castle Combe it seems to have been produced by the villagers themselves, but a different pattern was followed at Mells in Somerset. Here, Leland records that Abbot Selwood of Glastonbury had seen the wealth of the inhabitants 'and decided to rebuild it with modest houses of stone blocks', some of which still survive.[22]

Postan was also cautious in his assessment of the economic impact of church-building. He asked whether more stone and mortar had been used than in previous centuries, although we should also ask about the time taken for the elaborate carving and moulding. Church-building generated jobs, and the craftsmen and labourers themselves needed food and service industries. The latter provided a means whereby economic profits could be recycled into further jobs and growth, and in certain areas, the scale of new towers, refenestration or whole new churches (or at least of those parts under parochial responsibility) must have had a considerable impact on the local economy. Churches like Huish Episcopi and Middle Zoyland have to be seen not as isolated examples of employment, but as part of an area of extensive and lavish new church-building in south-east Somerset.[23]

The cloth industry was the most noticeable example of commercial and industrial growth but it was not the only industry that would have generated employment and markets. The leather industry was found in most towns, as in the Wiltshire poll-tax figures for 1379: at Marlborough it was more important than the cloth industry. In the countryside these returns also show the presence of large numbers of tailors. Then there were the building workers, the carpenters and the tilers, the latter reflecting in part the growing development of the tile-making industry.[24]

[20] E. M. Carus-Wilson, 'Evidences of Industrial Growth on Some Fifteenth Century Manors', *Essays in Economic History*, 2 (London, 1962), p. 166; G. P. Scrope, *History of the Manor and Ancient Barony of Castle Combe* (1852), pp. 227–30.

[21] Figures (excl. Berks) calculated from Gray, 'Production and Exportation'; R. B. Dobson, *The Peasants' Revolt of 1381*, 2nd edn (London, 1983), pp. 55–7.

[22] Scrope, *Castle Combe*, pp. 249–50; *Leland's Itinerary*, p. 430; E. H. D. Williams, J. and J. Penoyre, and B. C. M. Hale, 'New Street, Mells', *Proceedings of the Somerset Archaeological and Natural History Society*, cxxx (1987), pp. 115–25.

[23] N. Pevsner, *South and West Somerset* (Harmondsworth, 1958), and the buildings themselves.

[24] J. N. Hare, 'The Growth of the Roof Tile Industry in Later Medieval Wessex', *Medieval Archaeology*, xxxv (1991), pp. 86–103.

Economic trends in north Hampshire

The complex inter-relationship between the land, its ownership, population and expanding industry may be summed up by examining a single area. North Hampshire (approximately north of a line from Andover to Alton) has traditionally been seen as an area in clear decay. To Postan, this interpretation provided an explanation for the apparently conflicting conclusions of A. E. Levett. Her study of a group of manors belonging to the bishopric of Winchester showed that in the immediate aftermath of the Black Death, tenancies were refilled with little signs of any damage to the basic structure of demesne agriculture or to settlement. How could this fit with a view of the post-plague period as dominated by demographic decline? Postan explained this evidence of rapid recovery in terms of her choice of manors. By looking at the rich fertile manors in south Hampshire and elsewhere, she was looking at those places where decline would have been less visible. For him it was the marginal lands of north Hampshire, earlier examined in the *Victoria County History* by Shillington, that would be the more typical and more relevant to the impact of demographic decline than the richer lands where death could have been counterbalanced by immigration from poorer, less attractive land.[25]

There is indeed evidence to suggest that here demographic decline was significant; it therefore fitted into the model of agrarian recession postulated by Postan. Shillington had provided evidence of unfilled tenements and fallen rents in the immediate aftermath of the plague, and subsequently this area was to show more evidence of change than manors elsewhere. On the estates of the cathedral priory in north Hampshire, Wootton showed a dramatic decline in the size of the demesne, contrasting with the essential stability of the priory's riverine manors to the south. Froyle, belonging to St Mary's Abbey, also showed a decline in the demesne and was leased early, in 1381, long before the estate had leased its Wiltshire manors.[26] On the bishopric of Winchester estates, the north Hampshire manors were less successful in recovering the decayed rents than were the manors in the centre of the county, and also showed a high rate of shrinkage of the demesne compared with the position before the Black Death.[27] Thus at Overton, there was a considerable decay of rents in the latter fourteenth century which continued on a smaller scale in the early fifteenth century, and there were similar difficulties in some of the villages around. The effect was most dramatic at the settlement of Northington, part of the manor of Overton. The customary tenements fell out of use. Where once there had been twenty-eight virgators and five half virgators, by 1485 there were only four tenants left. What was then left of the village and its open fields was replaced by a single farm with four hedged fields.[28] At Burghclere, Bishop Wykeham had absorbed some of

[25] Postan, *Essays*, pp. 208–11; A. E. Levett, *The Black Death on the Estates of the See of Winchester* (Oxford, 1916); *VCH Hants*, v, p. 422.

[26] BL Add. Rolls 17490, 17495, 17496. Demesne cultivation was later and temporarily resumed at Froyle.

[27] J. Z. Titow, 'Lost Rents, Vacant Holdings and the Contraction of Peasant Cultivation after the Black Death', *AgHR*, 42 (1994), pp. 109–112; D. L. Farmer, 'Grain Yields on the Winchester Manors in the Later Middle Ages', *EcHR*, 2nd series, xxx (1977), pp. 555–66.

[28] Hare, 'Agriculture and Rural Settlement', pp. 166–7.

the former arable land into the park at Highclere, and the demesne and customary land had been partly replaced by pasture.[29] It was, however, a much less dramatic and depressed situation than that implied by Shillington, since much of the land lost to the park represented twelfth- or thirteenth-century changes rather than later medieval decline, and the reduced cultivation of a hundred acres reflected the stock and land lease rather than an accurate view of how much of the demesne was then cultivated.[30]

But there is also a great deal of evidence that does not easily fit in with such an interpretation of gloom and recession, and suggests the presence of growth, particularly generated by cloth production, that counterbalanced any shrinkage of opportunities in the agrarian sector. Such industrial expansion generated new demands for food, services and employment in the countryside. In North Warnborough, a long terrace of timber-framed houses with jettied first floors still survives. It would have graced any large urban development, and it parallels those familiar at towns like Battle and Tewkesbury. But here it appears to lie in the middle of nowhere, in a village on the fringes of the town of Odiham. The first part of the terrace, ninety-six feet long, was built in 1476, and was extended eighty-one feet in 1534–5.[31] It was clearly designed for multiple occupancy, a row of houses rather than a single property, and it was not a building for farming. The growth of an industry like that of cloth might provide one explanation. The presence of this range suggests a considerable and growing demand for housing or shops for non-farmers, sufficient to repay the considerable investment required.

Above all, the small towns of this area showed an economic resilience that does not easily fit in with the image of rural decline. At the top, the taxation records suggest growth and prosperity in Basingstoke and Alton. Dyer's listing of the fifty largest provincial English towns in the subsidy of 1524–5 included both of these towns, Basingstoke in forty-fifth place and Alton in forty-eighth, while the former also entered the rankings in the top fifty by taxable wealth (forty-fourth). We must not exaggerate the importance of these figures, for together the two towns had a taxable population of less than the long-declining city of Winchester, but it was an achievement, nevertheless, that provides an indicator of dramatic growth.[32]

This prosperity is also suggested by the surviving buildings of these towns. Dendrochronology is only just establishing building dates which are of sufficient accuracy for them to be to be used in quantifiable terms by the historian. Moreover, two of the most important towns of the area, Andover and Basingstoke, were largely destroyed by rapid development in the 1960s when the survival of earlier buildings behind later brick facades was not widely understood. In the former, extensive rescue recording took place prior to

[29] *Register of the Common Seal of the Priory of St. Swithun, Winchester*, ed. J. Greatrex, HRSer, 2 (1978), pp. 19–20; *VCH Hants*, v, p. 422.

[30] *The Pipe Roll of the Bishopric of Winchester*, ed. N. R. Holt (Manchester, 1964), p. 93; *The Pipe Roll of the Bishopric of Winchester, 1301–2*, ed. M. Page, HRSer, 14 (1996), p. 112; ibid. *1409–10*, 232–2; Hampshire RO 11M59 B1/191; for further evidence of difficulties in securing tenants at Highclere and Overton, see *AHEW*, p. 9.

[31] E. Roberts and D. Miles, 'Castle Bridge Cottages, North Warnborough, Hampshire', *Vernacular Architecture*, 28 (1997), p. 117.

[32] A. Dyer, *Decline and Growth in English Towns 1400–1640* (Basingstoke, 1991), pp. 66–7, 70–1.

Table 7. Number of dated buildings in the towns of north Hampshire

Period	*No. of dated buildings*		
1300–49	2		
1350–99	1		
1400–49	6	[2	1400–09]
		[4	1440–49]
1450–99	4		
1500–49	4		
1550–99	1		
1600–49	0		

These figures are based on the list of Hampshire tree ring dates produced by Edward Roberts, who has kindly advised on their use. They include buildings at Odiham, Alton, Andover, North Warnborough, Whitchurch, Overton.

destruction, but in the latter no serious examination seems to have been undertaken. Although the number of dated examples are still few, they raise some intriguing questions about the towns of this area. Most were built in the fifteenth and early sixteenth centuries, while twelve out of seventeen come from the period 1440–1550. Why was so much building taking place during this restricted time span?

Documentary evidence also reinforces this willingness to invest in urban property. During the period 1444–59, Winchester College financed a major programme of urban redevelopment at Andover, on the prestigious High Street. Three new houses were built together with a major inn, The Angel. The carpenters' contract for the inn was for £90, but total expenditure was much higher, the houses and inn together totalling £582 4s. 11¾d. The inn itself, parts of which still survive, probably cost in the region of £400. That such massive investment was begun shortly before the economic recession of the mid-century struck was particularly unfortunate, but the investment reflected the assumptions of the 1440s, in which urban investment seemed to make much sense. The three town houses were evidently expected to yield £5 in rent and the inn at least £10. Although these expectations were not fully realised, the college could normally anticipate an income of £14, comparable to the yield of its rural manor of Coombe Bisset.[33]

Other lords also invested in inns, a reflection of wider economic prosperity. Magdalen College, Oxford, followed Winchester College's Angel Inn with the construction of the Bell Inn, also in Andover, in 1534, at a cost of £191 4s. 8¼d.[34] Other inn-like structures were built at the George at Odiham in 1474 and 1486–7, the Swan at Kingsclere in 1448–9, and the George at Alton in 1501. Winchester College bought an inn at Stockbridge.[35] Men also made

[33] WCM 2678–91, 2694, 2704–10, 2714, 2726–35, 2739, 2742. For the Angel, see E. Roberts, 'A Fifteenth Century Inn at Andover', *PCFC*, xlvii (1991), pp. 153–70.

[34] R. Warmington, 'The Rebuilding of "La Belle" Inn, Andover, 1534', *Post-Medieval Archaeology*, x (1976), p. 139.

[35] Hyde Abbey's Pelican Inn in Alton can be dated stylistically *c.*1500; Stockbridge, *Winchester College Muniments*, ed. S. Himsworth II (Chichester, 1984), p. 909. On the economic role of inns, see Dyer, *Everyday Life*, pp. 297–8.

other long-term purchases in these towns. When Archbishop Warham wished to endow Winchester College, he bought for it the property in Kingsclere that later became the Falcon Inn. When the shrewd and well-informed Bishop Fox was buying land for his Corpus Christi College, he included several tenements in Overton. On a lesser scale, men from Newbury invested in land in Kingsclere.[36]

Some of these towns, such as Andover and Basingstoke, benefited from their presence on a main route to London. A key element in their prosperity, however, was probably the growth of the cloth industry which here concentrated on the production of kerseys, and which probably represented an extension of the Thames valley industry.[37] The aulnage accounts, which record a tax on the sale of cloth, give an idea of the transformation that was taking place. They record the returns on a tax on cloth marketed, and despite the unreliability of some of the later accounts where forgery has been shown, the early ones seem to be reliable and many of the latter ones may be used with caution.[38] In 1394–5, Hampshire's cloth industry was dominated by Winchester, which then marketed three-quarters of the county's cloth. Alton and Andover in north Hampshire were accounted for separately while Basingstoke was not, but together they marketed under 4 per cent of the county's total. North Hampshire was thus unimportant. But by 1467, the situation was being transformed. Winchester remained the largest single centre, but it had lost its overwhelming pre-eminence. The small towns of north Hampshire (Andover and Whitchurch; Basingstoke and Odiham; Alton with the eastern centres of Petersfield, East Meon and Headley) marketed almost a fifth of the county's recorded cloth, reflecting the production of the towns and the villages immediately around.[39]

New cloth-producing centres had emerged, while other traditional centres had expanded and shifted from the production of broad cloths to that of kerseys. One very large entrepreneur had appeared at Basingstoke, where Nicholas Draper with his 140 kerseys controlled nearly 60 per cent of the cloths sold in Basingstoke and Odiham. The expansion of kersey production in this area had occurred after the 1390s and is unlikely to have occurred recently during the mid-century recession. It would seem to have been a product of the first half of the century, perhaps of the second quarter. But change and development were to continue and by the sixteenth century other new centres had also been added: Kingsclere, Overton and Mattingly.[40] As we have seen, such industrial growth would also have generated demands for labour both for agricultural produce and for consumer goods, whether for buildings or for more transient products. North Warnborough had some clothiers resident in the fifteenth century and it is perhaps to this industry and its associated demands that we should look for an explanation for that fine terrace of houses or shops.

This is not to suggest that the fifteenth century was a period of uninterrupted

[36] S. Waight, 'The Hampshire Lands of Corpus Christi College, Oxford, and their Management, 1500–1650', *PCFC*, li (1996), pp. 174–8.

[37] E. M. Carus-Wilson, 'The Woollen Industry', *Cambridge Economic History of Europe*, ed. M. M. Postan and E. Miller, ii, 2nd. edn (Cambridge, 1987), p. 679.

[38] E. M. Carus-Wilson, 'The Aulnage Accounts: A Criticism', *Medieval Merchant Venturers*, 2nd edn (London, 1967); for subsequent discussion, see Hare, 'Growth and Recession', pp. 2–3.

[39] D. Keene, *Survey of Medieval Winchester*, 2 vols. (Oxford, 1985), i, p. 316; PRO E 101/344/17 m.18.

[40] PRO E 101/347/17; see also *VCH Wilts*, v, p. 484.

Table 8. Cloth production in Hampshire

Location	1394–5	1466–7
Winchester	76.6	53.3
Romsey	6.3	13.6
Isle of Wight	6.8	11.7
Andover	2.0	6.1
Alton	1.8	7.1
Basingstoke		4.8
N. Hampshire (Andover, Alton and Basingstoke)	3.8	18.0

Notes The marketing of each centre is represented as a percentage of the total for the whole county in the same year.

In 1466–7, other centres are incorporated with the main towns: Andover includes Whitchurch; Alton includes Headley, Petersfield and East Meon; and Basingstoke includes Odiham. Other centres recorded in the aulnage figures are for 1394–5: Alresford, Southampton, Havant and Fareham; and for 1466–7: Southampton, Fawley, Lymington and Christchurch. Winchester is divided in the latter year between the city and the soke.

The aulnage account recorded whether the cloths are the full or broad cloth, a kersey (or a straight in Southampton), and then converted the kerseys and straights into the equivalent number of cloths of the assize (3 kerseys = 1 cloth).

growth in north Hampshire. Winchester College's capacity to collect its rent at Andover varied, and showed signs of short-term difficulties. The difficulties of the bishop of Winchester's rent collectors at Newtown also show the problems brought about by the mid-century recession, with dramatically higher arrears in the 1460s.[41] The presence of financial difficulties also varied from manor to manor as shown in the neighbouring bishopric manors of Highclere and Burghclere, with the main drop in rents occurring before 1442 in the former manor and after this date at the latter.[42] But the evident willingness of lord and tenant to build, and the expansion of the cloth industry, suggests the presence of elements of growth in the market towns, and thus of increased prosperity in their rural hinterlands.

The lord, the peasant, and the wider economy

Postan provided a view of the period that emphasised the difficulties for the lord, and with them the difficulties for the wider economy. The decline of the population had transformed the balance of the market in favour of the tenant and the worker and to the detriment of the lord, who now received less for his land and had to pay out more for labour.

> The real sufferers from the agricultural depression were therefore the landlords. The depression of prices and the rising cost of labour made the cultivation of the demesne unprofitable; the revenue from

[41] Hampshire RO 11M59 B1/182, 191, 192, 193, 197, 200, 216.

[42] *Winchester Pipe Roll 1409–10*; HRO 11M59 B1/182, 191, 192, 197.

> rents which at first grew with the letting out of the demesne was in the end affected by the 'vacancies' and the general fall in agricultural values. In short in the countryside the main burden of economic change was borne by the upper ranks of society.

But the damaging impact on the lords also affected the wider economy. The lords had been large-scale producers of grain for the market. As Postan remarked,

> The large estates of the great secular or ecclesiastical landowners like the Duchy of Lancaster or the Bishop of Winchester used to produce very largely for the market. From the economic point of view large estates of this kind in the late thirteenth century were capitalist concerns: federated grain factories producing largely for cash.

The leasing of the demesnes did not stop commercial sales,

> but in so far as the peasant holding represented a more self-sufficient type of economy the multiplication of peasant leases represented a tendency towards natural economy and a relative contraction of agricultural exchange.[43]

The peasants might benefit, but the economy suffered. It could be justifiably considered 'as a time of economic decline and as the golden age of the English peasantry'.[44] It was a world of contracting markets. But how far was it such a period of doom and gloom for the landlord and the wider economy beyond? How far did it see a replacement of a large-scale capitalist production by a more peasant-based agriculture? How far does this area justify the pessimism implicit in Postan's approach to the period?

By 1400, the leasing of the demesnes was well under way in much of England. But it had not gone far in parts of Wessex. It had taken place in the claylands and Cotswold fringe of Wiltshire, and in the chalklands on many of the lay estates and particularly those of the great national estates such as the duchy of Lancaster. But on ecclesiastical estates, both monastic and episcopal, it made little progress within the chalklands, as on the manors of Romsey Abbey, St Swithun's Priory, St Mary's Abbey or the bishopric of Winchester. In the chalklands of Hampshire and Wiltshire the main period of such leasing seems to have been in about the 1420s and 1430s. On the estates of the bishopric of Winchester in the early 1440s, there were still twelve manors that continued direct cultivation, but of these, only one Wiltshire manor and three Hampshire ones retained direct cultivation in 1449. By the middle of the century direct cultivation was unusual and probably reflected the need for a home farm or short-term difficulties in finding a tenant.[45] It is

[43] Postan, *Essays*, pp. 48, 44.

[44] M. M. Postan, *Medieval Economy and Society* (Harmondsworth, 1975), p. 158.

[45] J. N. Hare, 'The Monks as Landlords: The Leasing of the Monastic Demesnes in Southern England', *The Church in Pre-Reformation Society*, ed. C. M. Barron and C. Harper-Bill (Woodbridge, 1985), pp. 88–9; *AHEW*, p. 143.

difficult in this area to support the view that the lord was seeing a continuing and substantial squeeze, and to find a purely economic explanation for leasing.

Why had this development taken place? Economic factors were clear and the rise in wages together with falling grain prices and yields since the late fourteenth-century boom put the finances of the demesne under pressure, although they still made a profit.[46] Many manors on the estate of the bishopric of Winchester showed evidence of declining profits of arable farming from the second decade of the fifteenth century.[47] Demesne agriculture involved high costs and administration, for a relatively small part of the manor's income. When the demesnes were leased on three Wiltshire manors of the duchy of Lancaster (Aldbourne, Collingbourne and Everleigh) and at Somborne (Hampshire), they only generated between 10 and 14 per cent of the manorial valor. Falling yields seem to have generated crucial damage at Bromham, falling by about a third between the 1380s and 1420–39, and on some manors there was evidence of a fall in demesne rent.[48] But it was not such that economic trends forced lords to give up demesne agriculture, rather they destroyed the justification of the exceptional and bureaucratic system that England had adopted in the thirteenth century, that of direct cultivation. Instead the simpler pattern used by lords before and since – renting out the land for a fixed and negotiable sum – became the norm. Leasing made things much simpler for the lord and he could escape the minor details of each item of cost. It is an attraction for the lord which any reader of account rolls from the two periods will instantly recognise. But it was not a process that was here adopted in the chalklands with any speed or enthusiasm.

Even when the arable had been leased, the lord frequently remained involved in his chalkland demesnes, above all in pastoral farming. Often, he continued to maintain a sheep flock at almost the same level. The duchy of Lancaster continued large-scale sheep farming until 1443, with flocks on nine or ten manors in Wiltshire, Dorset, Hampshire and Berkshire totalling over four and a half thousand sheep.[49] Wool sales on its Wiltshire manors were an important part of the revenue of the manor, yielding about a third of the annual valor.[50] Although sheep farming now ceased, it was later resumed on some of the manors in Hampshire and Dorset, as in 1462, although not in Wiltshire. The barons Hungerford possessed large flocks including over a thousand sheep at Winterborne Stoke and at Heytesbury (Wiltshire). At Watterson in Dorset, later a deserted village, flocks of between 814 and 1823 were maintained in the

[46] J. Z. Titow, 'Le Climat à travers les rôles de comptabilité de l'évêché de Winchester (1350–1458)', *Annales*, xxv (1970), pp. 344–7; London School of Economics Library, Beveridge collection, Box B2, figures from the bishopric manors in Wiltshire; Farmer, 'Grain Yields', pp. 355–66.

[47] Personal communication from Dr J. Z. Titow.

[48] Hare, 'Lord and Tenant', p. 350; 'Monks as Landlords' pp. 88–9; *AHEW*, p. 143.

[49] 1432, 4864 (PRO DL 29 /732/12034); 1439, 4619 (DL 29/733/12041); 1441, 6140, and 1442, 4573; E. M. Fryde, *Peasants and Landlords in Later Medieval England c.1380–1525* (Stroud, 1996), p. 109.

[50] In 1400 and 1406 on the manors of Aldbourne, Collingbourne and Everleigh it ranged from 27 to 44 per cent of the *valor* (other than in the exceptional, but explicable, 9 per cent at Everleigh in 1406). By contrast the proportion rendered by the lease of the arable was much less (10–14 per cent). Figures tabulated in Hare, 'Lord and Tenant', p. 66. Kingston Deverill, belonging to Netley Abbey, produced figures of 41 per cent and 24 per cent 1401 and 1407, ibid. p. 64.

fifteenth century.[51] On the ecclesiastical manors sheep flocks were maintained on the estates of St Swithun's Priory, St Mary's Abbey, and Netley Abbey until 1460s and 1470s, and on some of those of the bishopric of Winchester, where flocks were retained late at Bishopstone and on a dozen or more manors in Hampshire.[52] On the latter estate, numbers were certainly down on their peaks in the late fourteenth century, but they remained at a level generally higher than that of most years before the mid-fourteenth century, and there was no sign of continuing long-term decline. The difficulties of wool prices during the mid-century depression may have been a factor in this final leasing and yields may have been falling, but lords had not rushed into leasing. They also continued for a time to manage directly that other erratic but lucrative aspect of downland agriculture, the rabbit warrens, as at Aldbourne, and on a smaller scale at Somborne (Hants).[53]

Moreover, some lords continued to maintain their flocks into the sixteenth century. This seems to have had a regional aspect to it, with a greater tendency for this to take place in Dorset than in richer Wiltshire. One of the peculiarities of the Dorset entries in the *Valor Ecclesiasticus* is its record of the demesne pastures, mainly in the chalklands. These probably represent an approximation of flocks that were maintained by the lord, and which by their very nature would have fluctuated considerably from year. They do not appear to be the record of stock and land lease. On the estate of Shaftesbury Abbey, comparison can be made with the flocks as recorded on the account roll for 1516, which shows that similar-sized flocks were still being maintained (Table 9).[54] The monasteries may not, however, have been exploiting the demesne possibilities to the full. Bindon had flocks about half of what it had had in the early fourteenth century. The abbess of Wilton would also seem to have been active as a sheep farmer in 1521.[55] Shaftesbury and Wilton were two of the richest monasteries in the area and their involvement may suggest that this was a practice being maintained in the chalklands of Dorset and south-west Wiltshire, but not elsewhere. There is no evidence from inter-manorial stock movements in 1516 that sheep were maintained on any of Shaftesbury's other Wiltshire manors, in the north or the west of the county. On the claylands in the north of the county Stanley Abbey had resumed its involvement in pastoral farming, although what was being kept is not clear.[56] We have few figures for lay estates in Wessex for the early sixteenth century, but in Dorset Sir Roger Newburgh possessed 4,000 sheep in 1515.[57]

When the chalkland demesnes were leased, they were transferred to a single tenant and thus the large-scale market-oriented pattern of agriculture was maintained. Elsewhere leasing had often been to a group of tenants, as at Castle Combe and Oaksey (Wiltshire), but not in the chalklands. The new chalkland

[51] PRO SC 6/853/24; 30; B. Reynolds, 'Late Medieval Dorset' (unpub. London Univ. MA thesis, 1958), p. 58.
[52] Hare, 'Monks as Landlords', p. 90.
[53] Hare, 'Agriculture and Rural Settlement', pp. 164–5.
[54] Wiltshire RO 1728/70; *Valor Ecclesiasticus*, ed. J. Caley and J. Hunter, 6 vols., Record Commission (London, 1810–34).
[55] Hare, 'Monks as Landlords', p. 86.
[56] PRO SC 6/Hen VIII/3958.
[57] Taylor, *Dorset*, p. 127.

Table 9. Sheep flocks on the estate of Shaftesbury Abbey

Manor	1517	1518	1535
Barton	283 e	307	300 e
Berwick	281 w	296	200 w
Donhead	297 w	234	250 w
Tarrant	249 w	236	200 w
	308 e	315	200 e
Hanley	519 w	530	600 w
	287 h	257	200 h
Encombe	374 w	459	350 w
TOTAL	2598	2634	2300

Note e = ewe; w = wether; h = hoggaster

Sources WRO, 1728/70; and *Valor Ecclesiasticus*, i, pp. 277–9

tenants could thus be responsible for a very large demesne, flock and rental. In the later fifteenth century the lessees of Urchfont, successively the two William Harvests and Robert Wylkins had to provide over £36 a year in payments for the demesne and rectory, although this excluded the main tenant rents which were collected separately. The lease of the sheep flock produced over £14, the arable £7 (although for most of the time it produced wheat and barley, for Winchester, the latter being turned into malt before dispatch), and the rectory produced £15. The family also leased elsewhere in the county, on the abbey's other giant manor of All Cannings, as well as at Durrington.[58] Such families often accumulated several demesnes in the same area, as with the Goddards. By the time of the 1525 lay subsidy returns, John Goddard who leased at Aldbourne was credited with goods worth £440 and Thomas Goddard who played the same role at the neighbouring Ogbournes was assessed at £640. The latter could sell £30 of wool in a single transaction, and was also referred to as a gentleman.[59] Richard Kingsmyll, father of a leading member of Henry VII's judiciary, leased the manor of Ashe (Hampshire) in 1472. The family had come from Barkum in Berkshire and possessed land and trading connections. Richard had moved to Basingstoke, a growing town in north Hampshire where he was later buried. He was variously described as grazier, gent and yeoman. He marketed four cloths at Basingstoke in 1467 and performed various professional roles as bailiff of Basingstoke, a Justice of the Peace, and assessor of the subsidy in Hampshire. He became Member of Parliament for Ludgershall.[60] Lords showed their assumptions about the continued large scale of demesne agriculture after leasing through their investment in rebuilding the great barns of the manor. The bishop of Winchester paid over £47 7s. 11d. in 1497–8 for a new barn at Overton (Hampshire), as well as providing the timber, while Winchester College spent £42 13s. 3d. on a barn at Durrington in

[58] BL Add. Roll 19722; J. N. Hare, 'The Demesne Lessees of Fifteenth Century Wiltshire', *AgHR*, 29 (1981), p. 12.
[59] *A History of Parliament*, i, *Biographies*, ed. J. Wedgwood (London, 1936), pp. 516–17; F. J. Baigent and J. E. Millard, *A History of the Ancient Town and Manor of Basingstoke* (London, 1889); HRO, M61/HMC202; PRO E 101/344/17 m.18.
[60] Hare, 'Demesne Lessees', pp. 9–11.

1412–13, and £56 9s. 6½ d. on one at Downton in 1410.[61] This was agriculture on a large scale, requiring much capital and labour, and it parallels the activities of Roger Heritage, so clearly delineated by Professor Dyer. It is difficult to see this as any less capitalist than the system it replaced or in any way, in Postan's words, a 'tendency towards natural economy'.[62]

Within the peasantry, developments also encouraged the growth of large holdings with a consequent need for labour and for market production. This was an area where the structure of the land market was dominated by the standard customary tenements of virgates and cottages, rather than by acres, whether held individually or in clusters. The initial impact of the Black Death may have been to enable peasants to upgrade themselves, to become holders of the standard virgate holdings when previously they had been restricted to being cottagers. It was these cottage tenements that tended to be vacated and decayed. But by the fifteenth century, peasants were using the increased availability of land and the declining family influence in landholding and succession to accumulate more standard holdings.[63] They thus required more wage labour and this was unlikely to lead to a higher proportion of the productivity of the tenancy being used to feed the family. If anything this should have ended with a higher proportion of production going to the market. At Durrington, in the fourteenth century, the sixteen virgates were all held by different peasants, constituting a broad-based village aristocracy. But by 1506, it was a very different situation. Two men held three virgates, and three held two, with the two leading figures being related to the demesne lessee of the neighbouring manor. Those who now possessed only a single virgate were now economically second-class citizens within their village.[64] Durrington shows an early and extreme example of a wider tendency found elsewhere, as at Coombe Bisset (Table 10), or at Ramridge (Hampshire), where by 1433 one-fifth of the tenant population held more than a virgate and a third held the standard virgate tenement, or in the 'peasant aristocracy' of Coleshill (Berkshire).[65]

Whether peasant agriculture was more efficient or productive than that of the demesne must be a matter of speculation, but the peasant community was highly responsive to the market. The sheep-rearing activities of the peasantry are reflected in countless court rolls particularly away from the extensive chalk downs, and where, therefore, pressure on the common pastures was at its most acute, as at Eastrop and Steeple Ashton.[66] But their trading activities were also reflected in the great demesne farms. Increasingly some of the large flock owners gave up breeding; their flocks were entirely of hoggasters or the wethers that were kept for wool. This was the case at All Cannings, Urchfont and Aldbourne. But such a practice could only operate where the peasantry produced large numbers of lambs for sale.

The brewing industry provides a further example of the links between the

[61] E. Roberts, 'Overton Court Farm and the Late Medieval Farmhouses of Demesne Lessees in Hampshire', *PCFC*, li (1996), pp. 102–3; WCM 5967–8; 5388.
[62] Dyer, *Everyday Life*, pp. 315–21; Postan, *Essays*, p. 44.
[63] *Agrarian History*, pp. 717–18; Hare, 'Lord and Tenant'; Faith, 'Berkshire', p. 132.
[64] Hare, 'Durrington', p. 146.
[65] J. P. Genet, 'Economie et société rurale en Angleterre au xve siècle d'après les comptes de l'hôpital d'Ewelme', *Annales*, xxvii (1972), p. 1465; Faith, 'Berkshire', pp. 157–8.
[66] Faith, 'Berkshire', pp. 171–3.

Table 10. Land-holding and tenant differentiation at Durrington and Coombe Bisset

Durrington

	Number of virgates							
	3+	2–3	2	1–2	1	½–1	½	<½
1334–5					17			19
1359			1	4	10		4	16
1411–12	1		1	3	8		2	12
1441		2	2	3	5	2		9
1505–6	2		3	3	2	2		10

Coombe Bisset

	Number of virgates							
	3+	2–3	2	1–2	1	½–1	½	<½
1307				1	12		2	14
1372				5	8	3	2	12
1411–12	1		1	2	6		2	11
1450				6	10		3	6
1552	1		3		6	2	10	

Sources Durrington: WCM 5601 Aa; 5601 Ca; 13373; 5603d; 5606 Aa; Coombe Bisset: WCM 4350, 4351b, 13373, 4353, 4354.

peasant and the market. It is rare to be able to compare the production of the lord and his tenants, but this can be done at Downton, where both the rectory accounts and the bishop's demesne accounts still survive. Barley production on the bishop's demesne had increased by the beginning of the fifteenth century, reflecting the increasing national importance of barley in demesne production in this period.[67] In 1410, 44 per cent of the sown acreage of the demesne was given over to barley, one of the highest percentages yet located in the county at any time in the Middle Ages. But at Downton demesne production of barley was still substantially less important as a crop than for the rest of the parish. Barley constituted 63 per cent of grain produced on the bishops' demesne, but about 77 per cent for the parish as a whole. The rector was even more closely tied to barley production: in 1406 he grew nothing but barley. This crop with extra labour could be converted into the much-needed ale required by the great city of Salisbury. Ale was less efficient in its use of calories as a food-stuff, so that it would have increased the demand for the grain. It also required extra labour to convert the grain to malt, but this added to its value, and the tenants showed a greater sensitivity to the market than did the policies of the bishop's demesne. The impact of peasant production of ale and malt in generating jobs would be underestimated by the records of the demesne. This contrast is one which seen on a lesser scale elsewhere both in earlier tithe returns for Wiltshire

[67] B. M. S. Campbell, K. C. Bartley, and J. P. Power, 'The Demesne Farming Systems of Post Black Death England: A Classification', *AgHR*, 44 (1996), pp. 133–4; J. A. Galloway, 'London's Grain Supply: Changes in Production, Distribution and Consumption during the Fourteenth Century', *Franco-British Studies*, 20 (1995), pp. 31–2.

Table 11. Downton: demesne and tenant production, 1407–12

Crop	*Parish crops %*	*Demesne crops %*
Wheat	16.8	17.2
Curral		1.5
Barley	75.4	62.8
Oats	7.8	15.5
Peas		1.5
Vesch		1.5

The production of the individual grain is expressed as a percentage of the total grain production of the demesne or the parish. The figures are calculated for the years 1407, 1410, 1411 and 1412. Parish figures are taken from the rectory accounts (WCM 5385, 5388, 89, 90) and therefore include produce of the bishopric demesne. The figures for the bishopric are taken from the pipe rolls (HRO 11M59 B1/154; *Winchester Pipe Roll 1409–10*, pp. 65–6; HRO 11M59 B1/157; /158).

and in the contemporary figures for East Meon (Hampshire). At Downton, under the influence of the Salisbury market, the contrast was much greater. East Meon (in east Hampshire) had different soils and was far distant from Salisbury. In 1410, 29 per cent of its tithes were in barley compared with 22 per cent of the product of the bishop's demesne, and in selected years during the period 1350–1441, barley made up 25 per cent of the parish production of grain, and 16 per cent of that of the demesne.[68] A similar emphasis on tenant barley production has also been seen in the West Midlands.[69]

The scale of demographic decline makes it likely that total production declined over the later Middle Ages as a whole, but this does not mean that there was any likelihood of a reduction of either the efficiency or the market orientation of agriculture. Crops might vary, but in the chalklands of Wessex the pattern of agriculture continued in its traditional way. The lord had retreated from direct involvement, but the large-scale nature of agriculture and its domination by sheep–corn husbandry was strengthened and passed on to later centuries. It was this world of capital-intensive farming that was to be at the heart of later agricultural change. In the short term, the signs of agricultural change seen in the erosion of the open field and of the customary holdings were to be more apparent away from the chalklands.[70]

Rent and the demand for land

Finally, in assessing the balance of lord and tenant we need to turn from the world of agriculture to that of the demand for land and the revenues that flowed from tenant to lord. How far was it the case that 'the values of land, however measured, were falling off'?[71] We must seek patterns of rent variations, whether

[68] Hare, 'Lord and Tenant'; calculations from Page, *Winchester Pipe Roll*; *AHEW*, p. 719.
[69] C. Dyer, 'Farming Practice and Techniques', *AHEW*, p. 229.
[70] Hare, 'Change and Continuity', pp. 9–10; *VCH Hants*, v, p. 421.
[71] Postan, *Essays*, p. 43.

they are regional or between estates. Such rents took a variety of forms. There was the annual rent, the entry fines, and other forms of payments from the tenant through the courts, as with the payments associated with serfdom. There was also the question of how much of the anticipated revenue could be collected: what were the level of arrears and were they good arrears that were simply late or bad ones that would never be received.[72] Finally comparison is made more difficult as a result of changes in estate policy. The leasing of the demesnes or the commutation of rents complicate the task. Such studies are time-consuming, but are important for understanding what was happening in this period. It has been done for Wiltshire and now needs to be extended.[73] This suggested that here it was useful to consider developments up to and including the 1440s, to look at the 1450s and 1460s, and then to look at changes in the later fifteenth century.

Here four major patterns of demand may be distinguished. Traditionally, and following on from Postan, the early fifteenth century has been seen as a period of declining rents and long-term agrarian depression, and parts of Wiltshire confirm this development, particularly the north of the county as at Oaksey or over the border in Berkshire at Coleshill.[74] There are also signs of difficulty in the south, as at Coombe Bisset and Downton. But elsewhere the growth of the cloth industry produced very different patterns of demand. In the cloth-producing areas of west Wiltshire rents might show some rises, as at Heytesbury, particularly in the latter part of the period, and lords could gain from the prosperity through the courts. A classic case would be that of Castle Combe where Sir John Fastolf benefited enormously from the expansion of the cloth industry, which he had himself encouraged.[75] Finally, there were the areas which did not have a cloth industry but which were dependent on the industrial areas for their own prosperity: they produced grain, malt, meat and wool for the growing industrial and urban parts of the county. Durrington was an example of this pattern, with easy access to both Salisbury and west Wiltshire.[76]

The middle of the century produces a very different picture. Those areas where there had been declining demand for land now seemed relatively immune. By contrast those areas that had hitherto prospered now showed evidence of severe decline. This was both in the manufacturing areas, where rent reductions particularly affected cottage rents, and in the agricultural areas that depended on industry, where rents were hit dramatically both by the industrial recession and by the related agricultural recession. Those parts of the county that had seen industrial growth in the early part of the century were now more than ever dependent on the cloth industry, whether through those directly engaged in the industry or those who served the needs of those who were. These were areas that showed wide-scale reductions in cottage rents, falls in court profits and difficulties in collecting the full and expected

[72] J. N. Hare, 'The Lords and their Tenants: Conflict and Stability in Fifteenth Century Wiltshire', *Conflict and Community in Southern England*, ed. B. Stapleton (Stroud, 1992), pp. 25–6; R. R. Davies, 'Baronial Accounts, Incomes and Arrears in the Later Middle Ages', *EcHR*, 2nd series, xxi (1968), pp. 211–29.

[73] Hare, 'Growth and Recession', pp. 1–26. This is the source of the next section.

[74] Faith, 'Berkshire', p. 117.

[75] Hare, 'Growth and Recession', pp. 13–15 and table II; Carus-Wilson, 'Industrial Growth', pp. 159–67.

[76] As reflected in the will of Robert Martyn, Hare, 'Durrington', pp. 146–7.

Table 12. Movements in rent totals on some Wiltshire manors

	1405–45	1445–65	1465–1500
Oaksey	–23.7	0.8	0.5
Coombe Bisset	–27.0	–4.3	3.6
Heytesbury	23.7	–12.9	6.8
Durrington	3.6	–16.0	7.5

Table 12 compares the total rent at the end of the period with that at the beginning, expressing change as a percentage of the total at the beginning of the period. For further details and other examples, see Hare, 'Growth and recession', pp. 1–25.

income. The dependence on industry made these areas ever more vulnerable to economic recession generated by problems arising in the export trade and the damaging effect of monetary shortages. Too often in the past evidence of declining incomes between 1400 and 1470 has failed to distinguish between long-term agrarian recession and the short depression that followed on from a period of industrial growth and prosperity. The result has been the view that while recession may not have been so deep in the southern counties as elsewhere, here too 'demand for land generally declined significantly in the course of the first half of the fifteenth century'.[77] Finally, from the 1470s there are signs of piecemeal growth in demand, both in industrial and rural areas: shown in rising court profits and rents, or in greater collection of income. Bromham provides an example of some of these trends evident from the 1490s.

Such an examination of land demand reinforces the signs of growth that have been noticed earlier. This is not to suggest that we should see the period as dominated by rising seigneurial incomes, and the patterns seem to be regional in character. That there was money to be made from the economy is clear, and Sir John Fastolf at Castle Combe is an extreme example of a prospering landlord. For the ruling classes, fortunes were not made and lost in the economy, but in marriage, politics and war as reflected in the rise and fall of one of the region's pre-eminent families, the Hungerfords. The manorial evidence from this part of England suggests that the fifteenth century might show signs of difficulty and short-term problems but not of continuous decline. The cash liveries also suggest that while there might be difficulties the period was by no means one of great crisis.[78]

Conclusions

Postan illuminated one aspect of the period for us, and his model of a society where change was driven by demographic fall remains of vital importance in understanding the economy of the period. It provided a unity to the period, 'a

[77] J. Hatcher, *Plague, Population and the English Economy, 1348–1530* (1977), p. 39; *VCH Wilts*, iv, pp. 40–1.
[78] Hare, 'Growth and Recession', table 7.

secular slump which began at some time in the fourteenth century . . . and continued . . . until the late seventies and eighties of the fifteenth century'.[79] But there now seems to be a need to disaggregate our figures both in space and time. We have for long been familiar with the idea that certain areas suffered less during this period than others, and are increasingly aware that there were also chronological variations. As Professor Hatcher has reminded us, 'the more that is discovered about the experience of the later Middle Ages, the more difficult it becomes to squeeze the emergent facts into a single descriptive or explanatory framework'.[80] Wessex shows the need for such sub-divisions. Chronologically, there was a period of expansion in the early fifteenth century and again at the end of the century with a deep recession in the middle. But even within these different periods, there were also geographical variations, as in early fifteenth-century Wiltshire, with areas of growth and of decline. In north Hampshire, agrarian recession could be counterbalanced by later economic growth. West Berkshire also shows regional contrasting patterns of economic growth in which the cloth industry was to play an important role.[81] The demands of this industry were to have an important impact on the local diversity throughout our region. But the growth of the textile industry was not the product of a single movement or a single moment. It did not stop in 1400, as has often been implied,[82] but continued with considerable expansion in some parts of this region. Society was changing and the more the economy grew on the basis of industrial production, the more it became subject to the vagaries of monetary pressures and the interruptions of trade, rather than to demographic factors. This was clearly seen in the in the mid-fifteenth-century recession. It was no longer so completely the agrarian society in which demographic factors were necessarily pre-eminent. It was not surprising that in 1450, alongside the evidence of political protest, many of the areas where discontent broke out into the open were united by being cloth-producing areas. These hitherto prosperous areas now suffered from the international monetary-driven recession as well as the interruptions of trade with the Hanseatic League, Burgundy and France. But now this society had become increasingly dependent on a wider markets and trade fluctuations.

In Wessex, fifteenth-century movements in prices, wages and land demand could be ascribed as much to monetary-led shifts or the increasing demand for labour and produce from the industrial areas, as to demographic factors. There were still areas where the absence of an expanding industry may have led to a pattern of long-term agrarian recession more appropriate to Postan's model, but in general this was a region which displayed prosperity and growth. The collapse of population in the mid-fourteenth century had cut total national agricultural and economic production, but this was over by the fifteenth, and population had now stabilised at a new and low level. In Wessex, signs of

[79] Postan, *Essays*, p. 43.

[80] J. Hatcher, 'The Great Slump of the Mid-Fifteenth Century', *Progress and Problems in Medieval England: Essays in Honour of Edward Miller*, ed. R. H. Britnell and J. Hatcher (Cambridge, 1996), p. 239. For a further attempt at chronological sub-division, see J. M. W. Bean, 'Landlords', *AHEW*, 579–86.

[81] M. Yates, 'Change and Continuities in Rural Society from the Later Middle Ages to the Sixteenth Century: The Contribution of West Berkshire', *EcHR*, 2nd series, lii (1999), pp. 617–37.

[82] For example Postan, *Essays*, p. 198.

further decline were more than counterbalanced by the evidence of growth. It was a time of increased mobility when village shrinkage in one part of the region led to the growth of population elsewhere, when industrial areas sucked in population from elsewhere in the region and beyond.

But we also need to look for a wider chronological pattern. Postan emphasised 'how little the economic development of the fifteenth century owed to it being sandwiched between the fourteenth and the sixteenth, it was population that provided the crucial driving force'.[83] But Wessex in the fifteenth century saw the development of the patterns of society and farming that were to dominate the next few centuries; the large scale capital-intensive agriculture of the chalk country and the family and pastoral farms of the cheese country. It saw the emergence of the gentleman farmer who was to prove so vital in the subsequent agrarian development of this area.[84] Here we need to go beyond the fifteenth century and to treat this and the following century together, as has been done by Professor Dyer, as a single period of transition.[85] There were developments influenced by demographic changes that distinguish the two centuries, but there were others which continued to develop both in the period of demographic decline and in the contrasting successor period of population growth.

Wessex both reinforces and challenges the traditional picture of the fifteenth century. It offers us evidence of growth and even of agricultural recession depending on when and where we look. But can it simply be dismissed as an exceptional region or does it suggest the need to look again at our generalisations about the period? Just as the economic historian of the twentieth century must consider regional and short-term chronological variations, so too should we. The challenge is there, and the evidence, however imperfect, allows us to establish such variations. To do so, we must first strive to integrate all our sources: manorial records with the results of dendrochronology, and lost villages with church rebuilding. Only in this way can we hope to understand the complexity, creativity and change that lay at the heart of the fifteenth century.

[83] Postan, *Essays*, p. 42. 'In a society so predominantly agricultural and in an agricultural system so predominantly peasant as those of medieval England, changes in population must *ex hypothesi* have had a direct effect on demands for land', ibid. 203.

[84] *VCH Wilts*, iv, pp. 43–64; Hare, 'Change and Continuity'.

[85] C. Dyer, 'Peasants and Farmers: Rural Settlement in an Age of Transition', *The Age of Transition: The Archaeology of English Culture, 1400–1600*, ed. D. Gaimster and P. Stamper (Oxford, 1997), pp. 199, 61–74.

The Trade of Fifteenth-Century Cambridge and its Region

John Lee

'Not a century of growth [but] an age of recession, arrested economic development and declining national income' was how Postan described the fifteenth century in 1939.[1] He pointed to a reduced population, falling land values, and a contraction of settlement and land cultivated, despite the increased prosperity of wage-earners.[2] Although since then the case has been put forward for viewing the fifteenth century as a period of 'economic growth',[3] many historians now accept much of Postan's argument, even if during the century, some areas saw periods of expansion.[4] The contraction of the economy reached its most intense and widespread during the 'great depression' of the mid-fifteenth century, when overseas trade collapsed and agricultural commodity prices reached their nadir. Recovery was slow and hesitant, and even the later fifteenth and early sixteenth centuries have recently been seen as a period of limited opportunities for economic development.[5]

The fifteenth-century economy has been likened to that of Britain between the two world wars, with areas of growth coexisting with areas of decline. But much of the growth that did take place was often at the expense of other areas. Textile production expanded in districts such as the Stour Valley of Suffolk, the West Riding of Yorkshire, the Cotswolds and around Exeter. But this was at the expense of older cloth-making towns such as York, Coventry and Norwich, and of other parts of the countryside. An increasing proportion of cloth exports were shipped through London, hitting other provincial ports, while the capital's network of trade and credit damaged provincial merchants. Even localised growth took place at the expense of decline elsewhere. The small town of Buntingford in Hertfordshire thrived as the established borough of Standon, one mile distant, decayed.[6]

Cambridge was a medium-sized county town of about 3,500 townspeople in

[1] This work is drawn from my doctoral research 'Cambridge and its economic region, 1450–1560'. I wish to thank my supervisor Professor John Hatcher, and the Economic and Social Research Council, for their support.

[2] M. Postan, 'The Fifteenth Century', *Essays*; 'Some Economic Evidence of Declining Population in the Later Middle Ages', *Essays*.

[3] A. R. Bridbury, *Economic Growth: England in the Later Middle Ages* (London, 1962).

[4] J. Hatcher, *Plague, Population and the English Economy 1348–1530* (London, 1977), pp. 35–54.

[5] J. Hatcher, 'The Great Slump of the Mid-Fifteenth Century', in *Progress and Problems in Medieval England*, ed. R. Britnell and J. Hatcher (Cambridge, 1996), pp. 237–72; R. H. Britnell, 'The English Economy and the Government, 1450–1550', *The End of the Middle Ages? England in the Fifteenth and Sixteenth Centuries*, ed. J. L. Watts (Stroud, 1998), pp. 89–116.

[6] M. Bailey, 'A Tale of Two Towns: Buntingford and Standon in the Later Middle Ages', *Journal of Medieval History*, 19 (1993), pp. 351–71.

1524–5, plus its university. It served a region of about ten to fifteen miles radius, roughly running along the county boundary, with no other major towns except at the periphery. This paper seeks to explore the principal areas of trade with the region during the later fifteenth century, and examine possible areas of growth.

In considering the supply and demand of the region, we need to look at three areas: the town of Cambridge, its surrounding countryside and London. On the basis of tax returns, Cambridge's population remained fairly constant between 1377 and 1524–5, but these returns do not include the university, which increased in size from between 300 and 700 scholars to around 1,300 between the late fourteenth and late fifteenth centuries.[7] This growth of the university generated an important increase in demand, and helped the town to avoid the worst of the effects of general population decline that hit many late medieval towns. The countryside around Cambridge was unlikely to have provided a source of growing demand in the later fifteenth century. In terms of population and taxable wealth the county was outstripped by the growth of neighbouring counties, and it suffered a retreat from cultivation in the western clay uplands. The county was not a significant cloth producer. But there were opportunities, as will be explored later, for the region to supply the town with foodstuffs. Finally, there was the impact on Cambridge of demand from London, which lay fifty miles away, and was considered a day's journey in parliamentary writs.[8] London was not immune to the population decline of the fifteenth century, but was able to compensate by increasing involvement in the marketing and distribution of goods across the country. London created demands for produce, but also supplied goods and services on a greater scale.

How did these three areas interact in the later fifteenth century? Firstly, it will be proposed that the growth of the university led to an increase in institutional and individual consumption demands in the town. These demands were met by suppliers within Cambridge, and from Lynn and London. Secondly, the demand of the town on the region will be illustrated by the agreements of King's Hall for food and fuel supplies. Thirdly, the development of trade in malt barley and saffron in the region, stimulated at least in part by the London market, will be explored.

1. Demand within Cambridge

The redistribution of wealth following the population decline of the later fourteenth and fifteenth centuries led to an improvement in incomes, diet, housing and possessions of many urban residents. Wage-earners and artisans increased their spending on clothes, household textiles, pewter and wooden furniture.[9] In Cambridge, the growing demand for these goods seems to have been intensified by the expansion of the university. As already mentioned, it has

[7] T. H. Aston, G. D. Duncan and T. A. R. Evans, 'The Medieval Alumni of the University of Cambridge', *Past and Present*, 86 (1980), pp. 11–27.
[8] *VCH Cambs*, iii, p. 1.
[9] Dyer, *Standards of Living*, pp. 207, 210.

been estimated that the number of scholars had more than doubled to around 1,300 by the later fifteenth century. Most scholars at the university did not come from the richest groups in society, but were men of modest wealth, coming from the more affluent peasantry, yeomanry, lesser gentry, leading urban merchants and property-owners. Even so, many accumulated some possessions. The wills of a King's College scholar, clerk, and three masters of arts in the 1460s and 1470s reveal a wide range of belongings, including coverlets, linen sheets, blankets, robes, surplices, hoods, a mantle, mazer bowls, salt-cellars, pieces of silver, a counter (i.e. a table) a feather bed, and books.[10] Institutional purchases also increased, with the foundation of seven new non-monastic colleges in Cambridge between 1350 and 1500, and as scholars began to reside in colleges rather than hostels.[11] This was at a time when demand for expensive luxury goods was generally fairly static, as seigneurial incomes fell, and some households cut back on expenditure. This combination of purchases by individuals and institutions produced a demand that was met by three principal sources in the fifteenth century: suppliers from Cambridge, Lynn and London.

Within Cambridge, a range of specialist trades developed to serve the academic community. A schedule survives from 1503 of sixty-eight people who held the university privilege, placing them under the authority of the university rather than the borough. These included manciples, launderers, bakers, barbers, surgeons, stationers, apothecaries and the university mason. An even wider diversity of specialist occupations is found in the tax returns of the 1520s including an organ player, freemason and collar-maker; a diversity of trades wider than would have been justified by the size of the town alone.[12] As well as a large number of the usual urban trades of baking, brewing, butchery, tailoring, carpentry and metal work, Cambridge had a few goldsmiths and pewterers. A large number of leather workers were supported by many alien immigrants in the 1440s.[13] But goods could also be obtained from two principal sources outside the town as college accounts show: from merchants at Lynn and from London.

Lynn, readily accessible from Cambridge via the Cam and Great Ouse, served as the town's seaport. Trade was hit during the fifteenth century through warfare, embargoes and sea-level changes, which caused the silting of the haven.[14] Like most provincial ports, it lost trade to London. The principal foreign traders at Lynn were the Hansards, who imported cheap bulk commodities from the Baltic like timber, timber products, iron, flax and wax. Gascon wine, Bay of Biscay salt, North Sea fish and grain from eastern Europe was also distributed through the port.[15] The port served a wide

[10] KCC Ledger Book, i, ff. 58, 70v, 77, 107v.

[11] Aston *et al.*, 'Medieval Alumni', pp. 14, 50.

[12] Cambridge University Library, University Archives, Luard 145b; PRO E 179/81/133.

[13] PRO E 179/81/85.

[14] E. M. Carus-Wilson, 'The Medieval Trade of the Ports of the Wash', *Medieval Archaeology*, vi–vii (1962–3), p. 201; S. H. Rigby, '"Sore Decay" and "Fair Dwellings": Boston and Urban Decline in the Later Middle Ages', *Midland History*, x (1985), pp. 47–61; A. Dyer, *Decline and Growth in English Towns 1400–1640*, 2nd edn (Cambridge, 1991), pp. 65–6.

[15] J. D. Fudge, *Cargoes, Embargoes and Emissaries. The Commercial and Political Interaction of England and the German Hanse 1450–1510* (Toronto, 1995), pp. 148–9.

hinterland, including local shipyards and the Norfolk textile industry, as well as Cambridge and its surrounding region. The bursar of King's College bought over 250 lbs of wax at Lynn in 1448–9.[16] Floor tiles for building work at Cambridge came to the Great Bridge there in 1478–9.[17]

London was the other important source of supply for Cambridge, both via the coast and Lynn, and overland. Carriers linked Cambridge with the capital, delivering goods such as pike and butts of malmsey.[18] King's College regularly purchased a significant amount of spices and fish from London suppliers, like a hogshead of white wine bought in 1472–3 with 4s. 4d. in carriage, or the six barrels of white herring carried from the Steelyard to Bishopgate and thence to Cambridge for 5s. 4d. in 1509–10. Smaller colleges like Peterhouse also bought some commodities in London, such as 28 lbs of wax in 1456–7 and 1 lb of pepper in 1458–9.[19]

Stourbridge Fair, held annually in late August and early September on the outskirts of Cambridge, was a major source of distribution for the goods of merchants from Lynn and London. This enabled even poorer customers, who could not otherwise have afforded the costs of search and transport, to purchase from these traders. The fair appears to have grown in size and importance during the late fifteenth and early sixteenth centuries. There is considerable evidence from many colleges and other local institutions in the area, including Thetford Priory and Peterborough Abbey, of bulk purchases of foodstuffs and hardware products at the fair.[20]

An unusual source strongly suggests that individual scholars also made purchases at fairs like Stourbridge. A school book of English prose passages with model Latin translations, probably composed by a teacher of grammar at Magdalen School, Oxford at the end of the fifteenth century, covers everyday activities of schoolboys in the town. One passage speaks specifically of Stourbridge Fair:

> Yff all thynge hade fortunede after my mynde I hade ben this day at stirbrige faire wher, as men say, a man may bye better chepe than enywher ellys.[21]

Remarkably, the fame of this fair was such that it was familiar to schoolboys in a rival university town. Other references probably refer to St Giles' Fair, the principal fair in Oxford, held in early September, but could equally apply to Stourbridge Fair. The presence of Londoners at the fair, and their deceptively attractive goods were subjects for translation:

[16] KCC, Mundum Books, i, f. 137v.

[17] *A Grace Book, Containing the Proctors' Accounts and Other Records of the University of Cambridge, 1454–88*, ed. S. M. Leathes, Cambridge Antiquarian Society Luard Memorial Series (Cambridge, 1897), i, p. 130.

[18] PRO C 1/19/469; C 1/232/32.

[19] KCC Mundum Books, vi, f. 70, x, 1509–10 account; Peterhouse, Cambridge, computus rolls, 1456–7, 1458–9.

[20] J. Lee, 'Fairs of Cambridge and its Region, 1450–1560', in Economic History Society Conference programme (1999), pp. 13–19.

[21] *A Fifteenth Century School Book from a Manuscript in the British Museum (MS Arundel 249)*, ed. W. Nelson (Oxford, 1956), p. 90.

> He that hath money enough to cast away lete hym pike hymselfe[22] to the faire and make a bargyn with the londyners, and I doubte not but er he depar thei shall make hym as clen from it as an ape fro tailys, for thei study nothyng in the worlde ellys but for to deceyve menn with fair spech.
>
> Many scholars of this universite wolde spende wast-fully all their fathers goodes in japys and trifulles at this faire yf they myght have it at their liberte. for thies londyners be so craftye and so wyly in dressynge their gere so gloriusly that they may deceyve us scholars lyghtly.[23]

Other passages mention a student who received a pen case and ink horn at the last fair from his uncle. Another schoolboy hoped that his mother and father would come when the next fair was to be held. At the fair he saw many of his acquaintances brightly apparelled in gold chains, brooches with gold, pearls and precious stones, probably bought at the fair.[24] For as well as stationery supplies, one gets the impression that the students were being tempted by a wide range of cheaper goods, perhaps objects like the straw hats, Nuremberg mirrors, imitation pearls and mistletoe beads which were imported into London in 1480–1, and similar items which came in through Lynn in 1503/4.[25]

The townspeople of Cambridge do not appear to have benefited greatly from the demand generated by colleges and individual scholars during the late fifteenth century. Many goods were produced outside the town, and many cheap consumables were imported, although the extent of imports reflected a general problem in the national economy. The distribution of goods was also largely outside the hands of the townspeople. Again, this was a not a problem unique to Cambridge: many provincial merchants faced competition from London traders during the fifteenth century.[26]

2. Cambridge's demand on the region

Although Cambridge had open fields, in which many townspeople and urban institutions held strips, the town relied on suppliers in the surrounding region for most of its food and fuel. Some colleges had estates which they cultivated directly for food, as King's College did at Grantchester during the 1460s and 1470s,[27] while other colleges may have taken some of their tithe income in kind. King's Hall bought some foodstuffs in the marketplace and at fairs, but

[22] pike hymselfe: be off.

[23] Ibid. p. 54.

[24] Ibid. pp. 14, 22, 90.

[25] *Overseas Trade of London. Exchequer Customs Accounts 1480–1*, ed. H. S. Cobb, London Record Society, 27 (1990), pp. xxxvi–xxxviii; J. L. Bolton, *Medieval English Economy 1150–1500* (London, 1980), p. 319.

[26] J. I. Kermode, 'Merchants, Overseas Trade, and Urban Decline: York, Beverley and Hull, c.1380–1500', *Northern History*, xxiii (1987), pp. 51–73; J. I. Kermode, 'Money and Credit in the Fifteenth Century: Some Lessons from Yorkshire', *Business History Review*, lxv (1991), pp. 475–501.

[27] J. Saltmarsh, 'A College Home-Farm in the Fifteenth Century', *Economic History*, xi (1936), pp. 155–72.

also drew up private agreements (*conventiones*) with suppliers covering the purchase and delivery of wheat, malt barley and fuel.[28] These state the supplier's name and often his residence, the quantity of the commodity, delivery date and terms of payment. The length of time between the date of the contract and delivery was generally between one and six months. The agreements can be used to show the extent of demand and the types of suppliers who met this demand.

In order to analyse these agreements, they were entered into a relational database and grouped by suppliers. Some assumptions had to be made, as spellings varied considerably. Suppliers were grouped by surname unless there were different recorded forenames or places of residence for that surname.

King's Hall, which later became part of Trinity College, was the largest and most important college in Cambridge until King's College was established. Its statutes provided for thirty-two fellows, just under half the total fellowships in the university. King's Hall received most of its income from the royal exchequer allowances farmed to various bodies, and from a number of appropriated churches.[29] The college had few estates that could supply its consumption needs, although it occasionally received rents in kind from its manor at Chesterton.[30] The college therefore depended on the market to a greater extent than other colleges with a larger landed endowment.

Figure 1 shows the geographical spread of the King's Hall contracts made between 1450 and 1500. Roughly half were made with farmers within five miles of the college, and few wheat or barley contracts were made with suppliers over ten miles distant. This hinterland is roughly comparable with the sources of agricultural supply of other towns of similar size,[31] and probably reflected the town's general supply area, with the possibility that as a larger institution, King's Hall could afford to look further afield for its supplies.

The geographical spread also reflected the geological differences within the county. The heavy clay soils of the south-west clay plateau were unsuited to barley-growing; relatively few barley contracts came from this area. Shown more clearly though, is the restricted availability of fuel supplies. Cambridgeshire had been sparsely wooded since the time of Domesday Book.[32] Reflecting this shortage of woodland, the King's Hall contracts for fuel dealt with suppliers further afield than those supplying the college with wheat and barley. Charcoal and other fuel, probably firewood, came from south-east Cambridgeshire, or from across the border into Essex and Suffolk. William Harrison described the same area as supplying Cambridge in the 1580s, although by then there were also regular shipments of coal.[33]

[28] Trinity College, Cambridge, King's Hall accounts, vols. xi–xxvi (1451–2 to 1543–4); A. B. Cobban, *The King's Hall within the University of Cambridge in the Later Middle Ages* (Cambridge, 1969), pp. 212–15.

[29] Cobban, *King's Hall*, pp. 44–5, 202–7.

[30] King's Hall accounts, vol. xxv, ff. 110, 142v.

[31] B. M. S. Campbell *et al.*, *A Medieval Capital and its Grain Supply*, Historical Geography Research Series, 30 (1993), p. 173.

[32] O. Rackham, *Ancient Woodland: Its History, Vegetation and Uses in England* (London, 1980), pp. 122–3.

[33] J. Hatcher, *The History of the British Coal Industry*, i: *Before 1700. Towards the Age of Coal* (Oxford, 1993), p. 44.

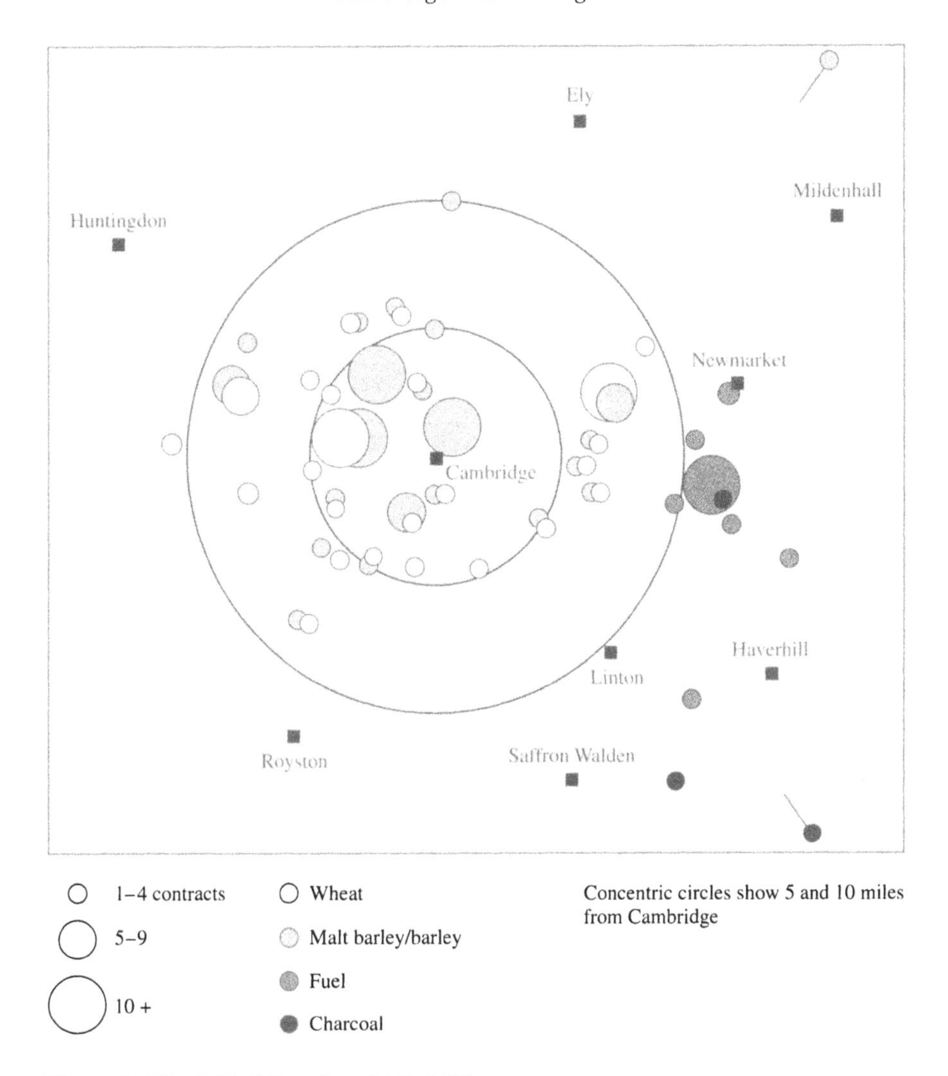

Figure 1: King's Hall Suppliers 1450–1500

The smallest wheat contract was for four bushels, and the largest for eighty and a half quarters, with a mean average of nine and a half quarters. Barley purchases varied from one to sixty-three quarters, with a mean average of just under nineteen quarters. A distinct feature of the contracts, which may have been one of their strengths, was their continuity. The most frequent suppliers are shown in Table 13. The sixteenth century saw a trend towards more contracts, more regularly with the same suppliers.

The names and places of residence given for many suppliers enable them to be traced further using the indexes of the *Victoria County History*, together with the 1524–5 taxation records, and other documents. This evidence provides a rare opportunity to examine the kinds of people who were marketing

Table 13. King's Hall, Cambridge: suppliers with largest number of contracts, 1450–1500

Name	*Residence*	*Contracts*	*Amount*	*Commodity*
Grene, John	Swaffham	11	204.5 qrts	wheat
Colyn, Robert	Madingley	7	136 qrts	malt barley
Harris, John	Elsworth	6	104 qrts	malt barley
Colyn, Robert	Madingley	6	58 qrts	wheat
Sutton, Thomas	not stated	6	23 qrts	wheat
Fane, John	Grantchester	5	81.5 qrts	malt barley
Vicar	Oakington	4	84 qrts	malt barley
Breton, John	Dullingham	4	2500	fuel
Stertour, William	Madingley	4	19.5 qrts	wheat
Attwoode, Thomas	Oakington	4	26 qrts	malt barley
Harris, John	Elsworth	4	34 qrts	wheat

agricultural produce. During the late fourteenth and early fifteenth centuries, many large land-owners abandoned the direct cultivation of manorial demesnes, and leased them out. The lessees appear to have come from several social groups, including the gentry, yeomen and husbandmen. For Postan, this marked a change from a market-orientated economy of great landlords selling grain to a more self-sufficient 'natural' economy.[34] But the King's Hall contracts show yeomen and husbandmen were participating in the market by supplying the college with their produce.

Several suppliers stand out as the wealthiest men in their community. A schedule of contributors to the first loan of 1522 lists those with more than £20 in goods or lands. Among them were suppliers such as Henry Cook of Chesterton, valued at £300, William Rouse of Swaffham, 200 marks, Robert Sewall of Bottisham, £42, and John Gotobed of Chesterton, £20.[35] These substantial men are not easy to classify. They are not recorded as possessing gentry status, and many seem to have had peasant origins. Many of these wealthy suppliers had taken up leases of demesnes. Thomas Baron of Comberton supplied twenty quarters of wheat and barley in 1474–5. He was farmer of Barnwell Priory's land there in 1498, and provided a window with a request for prayers in the parish church. He was succeeded by John Baron and another kinsman. Henry Cook, farmer of Chesterton, sent six consignments of wheat and barley between 1505 and 1529. His family rose from the yeomanry in the late fifteenth and sixteenth centuries. Henry Cook died in 1535 when he was lessee to Clare College, and probably held the Barnwell Priory demesne.[36] The *firmarii* of Bourn and Dry Drayton also supplied King's Hall.

Robert Colyn of Madingley supplied King's Hall with seven contracts of barley, totalling 136 quarters. His family occupied eighty-seven acres around Girton *c.*1500. John Fane of Grantchester supplied nine loads of cereals between 1498 and 1504. The family had a holding at Barton from the mid-

[34] Postan, *Essays*, pp. 162–3.
[35] *L&P*, iii(2), no. 2,640.
[36] *VCH Cambs*, v, pp. 183, 187; ix, p. 15.

fourteenth century and through the fifteenth century.[37] These yeomen usually held holdings on a variety of different tenures, often including leases of the lord's manorial lands. They were more likely to do physical work than the gentry, and produced a surplus which was marketed, using local wage labour or resident servants.[38]

Some fifteenth-century gentry took up demesne leases and Carpenter has pointed to the entrepreneurial role of this class in Warwickshire. But this was largely through specialised pastoral farming for the market,[39] and only a few Cambridgeshire gentry supplied the wheat, barley or fuel recorded in the King's Hall accounts. Edward Langley, lord of the manor of Lolworth, sold five quarters of wheat, and Richard Childe of Harlton, who sent five quarters of wheat in 1455–6, was probably lord of Huntingdon or Harlton manor at this time.[40] The gentry were not as heavily committed to the sale of produce as yeomen, because their own households often consumed a large proportion of their produce, and they had other preoccupations such as patronage and office-holding.[41]

John Atkyn of Haslingfield was one of another group of suppliers, assessed at between £10 and £19 in goods in the 1520s assessments. These husbandmen were likely to hold land by lease rather than own it outright. Some early sixteenth-century suppliers also came from poorer families, with individuals holding less than £10 in 1524–5. Such men were unlikely to be leasing whole demesnes, but perhaps leased part of a demesne, possibly under a sublease. They had enough surplus to be able to market their produce, at least in some years.

Suppliers of fuel also tended to come from these poorer groups, and on the whole, were less prosperous than suppliers of cereals. John Breton of Dullingham, a regular supplier of fuel in the 1480s and 1490s, may have been related to Thomas Bretyn of the same place, assessed at £7 in goods in 1524. Other fuel suppliers included Thomas Hithe of Dullingham, with £2 in goods, Thomas Keynd (?King) of Burrough Green, £1 in goods, and Richard Trewpenny of Reach, £2 in goods.[42]

Several clergy also supplied the college. John Petyt, vicar of Shudy Camps (1462–97), supplied two consignments of fuel in the 1470s. The vicars of Burwell and Oakington, rectors of Rampton, Chesterton and Girton, and the farmer of Wilbraham rectory also supplied wheat and barley. Clergy could supply agricultural produce that they had received either in tithes from their parishioners, or grown on their glebe lands. An investigation of the Lincolnshire probate inventories of the sixteenth century has shown that practically every parson was a farmer, with as much stock and farming equipment as the average husbandman, and in some cases, as a wealthier yeoman.[43]

[37] Ibid. v, p. 163; ix, p. 121.
[38] M. Bailey, 'Rural Society', *Fifteenth-Century Attitudes: Perceptions of Society in Late Medieval England*, ed. R. Horrox (Cambridge, 1994), p. 151.
[39] C. Carpenter, 'The Fifteenth-Century English Gentry and their Estates', in *Gentry and Lesser Nobility in Late Medieval Europe*, ed. M. Jones (Gloucester, 1986), pp. 36–60.
[40] *VCH Cambs*, v, p. 217; ix, pp. 158–9.
[41] C. Dyer, 'Were there any Capitalists in Fifteenth-Century England?', *Everyday Life*, p. 323.
[42] PRO E 179/81/134; E 179/81/163.
[43] F. W. Brooks, 'The Social Position of the Parson in the Sixteenth Century', *Journal of British Archaeological Association*, 3rd series, 10 (1945–7), pp. 34–5.

In years of particularly high prices, some grain was sought from more distant suppliers. In 1483–4 for example, the college purchased barley from Joanna Dutton, widow of Methwold in Norfolk, twenty-nine miles away. There was also a tendency at such times to resort to more unusual suppliers, not used in any other years. In 1482–3, the master of St John's Cambridge sold fourteen quarters of wheat at 8s. per quarter and Lord John Filay sold five quarters at the same price, while twenty-five quarters of wheat was bought from Gybson, baker in 1500–1, at 8.8 s. per quarter. Also in 1500–1, William Syre of Coton sold wheat described as *frumento antiquo*, possibly because the college was unable to secure better quality supplies.

The colleges provided a source of demand for agricultural products of the surrounding countryside at a time when commodity prices were generally low, and it was often difficult to sell cereals in bulk. Another market for agriculture was provided by demand from outside the region, and particularly from London.

3. London demand: malt barley and saffron

Debt cases give some indication of important trading links. Pardons to individuals in the patent rolls for not appearing to answer pleas of debt in the royal courts, listed in the calendars of patent rolls between 1450 and 1509, give a rough indication of the pattern of credit.[44] London was the single most frequently stated place of residence of creditors, and debts owing to Londoners tended on average to be larger than to creditors elsewhere. The most frequently recorded occupations of Cambridgeshire debtors were yeomen and husbandmen, suggesting that the source of the debts, which are not recorded, was probably in many cases transactions in agricultural commodities. Two commodities for long-distance trade seem particularly significant in the region in this period: malt barley and saffron.

Total demand for cereals fell in the later Middle Ages as the population declined. However, at the same time, rising living standards and greater leisure time led to increased ale consumption. This raised per capita consumption of grain so that overall demand did not fall by as much as population. It also prompted major shifts in the grain supply of urban hinterlands, most notably those areas supplying London. So while contacts between London and East Anglia were neither strong nor regular at the turn of the fourteenth century, after the Black Death, increasing ale consumption meant that East Anglia probably supplied barley more regularly to the capital. A parliamentary ordinance of 1394 named Cambridgeshire as a source of malt, which should be carried to London and sold there for the benefit of the royal household, noble households and the whole population.[45]

With fertile soils, more hours of sunshine than the national average, and accessible waterways for transport, Cambridgeshire was an ideal cereal-growing region. 'If any district in medieval England were able to ship corn in

[44] *CPR 1446–1509*.

[45] J. A. Galloway, 'Driven by drink? Ale Consumption and the Agrarian Economy of the London Region *c.*1300–1400', *Food and Eating in Medieval Europe*, ed. M. Carlin and J. T. Rosenthal (London, 1998), pp. 92–9; Campbell, *Medieval Capital*, pp. 70, 181.

a continuous stream to feed the population of other districts, it was this Cambridge area', wrote Gras, who identified the region as one of below average prices in the period 1401–1500.[46] Grain could be taken from Cambridgeshire to London by one of two routes. It could be shipped downstream to Lynn, and then via the coast to London. At least in the thirteenth and late sixteenth centuries though, Boston and Lynn were shipping grain from Cambridgeshire and East Anglia to northern England, garrison towns, and Flemish cities rather than to London.[47] Grain from Cambridgeshire could also be taken overland and then along the river Lea, and towns along this route like Enfield, Ware and Royston show increasing involvement in the malt trade during the late fifteenth and early sixteenth centuries.[48]

Disputes arising from the malt trade show that Cambridgeshire malt was being both brought into Cambridge for local brewing, and transported out of the region to other customers. For example, Richard Robynson, clerk, was to have supplied John Bell of Cambridge with two hundred quarters of malt, but only ninety quarters were delivered, while William Richardson of Cambridge agreed to supply sixty quarters of malt to William Cokkes and Thomas King, grocers of London, at Lynn.[49]

Evidence of barley being supplied to London brewers comes from accounts of the 1430s and 1440s from Grantchester manor, situated two miles south-west of Cambridge. Henry Somer, Chancellor of the Exchequer, bought this manor and resumed direct farming of the estate.[50] In 1435–6, 127 quarters of malt barley were bought by London brewers Thomas Yole and John Stone, of a total of 140 quarters sold by the bailiff. In 1436–7 and possibly in 1444–5, most of the malt barley sold again went to London brewers. These sales were undoubtedly facilitated by Somer's residence in London and the links between the manor and the capital. Costs were probably reduced because manorial transport and labour was being used. Such sales came to an end in 1452 when King's College purchased the manor and used it to provision the college.[51]

The late fifteenth century also saw the spread of saffron cultivation across many parts of southern Cambridgeshire. The saffron crocus was grown for its deep orange stigmas that were dried. Saffron was used as a medicine, as a dye, a pigment in manuscripts and as a flavouring and colouring in cookery. Its high cost, however, restricted its use. The crop emerged after the Black Death as one of a number of alternative uses for land when the demand for cereals sagged. Although its cultivation used small amounts of land and was highly labour intensive, at a time when land was abundant and labour scarce, it commanded very high prices, and seems to have been profitably cultivated as a horticultural crop.[52]

[46] N. S. B. Gras, *The Evolution of the English Corn Market from the Twelfth to the Eighteenth Century* (Cambridge, Mass., 1915), pp. 41–9, 62–3.

[47] Campbell, *Medieval Capital*, p. 181; N. J. Williams, *The Maritime Trade of the East Anglian Ports, 1550–1590* (Oxford, 1988), pp. 72, 112, 150–9.

[48] D. O. Pam, *Tudor Enfield. The Maltmen and the Lea Navigation*, Edmonton Hundred Historical Society, Occasional Papers, n.s. 18 (not dated), pp. 1–9.

[49] PRO C 1/66/414; C 1/293/59; C 1/341/31; C 1/687/35.

[50] *VCH Cambs*, v, p. 206; KCC, GRA/656–9, 661, 676, Grantchester bailiff's accounts 1435–46.

[51] Saltmarsh, 'Home-Farm'.

[52] J. Thirsk, *Alternative Agriculture. A History from the Black Death to the Present Day* (Oxford, 1997), pp. 7, 16–17.

Saffron was cultivated in many of the parishes in north-east Essex, and in southern Cambridgeshire, where they extended from Steeple Morden in the west to Shudy Camps in the east, with a particular concentration in the central southern part of the county. Saffron-growing first appears in the late fifteenth century, mentioned in wills and rentals. In several parishes, the introduction of saffron caused disputes over tithes.[53] In Cambridge, saffron was grown in several college gardens,[54] and in the 1530s the treasurers of the town corporation took just over twenty rents for the liberty to plant saffron in Barnwell and Cambridge fields.[55]

London marketing links were evident in the saffron trade. Thomas Hodylston, haberdasher of London, purchased 'English' saffron from a John Wode at Fulbourn in Cambridgeshire. John Capon, stockfishmonger of London, made a contract with William Elyott of Cottered in Hertfordshire at Stourbridge Fair to obtain saffron. John Gottis failed to deliver saffron to John Wodeward although an agreement had been made at the Swan Inn, Newmarket.[56]

Despite the spread of saffron cultivation across much of southern Cambridgeshire in the late fifteenth century, and even the sale of saffron at Stourbridge Fair, it was the small Essex town of Walden that became the centre of this industry, rather than Cambridge. Why this should have been so is not clear, and for Cambridge, this appears to have been something of a missed opportunity. It may be that saffron cultivation began in Walden, stimulated by a number of dye works that existed in the town in the 1380s.[57] But it was only during the later fifteenth and early sixteenth centuries that the industry really seems to have flourished and when the town adopted the flower as its symbol and as the prefix to the town's name.[58] As in the textile industry, growth centred on small towns and villages rather than within established provincial towns. This may in part reflect the ease in which London entrepreneurial links could infiltrate settlements free from the regulations imposed by borough governments and existing mercantile networks.

Conclusion

There were significant developments in the trade of Cambridge and its region in the late fifteenth century, but these are difficult to quantify, and we should be careful of presenting these in too optimistic a light.

The growth of the university seems to have offered the greatest opportunities for the town and surrounding region. Within Cambridge, specialist trades appeared to serve the academic community. The King's Hall contracts show

53 *VCH Essex*, ii, p. 360; *VCH Cambs*, v, vi, viii, ix, see indexes under crops, saffron.

54 R. Willis and J. W. Clark, *The Architectural History of the University of Cambridge and of the Colleges of Cambridge and Eton*, 4 vols. (Cambridge, 1886), iii, pp. 578–81.

55 Downing College, Cambridge, Bowtell MS 1, Cambridge Corporation treasurers' accounts (1515–60), ff. 122, 132v.

56 PRO C 1/264/8; C 1/489/28; C 1/596/37–9.

57 D. Cromarty, 'Chepying Walden 1381–1420: A Study from the Court Rolls', *Essex Journal*, 2 (1967), pp. 109–11.

58 *VCH Essex*, ii, pp. 359–64.

how a wide range of farmers from different localities and social classes in the region were supplying the college at various times. But many higher-value goods appear to have come from outside the region, and London suppliers and distributors appear to have been increasingly dominant.

Opportunities existed to supply the London market with barley, prefiguring the role of the eastern counties as major suppliers of cereals to the capital in the early modern period. But agricultural commodity prices were low through much of the fifteenth century, and recourse to more distant markets was often necessary. The Paston family in Norfolk sold malt to London merchants and to Flanders when they could not sell grain locally on favourable terms, and bore more of the expenses of marketing themselves. London demand and marketing may well have been behind the growth of the saffron industry in this period.[59] It is unlikely that local demand alone would have been sufficient to cause the spread of cultivation of the crop.

Cambridge and its region shows that within the darkness of stagnation and decline of the fifteenth-century economy there were brighter patches of growth – but these were dim, scattered and in several cases linked to London.

[59] R. H. Britnell, 'The Pastons and their Norfolk', *AgHR*, 36 (1988), p. 139.

Durham Cathedral Priory's Consumption of Imported Goods: Wine and Spices, 1464–1520

Miranda Threlfall-Holmes

This paper assesses Durham Cathedral Priory's purchasing and consumption of luxury imported goods, that is, wine and spices, in the late fifteenth and early sixteenth centuries. Wine and spices were not the only imported goods which entered the priory, but they are of particular interest for two reasons. Firstly, the other imported goods bought by the priory, primarily linen and iron, were not always imported; imports in these areas supplemented or were supplemented by local supplies and so the question of who supplied imported goods is obscured in these cases. Secondly, as luxuries, the priory's consumption of wine and spices is indicative of its relative standard of living.

This paper begins by looking briefly at the accounts on which this research is based, and then examines first the wine and then the spices bought by the priory, discussing the varieties bought, prices, the priory's purchasing policy and consumption. Finally some more general conclusions are drawn, including price trends, the changing locations from which the priory sourced its imported goods and the implications for the regional economy.

This research is based on the expenditure sections of the Durham obedientiary accounts, from 1464 to 1520 – the years for which the most comprehensive selection of the accounts has survived. Eleven of these accounts were compiled annually, one by each of the main officers of the monastery, and a great many of these still remain in the archive. In particular, the important bursars' accounts have survived in substantial series from as early as the fourteenth century, and forty-seven survive from the fifty-five–year period under consideration here. These provide much of the evidence used here, for the bursar was responsible for purchasing by far the greatest part of the wine bought by the priory. Smaller wine purchases were also made by the hostillar (for the guest-house), and by the sacrist (for communion wine). Spices were primarily purchased by the cellarer, with smaller amounts being bought by the bursar (for the prior's table), the hostillar (again, for the guest hall), and by the communar.[1] An important part of the latter's job was described in the 1593 *Rites of Durham* as being 'to provide for all such spices against Lent as should be comfortable for the said monks for their great austerity both of fasting and praying'.[2]

In addition to these purchases, it should be noted that most of the other

[1] I am grateful to the Dean and Chapter of Durham Cathedral, and to Alan Piper their archivist, for allowing me access to these records. All manuscript references relate to this archive (DCD).

[2] *The Rites of Durham*, ed. J. T. Fowler, Surtees Society, cvii (1903), p. 101.

obedientiaries contributed a few shillings each to the cost of wine for the prior's four annual *ludi* or holiday days, and often paid for occasional pittances or gifts of additional food and spices to the monks. However, this expenditure has been excluded from the present analysis: the amounts involved are small, payments made for different commodities are grouped together in the accounts and cannot be separated out, and no details are given in these entries of the quantity, quality or type of wine or spices purchased.

It is also possible that the purchases recorded in these accounts may have been supplemented either by gifts to the priory or by the individual purchases of monks in a personal capacity (since it was usual for monks to receive cash allowances by this period). Whilst it is unlikely that these would have constituted a significant part of the provisioning or consumption of the priory on a regular basis, it should be remembered that only the purchases of the priory as an institution, as recorded in the accounts, are under consideration here.

The level of detail recorded in the accounts varies between the different obedientiaries and commodities, and from year to year. Both the bursar and the hostillar regularly (although not invariably) record wine purchases by giving the price and quantity purchased from each merchant, the variety of wine, the name of the merchant and sometimes the place of purchase or the home town of the merchant concerned, whereas the sacrists' accounts tend to give only the quantity purchased and the price paid. In the case of spice purchases, the hostillar gives only a total cost for all the spices purchased that year, with no greater detail. Thankfully the cellarer, the communar and the bursar give costs for several individual spices, together with the quantities of each purchased, and often the merchant from whom or the place where they were bought, although both the communar and bursar also include a lump sum paid for 'diverse spices this year'.

Wine

Durham Cathedral Priory bought a consistently large volume of wine each year, seemingly regardless of any fluctuations in either supply or price, in quantities which were based on the vast barrel or 'tun' which held 252 gallons.[3]

Most of the wine purchased by the priory was ordinary red wine, with some white wine and claret also being bought in several years. It should be noted that the 'claret' referred to in these accounts was not the superior red wine that the term denotes today; rather, it was a spiced wine preparation, similar to mulled wine but not necessarily drunk warm. Several recipes for the making of this 'claret' have survived from the medieval period, the main elements being a sweetener (usually honey), and spices. One of the more elaborate recipes to

[3] The standard wine measures were tuns, pipes and hogsheads: 1 tun = 2 pipes = 4 hogsheads = 252 gallons. Non-standard measures in these accounts are the butt (assumed for the purposes of this study to have contained 126 gallons), the roundlet (18.5 gallons) and the barrel (31 gallons). These measures are discussed in *The Customs Accounts of Hull 1453–1490*, ed. W. Childs, Yorkshire Archaeological Society Record Series, cxliv (1986), pp. 253–6; and under each term in the full *Oxford English Dictionary*.

have survived includes cinnamon, ginger, pepper, long pepper, grains of paradise, cloves, galingale, caraway, mace, nutmeg, coriander, honey and brandy (which was itself probably a distillate of a spiced wine).[4]

These red, white and claret wines were the staple wines of the priory, and tended to share a common price and (presumably) a common quality. There was a tendency for these three varieties to be classed together in the accounts, suggesting that the accountant, at least, saw little to choose between them. In particular, there are frequent entries in the accounts which give a standard price for all three; for example, in 1499–1500 the bursar bought 'five tuns and one hogshead of red wine, a pipe of claret and a hogshead of white wine at £5 [per tun]'. Sometimes even the respective quantities were unspecified, as in 1504–5, when the bursar's purchases included 'two tuns of red, claret and white wine . . . at £5 6s. 8d. [per tun]'. Entries such as these, together with the large quantities purchased, strongly suggest that the monks of Durham viewed most wine as a commodity rather than a luxury, to be purchased in bulk, and to be discriminated between largely by price rather than by considerations of taste.

The exceptions were the particular types of wine purchased less frequently or in smaller amounts; most prominently the sweet wines that were increasingly fashionable in the latter half of the fifteenth century.[5] These were sometimes referred to generically simply as 'sweet wine' in these accounts, and were sometimes described as being specific varieties, of which malmsey is most frequently mentioned. Other varieties are each mentioned only occasionally – bastard and muscatel once each, and romney twice.[6] 'Sweet wine' is occasionally mentioned in small quantities in the 1460s to 1480s, but a trend towards buying this type of wine on a regular basis can be seen towards the end of the century, with a butt of malmsey being a regular annual purchase by the 1490s. For the most part, these varieties were significantly more expensive than the monks' usual wines. 'Sweet wine' or malmsey was consistently around twice the price of normal wine, as was the bastard bought in 1464–5. Romney was the exception, being only slightly more expensive than claret at £5 6s. 8d. per tun compared to £5.

These sweet wines were almost certainly significantly stronger – that is, more alcoholic – than the staple wines of the priory.[7] Unfortunately, specific alcohol contents are unknown and virtually impossible to calculate. However, it is known that three qualities of wine were produced by most vineyards, using the juice from the first, second and (diluted with water) third pressings of the grapes respectively. The last, third pressing wine was the common drink of the peasantry in wine-producing regions, and has been estimated to have contained perhaps 5 per cent alcohol by volume.[8] It is probable that the monks of Durham, in common with other wealthy and middling households, would have drunk the first pressing wine, which would have been much stronger. A rough estimate for the alcohol content of the usual wines might be made on the basis of the weakest wines common today, containing around 8 or 9 per cent alcohol by volume, but this can only be speculative.

4 T. Scully, *The Art of Cookery in the Middle Ages* (Woodbridge, 1995), pp. 149–51.
5 Dyer, *Standards of Living*, pp. 62, 105.
6 DCD, Burs.1464/5 (Wine); Burs.1503/4 (Wine); Burs.1514/5 (Wine).
7 Andrew Boorde, *Dyetary (1542)*, ed. F. J. Furnivall, EETS, e.s. 10 (1870), pp. 254–5.
8 Scully, *Art of Cookery*, pp. 141–2.

Wine prices and purchases

As a cash purchaser of large quantities of wine, the priory was highly exposed to fluctuations in price. However, all the evidence from these accounts demonstrates that the monks absorbed these cost differences rather than adapt their consumption in the affected years (Table 14). Despite the presence of large peaks in price in some years, however, the overall trend was for wine prices to decrease, as the graph demonstrates (Table 15).

Table 14. Wine prices over time and amount bought by the bursar

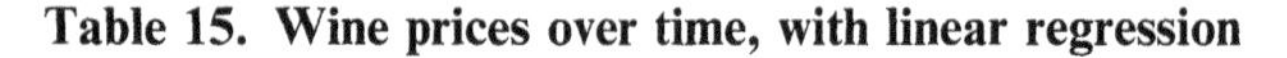

Table 15. Wine prices over time, with linear regression

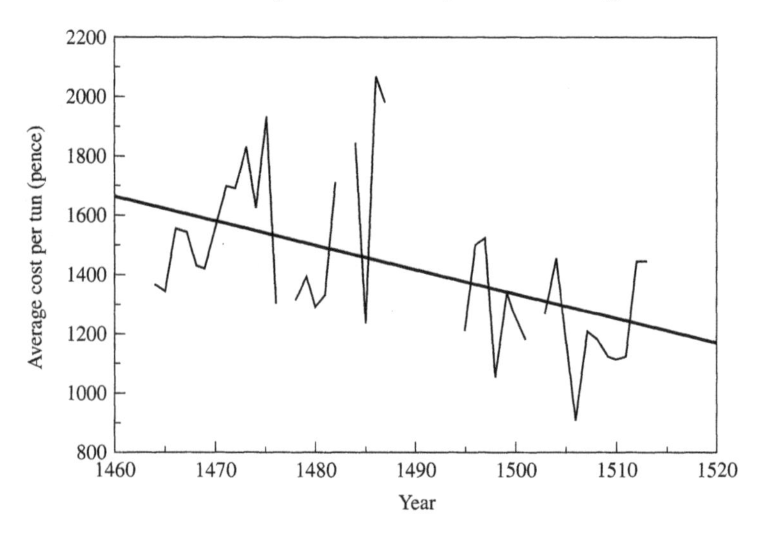

The effects of the loss of Bordeaux and the political manoeuvring caused by the instability of English politics in the third quarter of the fifteenth century had a direct impact on wine prices in this period, and these events are reflected in the prices paid by the priory. Prices increased to a peak in 1475–6, but then dropped dramatically following the removal of heavy French duties in January 1476. Apart from the brief but violent rise in the mid-1480s, which may have been a result of Henry VII's order that all wine be carried in English ships, prices generally remained at a consistently lower level between 1490 and 1520 – between 4d. and 6d. a gallon – than they had done in the previous quarter-century, when prices had fluctuated between around 5d.–8d. per gallon.[9]

In those years when wine prices rose particularly steeply, particularly 1475–6 and 1487–8, it is possible that the quantities purchased by the bursar may indicate some minor degree of retrenchment. The bursar bought five and a half tuns in 1475–6, compared to eight tuns in the previous year; and seven and a half in 1487–8, having bought nine tuns in the preceding two years. However, differences of these magnitudes are clearly not confined to years when there was a major price rise; the volumes purchased by the bursar regularly fluctuated by as much as a tun. In addition, it must be noted that there are some years when the amount spent by the bursar rose dramatically because of an increase in the price of wine, rather than volume being cut back to keep spending level. For example, in 1484–5 the amount spent on wine was £69 4s. 4d., 144 per cent of the average yearly spend of £48; and in 1486–7, the amount spent went up to the highest in this period, £75, 156 per cent of the average. This readiness to pay the highest prices for wine rather than retrench may be seen also in the first half of the century, when the bursar spent as much as £89 14s. 1½d. on wine in 1443–4.[10] But while it would not be true to say that the priory's demand for wine was truly elastic, since from year to year their purchases did not respond even to the most pronounced price fluctuations, over the whole of this period wine purchases did increase as prices decreased, as the graph shows. This can be seen even more clearly if we look at the best fit lines for prices and quantities bought, to iron out yearly fluctuations (Table 16).

There is some evidence to suggest that the bursar shopped around over a wide area for his wine, buying in Hull rather than Newcastle if prices there were more favourable. Overall, 6 per cent of the amount spent by the bursar on wine between 1464 and 1520 is recorded as having been spent in Hull, and this was concentrated across a few years in which wine bought at Hull accounted for a significant proportion of the priory's purchases. In particular, in 1481–2, 93 per cent of the wine bought by the bursar was purchased at Hull; as was 65 per cent in 1487–8. An explanation for this unusual concentration of purchasing away from Newcastle might be found in the fact that in 1486–7 (when the bursar bought three tuns of wine in Hull), and in 1487–8, the Hull wine cost £8 per tun compared with £9 per tun for that bought at Newcastle. Wine prices in Newcastle had nearly doubled since the previous year: in 1485–6, Thomas Swan sold four tuns to the priory for

[9] M. K. James, *Studies in the Medieval Wine Trade*, ed. E. M. Veale (Oxford, 1971), pp. 38–49.

[10] Here and elsewhere, figures for the first half of the century are taken from N. Morimoto, 'The Demands and Purchases of Wine of Durham Cathedral Priory in the first half of the 15th Century', *The Nagoya Gakuin University Review*, 20 (1983), pp. 81–117.

Table 16. Wine prices and amount bought: linear regressions

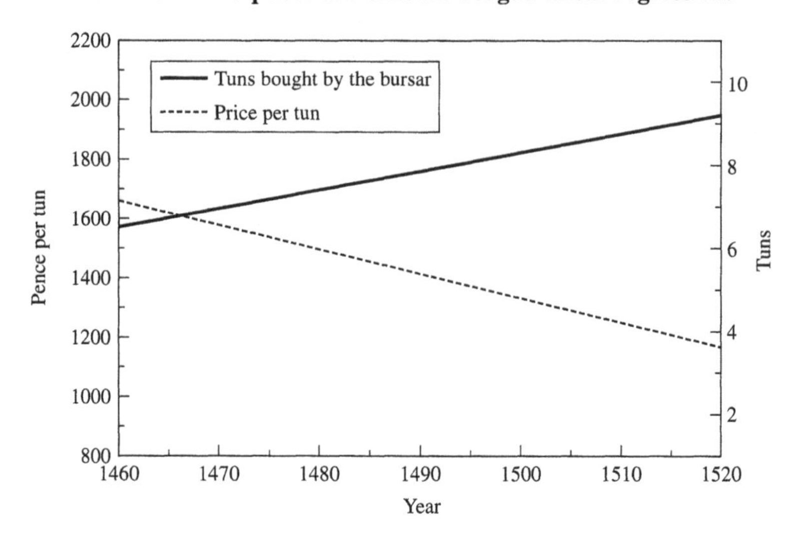

£5 6s. 8d. a tun, whilst in 1486–7 the same merchant's price for a similar quantity (five tuns) had risen to £9 a tun. It seems unlikely that the same merchant would sell to the same corporate customer in consecutive years two wines of such widely different quality as to account for such a difference in price without a note to that effect being included in the accounts. In 1486–7, the year this increase occurred, the bursar bought three tuns of wine from Robert Chepman of Hull for £8 each; the discovery of such a large difference in price between Hull and Newcastle in this year may well explain his decision to purchase the majority of his wine in Hull the following year.

Wine consumption

On average, the bursar purchased 7.7 tuns of wine per year in the years between 1464 and 1520 for which accounts remain. This was made up of about 0.4 tuns of sweet wine and 7.3 tuns of normal wine, with sweet wines becoming more common towards the end of this period, as has been seen. In addition, each year the sacrist purchased a pipe of wine for use in the communions celebrated in the cathedral, and the hostillar bought around a tun, most of which would have been drunk by the frequent guests that the priory was under an obligation to entertain.

If communion wine and guest wine are disregarded, to give the wine drunk by the monks as a part of their communal diet, then the priory consumed an average of 15,523 pints of wine each year. Calculating the consumption of an individual monk is far from being an exact science, since it is impossible for us to know how many other people (such as corrodians, seculars or guests) shared in this amount, or how it was distributed between the monks themselves. However, a rough estimate might be made on the assumption that absenteeism and additional shares might have effectively cancelled each other out, and that the wine was shared equally between the monks. The average number of monks residing at the priory at any one time was around forty,[11] which leads to the tentative conclusion that the average daily allowance of a monk was 1.1 pints (0.6 litres) of wine.

However, it should be noted that this allowance would have been spread very unevenly across the year. In the fast seasons of Advent and Lent wine is extremely unlikely to have been drunk, and the same probably applied to Wednesdays and Fridays throughout the year. In her study of Westminster monks in this period Barbara Harvey concluded that wine would only have been drunk on a hundred days of the year, comprising various saints days, anniversaries and other celebrations.[12] This would mean an average consumption per monk of 3.9 pints (2.2 litres) on these days, the equivalent of nearly three modern bottles. If this is spread over a larger part of the year, the 193 days that are left after the removal of the fast days noted above, then the allowance would have averaged just over two pints (just over a litre) on those days.

These levels of wine consumption are much higher than those suggested by St Benedict as reasonable provision. The exact quantity of wine recommended as a daily allowance in the rule was a *hemina*, which contained 0.273 litres, or about half a pint. St Benedict certainly allowed for this amount to be varied at the discretion of the prior, but almost certainly envisaged such variations as decreasing, not increasing, the allowance; the rule explains that the half-pint or so that is suggested is deemed 'sufficient' having taken the 'infirmities of the sick' into account; and goes on to discuss how

> We read that monks should not drink wine at all, but since the monks of our day cannot be convinced of this, let us at least agree to drink moderately, and not to the point of excess . . . [and] where local circumstances dictate an amount much less than what is stipulated above, or even none at all, those who live there should bless God and not grumble.[13]

It should also be noted that in addition to this wine, each monk received a daily allowance of around a gallon of ale. The volume of alcohol that they must have consumed is thus startling to modern dieticians, and can hardly be said to have met St Benedict's guideline of moderation.

It is interesting in this context to note that the report compiled by Bishop Neville of Durham following his 1442 official visitation of the priory did contain several criticisms of illicit drinking, although it concluded that the monks were 'men of worthy lives, chaste and sober, suffering neither the shame nor the chains of fleshy faults'. Certain sections of the report make it clear that drinking to excess was recognised as undesirable; but equally, the priory's replies do not suggest that any great seriousness was attached to such criticisms. Article 20 of the report concerns the chamberlain, whom over twenty of the monks had accused of not carrying out his duties satisfactorily;

[11] R. B. Dobson, *Durham Priory, 1400–1450* (Cambridge, 1973), p. 54. The monastic population of the priory was relatively stable throughout the fifteenth century.
[12] Harvey, *Living and Dying*, pp. 44, 58.
[13] *The Rule of St. Benedict*, ed. T. Fry (Minnesota, 1981), pp. 238–41.

'and when accusations are laid before the lord prior on this matter, the latter does not take steps to correct it, but says to the monks that this man is a drunkard, and so nothing is done'. Articles 45 and 46 both concern illicit drinking-sessions, involving both the monks themselves and also laymen entering the dormitory to join them. The reply made by the priory was that such sessions were not known of and would be prohibited; neither statement being entirely convincing.[14]

Whilst the differing size and composition of different households complicates the task of making relevant comparisons, it is clearly desirable to obtain some idea of how the wine consumption of the Durham monks compared with that of other similarly wealthy men. Barbara Harvey's analysis of the calorific make-up of the diet consumed by the monks of Westminster in this period revealed that, on average, they received an allowance of just over a quarter of a pint of wine each day, much less than the figure of just over a pint calculated for Durham.[15] At Battle Abbey few accounts remain, but in 1412–13 the daily allowance per monk can be estimated to have been 1.4 pints. Seven tuns of wine were bought in that year; it is unclear exactly how many monks were then in residence, but in 1394 there were twenty-seven, and twenty-five to thirty was the standard range. If there were twenty-seven, this would give 1.4 pints per monk per day assuming no other sharers in the wine; if thirty, this would become 1.1 pints, matching the Durham figures.[16] Dyer estimated that at both Battle Abbey and the household of the countess of Warwick (for which the 1420–1 accounts remain) 'the superior members of the household' probably received an allowance of about two-thirds of a pint of wine each per day.[17]

It should be noted that wine was almost certainly drunk much more commonly, and in greater quantities, in the first than in the second half of the fifteenth century.[18] Decreasing imports after the English loss of Bordeaux indicate that this was the case throughout the country, and Dyer has suggested that the practical effect of this decreasing consumption was spread across all wine-drinking ranks, with rich households cutting back daily allowances and lesser households no longer drinking wine on a regular basis.[19] The more usual drink in England at the end of the fifteenth century at least was ale: in 1497, an Italian visitor to England noted that 'the majority, not to say everyone, drink [ale]'. Another Italian, around 1500, commented that the English were 'very sparing of wine when they drink it at their own expense . . . not considering it any inconvenience for three or four persons to drink out of the same cup. . . . The deficiency of wine, however, is amply supplied by the abundance of ale and beer'.[20] This picture is confirmed by a comparison of the wine purchases of Durham Cathedral Priory in the first and second halves of the century. The

[14] Bishop Robert Neville's visitation report (9 July, 1442) in the appendix to R. B. Dobson, 'Mynistres of Saynt Cuthbert', *Church and Society in the Medieval North of England* (London, 1996), ch. 3.

[15] Harvey, *Living and Dying*, p. 64.

[16] *Accounts of the Cellarers of Battle Abbey, 1275–1513*, ed. E. Searle and B. Ross (Sydney, 1967), p. 105.

[17] C. Dyer, 'English Diet in the Later Middle Ages', *Social Relations and Ideas*, ed. T. H. Aston *et al.* (Cambridge, 1983), p. 194.

[18] James, *Wine Trade*, pp. 58–9.

[19] Dyer, *Standards of Living*, p. 105.

[20] *English Historical Documents*, v, *1485–1558*, ed. C. H. Williams (London, 1967), pp. 190, 195.

average yearly wine purchase of the Durham bursar was 15.1 tuns in the period from 1415 to 1440,[21] which was twice that recorded for 1464 to 1520. The number of monks inhabiting the priory remained stable throughout the fifteenth century, so that, high though the levels of the latter part of the century may seem, they would appear to represent a halving of the amount that was being drunk by the Durham monks half a century previously.

The large, though differing, quantities of wine that all these households consumed may be partially explained when it is realised quite how beneficial to health wine was believed to be. Andrew Boorde's *Dyetary*, a manual on the healthful qualities and dangers of all sorts of food, with diet suggestions for various complaints, which was first published in 1542 and widely read, devotes a long paragraph to a panegyric on the benefits of drinking good wine – albeit in moderation. Wine was alleged to

> quicken a man's wits . . . comfort the heart . . . scour the liver . . . rejoice all the powers of man, and nourish them . . . engender good blood . . . comfort and nourish the brain and all the body, and resolve phlegm . . . it is medicinable, especially white wine, for it . . . cleanses wounds and sores.

'Furthermore', Boorde adds, 'the better the wine is, the better humours it engenders.'[22]

In addition, it has been asserted that different levels of wine drinking helped to define the internal hierarchies of the medieval aristocracy.[23] In particular, the laying in of casks of wine was a mark of the richest households.[24] Buying a tun, pipe or hogshead of wine, rather than purchasing it by the gallon as required, entailed a considerable capital investment. It also meant that that volume of wine had to be drunk in the next few months or be wasted: at best, wine began to deteriorate after six or seven months, due to the hardly sterile processing conditions of the Middle Ages.[25] One of the features of the stronger sweet wines was that they kept for longer due to their higher alcohol contents: Andrew Boorde noted in his *Dyetary* that 'high wines, such as Malmsey, may be kept long'.[26] By buying and drinking wine in these quantities, the monks of Durham were clearly showing that they considered themselves to be near the top of the social ladder.

Spices

In addition to wine, the priory also bought a wide range of other luxury imported comestibles, which were grouped together under the title 'spices' in the accounts. The range of spices that the monks purchased was fairly constant

[21] Calculated from the table in Morimoto, 'Demands and Purchases', p. 101.
[22] Boorde, *Dyetary*, p. 254.
[23] Dyer, *Standards of Living*, p. 62.
[24] An Italian reporting on England in *c.*1500 specifically noted that 'few people keep wine in their own houses, but buy it, for the most part, at a tavern'. Williams, *English Historical Documents*, p. 195.
[25] James, *Wine Trade*, p. 165.
[26] Boorde, *Dyetary*, p. 254.

over this period, including sugar, aniseed, licorice, ginger, cinnamon, nutmeg, cloves, mace, pepper, figs and raisins. Nuts and saffron were also bought in several years, and in addition some more miscellaneous items were occasionally accounted for under the heading of spices, such as sweetmeats, cakes and elaborately designed pastry-sculptures for important feasts.[27] The spices for which most information can be gleaned from these accounts are dried fruit, sugar and pepper, and the following section looks at the priory's purchasing and consumption of each of these in turn, and then at the total spice consumption of the priory in relation to that of other comparable households at the time.[28]

Dried fruit

Dried fruit accounted for by far the largest part of the priory's spice purchases each year, in terms of both quantity purchased and amount spent. In all, 14 per cent of the priory's spice expenditure went on dried fruit, split between the cellarer, who spent an average of £2 6s. 5½d. (which was 10 per cent of his spice spend), and the communar, who spent an average of £1 3s. 8½d. (around half his total outlay on spices). The dried fruits that were bought included figs, raisins, 'big raisins', currants and prunes, and are measured in a bewildering variety of ways: in pounds, dozens of pounds, frails, toppets, pecks and sorts.[29]

The prices paid by the priory for dried fruit varied widely in the first half of this period, but they both dropped and became much more consistent after 1500. (The graph, Table 17, has fewer data points than the total number of purchases made by the priory for clarity.)

The average amount of dried fruit bought by the priory was 538 lbs per year, but this was not spread evenly across this period. The communar bought an average of 120 lbs in the 1470s and 1480s, which increased to over 300 lbs by the first decades of the sixteenth century. The cellarer bought an average of 255 lbs throughout the later fifteenth century, but by the second decade of the sixteenth century was purchasing much greater amounts – 692 lbs in 1515. It would seem likely, therefore, that the priory's demand was elastic, and that the major drop in prices that took place around 1500 stimulated increased demand.

It can be seen that considerable volumes of dried fruit were entering the monastery, especially towards the end of this period. However, the implied consumption is not actually that large when divided into forty monk-portions. The average 538 lbs gives just over 4 oz. per monk per week over the whole year, rising to around 7.5 oz. at the end of this period. However, dried fruit was an essentially Lenten aspect of the monastic diet; in Westminster, it accounted for 2.5 per cent of the calorific value of the monk's food in that season, and was

[27] Scully, *Art of Cookery*, p. 109.

[28] Two useful collections of medieval recipes have been used to compare the priory's consumption with other households: *Two Fifteenth Century Cookery Books*, ed. T. Austin, EETS, o.s. 91 (1888), and *Curye on Inglysch*, ed. C. B. Hieatt and S. Butler, EETS, s.s. 8 (1985).

[29] These measures have been standardised by combining documentary references, secondary literature and the relative prices paid by the priory as follows: a frail = 40 lbs, a toppet = 20 lbs, a peck = 80 lbs and a sort = 120 lbs. Key secondary sources are *The Oxford English Dictionary*, vi, p. 138; xi, p. 140; *The Customs Accounts of Newcastle upon Tyne 1454–1500*, ed. J. F. Wade, Surtees Society, ccii (1995), p. 311; also J. E. Thorold Rogers, *A History of Agriculture and Prices in England*, iv (Oxford, 1882), pp. 668–9.

Table 17. Prices paid for dried fruit by the cellarer and communar

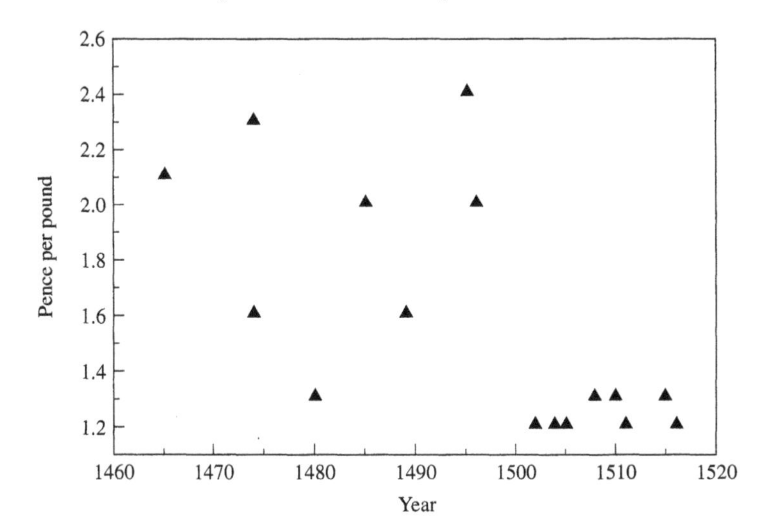

absent from their diet for the rest of the year. Averaged only across Lent, the average quantity purchased would have given each monk around 5.5 oz. per day. This is significantly higher than the comparable allowance received by the monks of Westminster in this period, who even in Lent received only 4 oz. of raisins each per week;[30] but is not excessive by modern standards.

It is worth noting that the great increase in the amount of dried fruit bought by the priory over this period reflects a general trend throughout medieval Europe to include more dried fruit in cookery as time went on, as can be seen in a comparison of fourteenth- and early fifteenth-century recipes with those of the later fifteenth and sixteenth centuries.[31] Figs in particular are a ubiquitous ingredient in the fifteenth-century recipes that have survived, being used in both sweet and meat dishes.[32]

Sugar

As with dried fruit, the majority of the spices bought by the priory are familiar today and need no further explanation. However, the forms in which sugar was purchased were rather different in the medieval period. Powdered sugar, such as is most common now, was perhaps the rarest and certainly the most expensive form in which sugar could then be found. Most sugar was bought in loaves – solid blocks from which sugar was scraped or broken off as required for use; alternatively, as was the case in Durham, it could be bought in plate form – plates of brittle sugar, rather like the hard toffee that

[30] Harvey, *Living and Dying*, pp. 57, 64.

[31] *Curye on Inglysch*, p. 12.

[32] *Two Fifteenth-Century Cookery-Books*. Dried fruit appears in the vast majority of recipes listed here. Typical sweet recipes based on figs, raisins and dates include 'Fygeye' (p. 24), and fruit-filled pies (pp. 15, 112). Fruit was also included in meat and fish tarts (p. 47), and several other savoury dishes.

covers toffee-apples. The other main form in which sugar was bought at Durham was as comfits, or confectionary, a term which covered a wide range of flavoured sugars and sweetmeats, from sugared almonds and similar sugar-coated seeds and spices, to sugar that had been delicately flavoured with rose-water. A very wide variety of spices, nuts, seeds and flavourings were used in making comfits: the 1482 *Regimen Sanitatis* of Magninus Mediolanensis listed the best and most delicious comfits then in use as being candied, sugar- or honey-coated ginger; candied pine-nuts, pistachios and filberts; candied aniseed, coriander, fennel and juniper seeds; crude dragees; fine table dragees; rose-sugar; marzipan and walnuts candied in sugar or honey. Similarly, Platina described in the 1475 *De Honesta Voluptate* how 'by melting [sugar] we make almonds . . . pine-nuts, hazelnuts, coriander, anise, cinnamon and many other things into candies'.[33]

Table 18. Sugar prices in the bursars' and communars' accounts

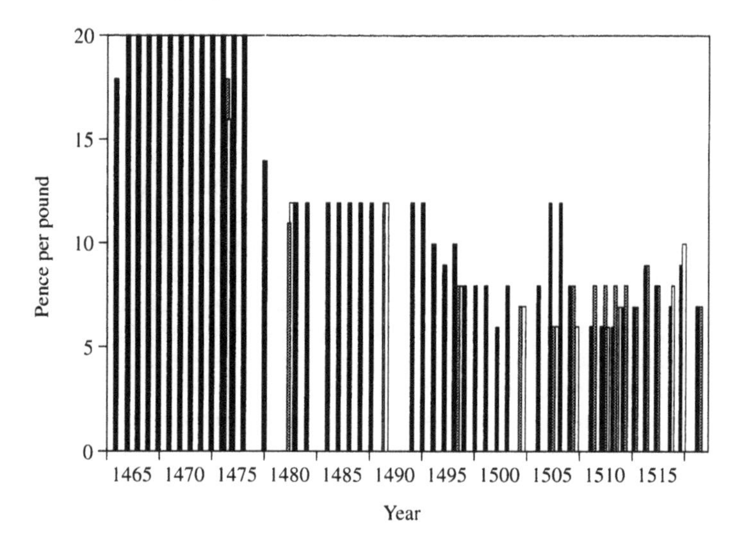

An excellent series of sugar prices is recorded in these accounts, showing some dramatic changes, with the prices paid by the priory more than halving over the period.

Between 1478 and 1482, the price of sugar dropped dramatically from a mode price of 20d. per pound to 12d.; and it then dropped again to around 7d. per pound around 1495. The increased variation in price which occurs towards the end of this period was probably in fact a characteristic of prices in the earlier decades too: the data sources proliferate in the accounts in the later years, so that less uniformity in the data is to be expected.[34]

Sugar prices seem to have been dropping throughout Europe in these years

[33] Scully, *Art of Cookery*, pp. 129–31, 57.
[34] This graph omits the prices recorded in the cellarer's accounts, since these occur much less regularly.

as a result of the new Portuguese navigations,[35] and comparable price series for this period can be found for Flanders, Brabant and Cambridge, in the archives of hospitals and colleges.[36] The specific forms of sugar referred to do vary in these accounts, but prices for all the different types and grades of sugar appear to have risen and fallen together (Table 19).

Table 19. Prices of sugars at Cambridge, Flanders, Brabant and Durham

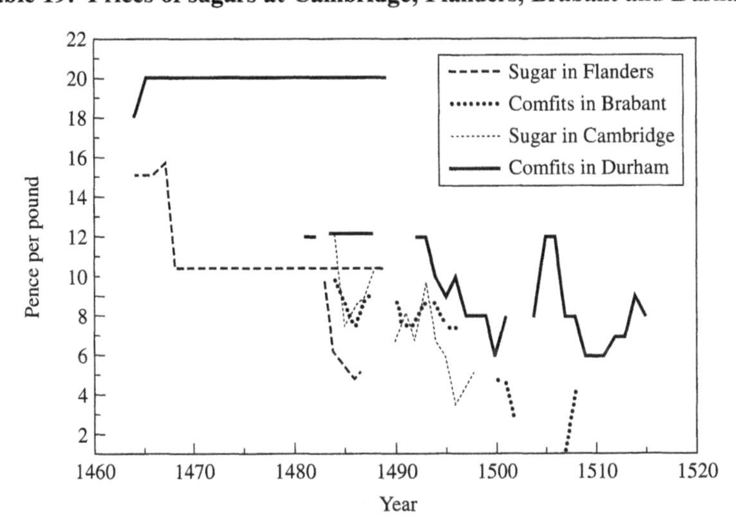

Two very interesting points can be drawn from a comparison of the evidence from these accounts with the Durham information. Firstly, the drop in price in Durham came over a decade later than in Flanders. Sugar prices in Flanders dropped significantly in the late 1460s, a fall that did not register at all in the prices paid by the monks of Durham until the years around 1480. Secondly, it is clear that prices in Durham (and presumably in the north-east in general) were consistently higher than elsewhere for the whole of this period, and up to double the price in the Low Countries. This may well reflect the additional transport costs involved in either importing sugar to Newcastle, or transporting it via London. It is also possible that low demand for the spice trade in the Durham and Newcastle area pushed prices up, a tendency that would have been reinforced by low levels of competition in the trade: only a handful of merchants appear supplying the priory with spices compared to nearly a hundred selling wine.[37]

[35] H. van der Wee, *The Growth of the Antwerp Market*, 3 vols. (The Hague, 1963), ii, pp. 127–9; J. A. van Houtte, *An Economic History of the Low Countries* (London, 1977), p. 176.

[36] Prices in Cambridge may be found in Rogers, *Agriculture and Prices*, iii, pp. 528–535. Prices in Flanders and Brabant are taken from *Documents pour l'histoire des prix et des salaires en Flandres et en Brabant*, ed. C. Verlinden (Bruges, 1959), pp. 47–8, 330. Prices given in Flanders and Brabant coinage have been converted into the equivalent English currency using the Flanders/sterling conversion table in *Cloth and Clothing in Medieval Europe*, ed. N. B. Harte and K. G. Ponting (London, 1983), p. 70; Brabant currency has been converted on the principal that £1 10s. Brabant = £1 Flanders, as stated in P. Spufford, *Handbook of Medieval Exchange* (London, 1986), p. 230.

[37] M. Threlfall-Holmes, 'Provisioning a Medieval Monastery: Durham Cathedral Priory's

The bursar, the cellarer and the communar all list sugar purchases in their accounts. The bursar purchased between 3 lb and 8 lb each year (averaging just over 5 lb), and the communar between 3 lb and 7.5 lb (averaging just over 6 lb). The cellarer did not buy sugar on a regular basis until after 1478, and the amount that he purchased was much more varied, being between none and 64 lbs thereafter. His purchases averaged around 20 lbs per year, although an average for these purchases is less meaningful than for those of the bursar and communar due to the much greater variation which existed from year to year. Nevertheless, the average sugar consumption of the monastery as a whole can be calculated to have been slightly more than 21 lb each year, or 8.5 oz. per monk per year.

As with dried fruit, the priory's purchases of sugar show a marked increase over the period under consideration here, rising from around 6 lb per year in the 1460s and 1470s, to 60 or 70 lb by the first decades of the sixteenth century.[38] By the 1520s and 1530s, over 100 lbs of sugar were being bought each year, and the average per monk had thus risen to 2.5 lbs per year, much higher than the average for the period, but still relatively small by today's standards. It should be stressed that the volume of sugar purchased by the priory in these years more than doubled over the period as the price halved. A detailed look at the purchases made by the bursar demonstrates the close relationship between price and amount purchased over this period. The bursar bought 3 lbs per year in the 1470s, when sugar cost 20d. per pound, and was buying around 6 lb per year by the 1490s, when the price had dropped to 10d. per pound or less. In 1505–6 and 1506–7, the price briefly rose from 6d. per pound to 12d. per pound, and the volume purchased by the bursar immediately dropped to 5 lb., rising to 6 lb. again in 1507–8, when the price dropped to 8d. per pound. The quantities bought by the cellarer make the same point more dramatically; he bought no or virtually no sugar in the 1460s and 1470s, and only small amounts (6–26 lbs) in the 1480s. By the 1500s much more was being bought: 49 lb in 1503, 50 lb in 1504, and 42 lb in 1506, whilst the four surviving accounts from 1520–36 show the purchase of between 63 and 104 lbs per year.

Pepper

After sugar, the most common spice in the medieval world was pepper. This was the staple commodity of the spice-dealers in the middle ages, accounting for over four-fifths of the cargoes brought to Europe from Alexandria by the Venetian galleys at the beginning of the fifteenth century.[39] Sellers of spices and aromatics were generally known simply as pepperers.[40] This is illustrated by the case of a French 'pepperer' found guilty of selling adulterated saffron, and banned in perpetuity from following the trade of pepperer; the judgement

Purchases of Imported Goods, 1464–1520' (unpub. MA thesis, Durham Univ., 1997), pp. 58–9, 95–6.

[38] As with dried fruit, sugar consumption was rising throughout Europe in this period, *Curye on Inglysch*, pp. 9–12.

[39] C. H. H. Wake, 'The Changing Pattern of Europe's Pepper and Spice Imports, ca.1400–1700', *Journal of European Economic History*, 8 (1979), p. 368.

[40] S. Thrupp, 'The Grocers of London', *Studies in English Trade in the Fifteenth Century*, ed. E. Power and M. M. Postan (London, 1966), p. 283; P. Nightingale, *A Medieval Mercantile Community* (London, 1995).

specifically banned the man from selling 'saffron, ginger, pepper, cloves, sugar or any subtle substance pertaining to the pepperer's trade'.[41] European imports of pepper increased by between 30 and 55 per cent over the fifteenth century, due at least in part to the progressive impoverishment of the Moslem Levant, which kept prices low on the Eastern markets throughout the second half of the century.[42] However, imports of other spices increased by much greater amounts over the same period, so that in relative terms the trend was for reduced consumption of pepper and increased consumption of other spices. For example, imports of ginger increased by 257 per cent, cinnamon by 395 per cent, and other spices by 561 per cent in the fifteenth century. Imports of Moluccan spices – cloves, nutmeg and mace – increased by 292 per cent in the fifteenth century and by a further 500 per cent between 1500 and 1620.[43] The greatly increasing quantities of all these spices being imported into Europe may well have reflected a widening of the strata of society that consumed such spices.

Pepper prices and quantities purchased are only specified in the cellarer's accounts until after 1502–3, when the communar began to separate pepper out in his accounts. Both clearly bought pepper throughout this period, as it is frequently mentioned by name in the communar's miscellaneous list of spices purchased but without individual details being given. The lack of more than a single data source until 1502–3 means that fewer conclusions can be drawn for pepper than for the spices looked at so far. It would seem, however, that no great changes took place in the priory's purchasing of pepper. The price paid varied from year to year, with a low of 13d. per pound paid by the cellarer in 1465–6, and a high of 24d. per pound paid by the communar in 1502–3. However, these fluctuations were not indicative of any trend, and in general pepper prices appear to have remained around the 16d.–20d. mark throughout this period.

The amount bought, too, appears to have remained stable. The cellarer bought between 6 and 16 dozen pounds in these years, but the latter figure was unusual and occurred right at the end of the period. From the 1460s to the first decade of the sixteenth century, the cellarer bought between 72 and 108 lbs of pepper per year, averaging 92.5 lbs. The cellarer thus provided the vast majority of the priory's pepper, the communar purchasing only between 0.5 and 1 lb per year after 1502–3 when his accounts reveal the details of his purchases. On average, then, the priory purchased around 93 lbs of pepper per year, and this amount remained steady throughout this period. The amount of pepper consumed by an average monk in a year was thus about the same as the maximum amount of sugar reached by the end of this period, around 2.5 pounds per year, thus confirming the impression gained from the recipes of the period that pepper was very much a staple of the medieval kitchen, and was used in far greater quantities then than now.

Comparative consumption

The total amount spent on spices by the priory in an average year was just over £25. This can be compared with what we know of the spice purchases of other

[41] K. L. Reyerson, 'Commercial Fraud in the Middle Ages: The Case of the Dissembling Pepperer', *Journal of Medieval History*, 8 (1982), p. 67.
[42] E. Ashtor, *Levant Trade in the Later Middle Ages* (Princeton, 1983), pp. 469–70.
[43] Wake, 'Changing Pattern', pp. 372, 393–4.

late medieval noble households. The monks of Westminster, for example, spent around £9 on spices each year, excluding the costs of spices for the prior's table for which they accounted separately.[44] This is only just over a third of the total spent on spices by the monks and prior of Durham Cathedral Priory (£3), although the addition of the prior's spices to the Westminster total might make a half more accurate. The population of Westminster was if anything rather larger than that of Durham, averaging fifty as opposed to forty monks, and the amounts that the two monasteries spent on wine were roughly commensurate, so this is a striking difference.

Some comparisons can also be made with large secular households. The household of Humphrey Stafford, Duke of Buckingham, spent £4 12s. on spices in 1452–3, less than a fifth of the priory's average. Evidence such as this lends itself less easily to comparison with the Durham figures, but it may be observed that Stafford's wine purchases, at £13 18s., were somewhat less than a third of the amount spent by the priory each year.[45] The household thus used disproportionately fewer spices than wine than was the case at Durham. However, the *Northumberland Household Book* reveals a similar spend on wine to Durham priory – £49 per year – and a slightly higher spend on spices, at £25 19s. 7d. (not counting raisins and figs).[46]

Conclusions

The fine state of preservation of the priory accounts as a series allows some long-term trends to be seen, as well as enabling the actual goods purchased by the priory to be studied. Firstly, it is interesting to note that the price movements of the commodities looked at in this study differ from the general direction of inflation in this period. Whilst yearly fluctuations could be great, the general trend was clearly for the prices of wine and the principal spices to fall, or in the case of pepper to remain stable, over this period. These price movements contrast with those observed in the market more generally, which remained static or rose very slightly in the second half of the fifteenth century, began to rise after 1500, and rose more steeply as the sixteenth century progressed.[47] Whilst external factors, principally the Portuguese entry into the international spice trade, no doubt contributed to this deflation in the luxury goods market at a time of general price stability and mild inflation, it seems probable that this also reflects a slackening in demand for such goods as a result of increasing pressure on aristocratic incomes throughout the fifteenth century.

But perhaps the most important change that these accounts reveal is the increasing proportion of the priory's business that went to Newcastle merchants over the medieval period. Margaret Bonney's analysis of the early bursar's accounts has shown that in the late thirteenth and early fourteenth

[44] Harvey, *Living and Dying*, pp. 37, 57.
[45] Dyer, *Standards of Living*, p. 56.
[46] T. Percy, *The Northumberland Household Book*, 3rd edn (London, 1905), pp. 6, 19–20.
[47] Y. S. Brenner, 'The Inflation of Prices in Early Sixteenth Century England', *EcHR*, 2nd series, xiv (1961), p. 226: S. V. Hopkins and E. H. Phelps-Brown, 'Seven Centuries of the Prices of Consumables', *Economica*, n.s. 23 (1956), pp. 297–302.

centuries, merchants from Durham itself provided the majority of the priory's supplies, with a wide variety of luxury goods being available in the marketplace there. By the mid-fourteenth century, the emphasis had shifted to the great fairs, and by the late fourteenth century to the towns of Newcastle, Hartlepool, Darlington, York and Hull.[48] This evidence from the fifteenth century shows an increasing trend towards Newcastle which continued over the century, with Newcastle merchants claiming an increasing share of the priory's business at the expense both of other towns in the region and even of London.

Of the *c.*£2,250 that the bursar's office is recorded as spending on wine over the forty-seven years for which totals survive, 94 per cent was spent with Newcastle merchants. Nearly 6 per cent was spent with the merchants of Hull, and negligible amounts were spent with merchants of York (£36 3s. 4d.), London (£17 0s. 6d.) and Durham (£9 6s. 8d.). The proportion of the priory's trade that was given to York, in particular, had declined noticeably since the first half of the century, when 11 per cent of the wine bought by the bursar had come from there.[49] This reflects the decreasing numbers of York merchants participating in overseas trade over the fifteenth century,[50] an important feature of the recession that lasted there from *c.*1420 to the early decades of the sixteenth century. The pattern of the priory's purchases from York merchants suggests that their increasing focus on Newcastle suppliers was a response, rather than a contribution, to this decline; that is, there was no sudden abandonment of the York market (indeed in 1471–2, 49 per cent of the bursar's wine purchases were made there).

The increasing focus on Newcastle over this period narrowed considerably the range of towns from which the priory bought wine, and a considerable difference can be seen here between the beginning and end of this period. In the first half of the fifteenth century, the bursar had occasionally purchased wine not simply at the four towns used in the second half of the century, but also from Hartlepool, Shields and Beaurepaire; by the sixteenth century, no wine was bought from even Hull, York or Durham merchants. Apart from the purchase of a butt of malmsey from London in 1500–1 and 1506–7, Newcastle merchants supplied all of the priory's wine after 1497–8.

Several historians have argued that Newcastle stood out as a rare example of success and prosperity in this period; however, the chronic lack of evidence available for medieval Newcastle has made this a necessarily tendentious conclusion.[51] The evidence that the obedientiary accounts of Durham cathedral

[48] M. Bonney, *Lordship and the Urban Community: Durham and its Overlords, 1250–1540* (Cambridge, 1990), pp. 169–74. For the wide range of luxury goods available in Durham in the late thirteenth and fourteenth centuries, see also C. M. Fraser, 'The Pattern of Trade in the North-East of England, 1265–1350', *Northern History*, iv (1969), pp. 46, 50.

[49] Morimoto, 'Demands and Purchases', p. 101.

[50] J. I. Kermode, 'Merchants, Overseas trade and Urban Decline: York, Beverley and Hull, *c.*1520–1500', *Northern History*, xxiii (1987).

[51] W. G. Hoskins, 'English Provincial Towns in the Early Sixteenth Century', *TRHS*, 5th series, 6 (1956), p. 4, argued for the success of Newcastle despite this lack of evidence, concluding that 'there can be little doubt that *had Newcastle been taxed in 1523–7* she would have emerged as not lower than fourth among the provincial towns' (my italics). Dobson, whilst referring to Newcastle as the most successful of the medieval new towns, points out that 'the sparsity of evidence makes it almost pointless to put the question' of how it fared in the fifteenth century: R. B. Dobson, 'Urban Decline in Medieval England', *TRHS*, 5th series, 27 (1977), p. 19.

priory contain for the imported goods purchased by the priory cannot directly address the question of whether overseas trading activity through Newcastle declined. This is a question that it will always be difficult to answer confidently since few figures are available for the volume of such trade, the Newcastle customs accounts having survived only for isolated years. However, it has been seen that Durham Cathedral Priory did not merely continue to source luxury imported goods from Newcastle rather than London, but in the second half of the fifteenth century the priory came to rely almost exclusively upon Newcastle as a supply centre. This at least suggests that the range and availability of imported goods in Newcastle did not decrease in this period; indeed, a surprising range of the more expensive imported goods were to be found in Newcastle, including malmsey and other sweet wines, the trade in which was generally centred on London. The variety of goods being imported into Newcastle, and the large number of merchants who can be seen from the priory accounts to have been engaged in overseas trade through the town, do suggest that Newcastle was more successful than most east coast towns in competing for trade in the difficult economic climate of the fifteenth century.

The Impact of St Swithun's Priory on the City of Winchester in the Later Middle Ages

Winifred A. Harwood

St Swithun's Cathedral Priory was one of three important Benedictine foundations in Winchester. The cathedral priory had long been an important landlord in the town, in Hampshire, and in surrounding counties. This paper investigates the impact of this large-scale institution on the city, both as an employer and as a generator of trade. The priory has left a significant archive, but one which is in no way comparable with the comprehensive range of records which exists, for example, for Durham Priory or for Westminster Abbey. There are considerable gaps in the evidence which covers a wide and disparate time span; thus this study is most valuable for the fifteenth and early sixteenth centuries. Despite this, the collection is a useful one. If a reliable notion of the impact of monasticism in general is to be reached, then we cannot rely solely on the half dozen houses which possess truly comprehensive records.

In terms of wealth, St Swithun's Priory did not rank as highly as, for example, Westminster Abbey, but it was the wealthiest house in Hampshire and could certainly be included as a member of the premier league. In terms of size, it did not rival the community at Durham, where numbers were maintained at seventy throughout the later Middle Ages, a figure, however, which included monks in outlying cells.[1] In Winchester, although numbers had exceeded sixty in 1261 and in 1325, they did not regain this former level after the Black Death, remaining between forty and forty-five for most of the fifteenth century. This number held even into the final years of the priory, where there were forty-five monks in 1532–3.[2]

Authority at St Swithun's was decentralised as obedientiaries assumed responsibility for certain aspects of monastic life. Overall responsibility lay with the prior and his deputies. Care of the church buildings and services rested with officials, such as the master of works and sacrist. The domestic economy was the responsibility of others like the curtarian, cellarer and hordarian. Links with the outside world were maintained by the almoner and guest master. Each obedientiary was assigned an income, the greater part of which came from the monastic estates. *Valor Ecclesiasticus* provides a complete view of income in 1535 and shows how it was allocated to individual

1 R. B. Dobson, *Durham Priory 1400–1450* (Cambridge, 1973), p. 54.

2 J. Greatrex, 'St. Swithun's Priory in the Later Middle Ages', *Winchester Cathedral 1093–1993*, ed. J. Crook (Chichester, 1993), pp. 144–5; D. Knowles and R. N. Hadcock, *Medieval Religious Houses in England and Wales*, 2nd edn (London, 1971), pp. 80–1.

officials to carry out their specific duties.[3] These figures conform with surviving obedientiary accounts. Although, for some obedientiaries, accounts have survived, for others none at all remain. It is particularly unfortunate that none exist solely for the prior whose income in 1535 amounted to £1,190 6s. 9¾d. or 68 per cent of total gross income. The many expenses incurred by this person appear in the account of the receiver of the prior's treasury for whom only one complete record survives. Because this account relates to 1334–5, a year when the prior had assumed responsibility for certain departments which had fallen into debt, it may not be truly representative. However, since the range of sources is incomplete, the findings of this paper are also bound to be incomplete and, therefore, the 1334–5 account has been used, but with full awareness of its limitations.

The obedientiary accounts provide comprehensive detail of the range of commodities purchased, but seldom reveal where the purchases were made. While it has been possible to estimate obedientiary purchasing in Winchester, this may not be typical of total spending. Christopher Dyer drew attention to different patterns of marketing based on wealth.[4] Since the prior was the one person likely to have been involved in distance purchasing, the scant survival of his accounts is to be regretted. Fortunately the brokage books of Southampton do demonstrate that purchases by the priory in Southampton were limited.

This study relied on the substantial corpus of obedientiary rolls at Winchester printed by Dean Kitchin. A few discovered elsewhere, such as the infirmarian's account of 1399–1400, have also been consulted. Of course, the rolls do not tell us everything we would like: while they are useful when estimating the numbers of non-religious employed by the monks, they record only those lay servants who made a direct charge on official funds. The variable nature of the working week and of seasonal employment led many people to pursue more than one occupation. Consequently, a lay servant might appear in these records twice, providing two different services. Such factors have been borne in mind when assessing the value of monastic employment to the local population.

While *The Compotus Rolls of the Obedientiaries of St. Swithun's Priory*[5] provide my principal evidence, information from them is supplemented by other sources. For example, Derek Keene's *Survey of Medieval Winchester* helped identify local people;[6] *A Consuetudinary of the Fourteenth Century for the Refectory of the House of St. Swithun in Winchester* defined the customary responsibilities of the prior and other obedientiaries with regard to the refectory;[7] two diet rolls showed the range of consumables purchased or taken from store, on a daily basis; and finally, the manorial accounts, together with extensive and scholarly research concerning the manor as 'food-farm' by

[3] *Valor Ecclesiasticus*, ed. J. Caley and J. Hunter, 6 vols., Record Commission (London, 1810–34), ii, p. 4.

[4] C. Dyer, 'The Consumer and the Market in the Later Middle Ages', *EcHR*, 2nd series, xlii (1989), pp. 305–27.

[5] *Compotus Rolls of the Obedientiaries of St. Swithun's Priory*, ed. G. W. Kitchin, HRSoc, 7 (1892).

[6] D. Keene, *Survey of Medieval Winchester*, Winchester Studies 2, 2 vols. (Oxford, 1985).

[7] *A Consuetudinary of the Fourteenth Century for the Refectory of the House of St. Swithun in Winchester*, ed. G. W. Kitchin, HRSoc, 6 (1886).

Joan Greatrex,[8] contributed greatly to an understanding of the bulk feeding of a large-scale institution.

The priory manors were an important source of food, to a variable and generally diminishing extent throughout this period. At first sight, the collection of manorial accounts is impressive, but unfortunately, like the obedientiary accounts, they survive for different periods and contain virtually no uninterrupted series. It is neither possible to assess total manorial contributions sent to the priory in any specific year, nor to establish entirely accurate trends. However, the evidence they do contain is broadly compatible with that of the obedientiary accounts.

The only complete record of priory income, that in *Valor Ecclesiasticus*, refers to 1535, the end of the period, whereas many of the accounts studied relate to a much earlier date. Despite this discrepancy, the figures are invaluable to this study since they make it possible to estimate, in financial terms, the extent to which Winchester gained from the presence of the cathedral priory in respect of employment and consumption.

Finally, in taking employment and consumption as the two areas for consideration, this paper does not seek to minimise the impact which the priory had on the city in other ways, cultural, liturgical or religious. One of the most obvious visible signs to a visitor of the city was the physical dominance of the priory buildings. The great building schemes at the cathedral must have provided numerous employment opportunities. While it is possible that most of the workforce, such as masons, may not have been local people, during contract they were residing, and hence spending, in the town. In addition, there must have been many others in Winchester who gained either directly or indirectly, in terms of employment or through benefit to the service industries, as a result of the building campaigns.[9] Successive bishops financed the major building works at the cathedral, but the monks were similarly involved, not only with the repair, maintenance and rebuilding of the domestic buildings but also of the cathedral buildings, for which they were, after all, responsible. The precise extent to which Winchester gained from such projects, great or small, is not quantifiable nor is it included in this paper, but neither is it ignored. By the fifteenth century, any creation of employment opportunities or generation of trade, in a city which had lost status and where industry had declined, was clearly of considerable importance. Table 20 provides examples of the sort of work which was undertaken during the period. Work generated by the major building projects was not the only means by which local people benefited from employment at St Swithun's. And it is to employment which this paper turns first.

[8] J. Greatrex, 'The Reconciliation of Spiritual and Temporal Responsibilities: Some Aspects of the Monks of St. Swithun's as Landowners and Estate Managers (*c.*1380–1450)', *PCFC*, li (1995), pp. 77–87; 'St. Swithun's Priory'; 'The Administration of Winchester Cathedral Priory in the Time of Cardinal Beaufort 1405–1447' (unpub. Ottawa Univ. PhD thesis, 1973).

[9] For example, in 1371 Bishop Wykeham appealed for men and transport to bring stone from quarries on the Isle of Wight: *Wykeham's Register*, ed. T. F. Kirby, 2 vols., HRSoc, 11, 13, (1896–9), ii, p. 127.

Table 20. Building schemes at Winchester Cathedral Priory

Date	*Cathedral*	*Domestic*
1300–50	rebuilding choir and presbytery – (choir stalls c. 1308)	construction of building now known as 'Pilgrim's Hall'
1350–1400	building work on new west front of cathedral; transformation of Norman nave to perpendicular (started 1394); chantry chapel Bishop Wykeham (d. 1404) part of scheme remodelling nave	
1400–50		? rebuilding of prior's hall
1450–1500	construction and completion great screen behind high altar; creation of new shrine; from 1450 onwards construction of other chantry chapels – e.g. Cardinal Beaufort (d. 1447); Bishop Waynflete (d. 1486)	
1500–30	vaulting of north and south chancel aisles; reconstruction of east bay and roof vault of Lady Chapel; construction chantry chapel Bishop Fox (d. 1528)	building of new infirmary hall
		? stables

J. Crook, *Winchester Cathedral*, Pitkin Guides, 1998; J. Crook, 'Winchester Cathedral Deanery', *PCFC* 43 (1987), pp. 125–73; J. Crook, 'The Pilgrims' Hall, Winchester', *PCFC*, pp. 85–101; J. Harvey, *English Medieval Architects: A Biographical Dictionary down to 1550*, rev. edn (Gloucester, 1987), pp. 22 and 30.

Note Conventual buildings are largely lost; therefore the full extent of works and chronology are unknown.

I

At certain times throughout this period, the number of religious in the three Benedictine houses of Winchester is known,[10] but the numbers of non-religious who were present seldom feature in ecclesiastical records. For instance, on the eve of the dissolution, when commissioners visited St Mary's Abbey they listed a total of a hundred and two persons of whom only twenty-six were nuns.[11] The numbers of non-religious who acted as advisers, casual labourers, clerks or servants provided a workforce which, when combined with guests, pilgrims and visitors, was constantly fluctuating and added significantly to the numbers. By analysing the surviving accounts of each obedientiary in turn, it is possible to

[10] See Knowles and Hadcock, *Medieval Religious Houses*, pp. 80–1, 268.
[11] *VCH Hants*, ii, pp. 124–5.

estimate the number of lay servants who benefited from employment by the monks, in terms of board, wages or livery, to assess the amount of employment which the monastery offered to local people and the amount and percentage of monastic income from which the local population benefited. On this occasion two examples must suffice.

The first example is the prior, who was a figure of local and national significance. He had his own household and staff, kitchen and cook. He was surrounded by advisers, administrators, lay and clerical personnel; some can be identified as local men deriving benefit from the presence of a monastery within the town, others clearly were not. Some were themselves substantial citizens.[12] The receiver's account of 1334–5 lists fifty-nine personnel who received fees or stipends in return for services rendered to the prior.[13] These ranged from the prior's attorney, who may or may not have been a local person, to the washerwoman and Philip the candleman, who most certainly were. William, the smith, of South Gate was not included amongst the regular workers in the accounts, but was paid £2 18s. 9d. for a year's work, which suggests that the monastery used his services regularly.

Ranking, based on net income in *Valor Ecclesiasticus*, classifies the sacrist as a major obedientiary, the second example. In 1536–7 the sacrist was John Buriton. Despite being assisted by five monks, he also depended on a variety of lay servants. Evidence from the only extant roll for this office, that of 1536–7, shows that the three monks who looked after the holy relics were assisted by a servant who guarded St Swithun's shrine for an annual payment of £1 6s. 8d.[14] Four servants of the church received a year's wage of £1, the same men were paid a total of 13s. 0d. for guarding the cloister doors.[15] Two watchmen were paid a stipend of 13s. 4d. and, with the others, slept in the cathedral over which they kept watch. Others who benefited from this department were the warden of the clock, the washerwoman, various sewing women, servants who cleaned the cathedral, William Penycot[16] who made the Easter taper, Bartholomew Dove who collected the Pentecostals, and William Lomer who repaired the bell gear. Various artisans, carpenters, goldsmiths and sawyers found work repairing the shrine, the high altar and hangings in the choir, and a clerk was paid to write the account. Of the total expenditure made by the sacrist in 1536–7, 52 per cent went to numerous lay personnel in cash or kind.

II

Table 21 shows the number of lay personnel regularly associated with each obedientiary for whom records exist, but in differing years. It provides examples of the type of casual work from which others benefited, and the amount and percentage of obedientiary expenditure assigned to wages. It shows that

12 *Register of the Common Seal of St Swithun's Priory, Winchester*, ed. J. Greatrex, HRSer, 2 (1978), pp. 11, 200 [37, n. 4]; see also Keene, *Winchester*, ii, p. 68.

13 Kitchin, *Obedientiary Rolls*, p. 238, n. 1.

14 Ibid. p. 111; Greatrex, 'St. Swithun's Priory', p. 148.

15 *Winchester Cathedral Documents*, ed. G. W. Kitchin and F. T. Madge, HRSoc, 1 (1889), p. 31.

16 William Penycot is someone who can be identified as a local man; see Keene, *Winchester*, p. 131.

Table 21. Summary of lay employment in St Swithun's Priory, Winchester

Obedientiary	*Year*	*Total costs*	*% expenses on wages*	*Cash expenses on wages*	*No. of lay personnel regularly employed*	*% total expenses on charity*	*Other lay servants in casual work*
		£ s d		£ s d			
Almoner	1311–12	39 17 2¾	64%	25 7 11¼	4	49%	hay-makers, rent-collector, roofers
Anniversarian	1394–5	18 1 3	33%	5 19 3	4	18%	clerk writing account
Chamberlain	1416–17	88 9 1¾	8%	6 19 2	8		clerk, servants
Curtarian and cellarer	1484–5	23 10 4½	9%	2 3 2	2		man nesting swans, women making oatmeal
Hordarian	1336	277 11 3	3%	8 7 2	8		man sacking wool, other servants
Infirmarian	1399–1400	12 2 8	7%	0 17 1	5		candlemaker, clerk, rent collector
Master of Works	1408–9	66 0 2¼	29%	18 15 ½	8		conduit man, labourers, other servants assisting
Sacrist	1536–7	48 4 10	52%	25 6 3	9		carpenter, cleaners, collector of pentecostals, goldsmith, sewing women
Receiver of prior's treasury	1334–5	1,348 15 6½	13%	195 11 10	59	1%	candlemakers, carpenters, coopers, masons and smiths
					107		

Figures are approximate and concern only those mentioned directly in accounts, including manorial serjeants.

approximately 107 lay personnel gained employment in the priory. When a possible two salaried staff are added to this for the refectory, perhaps three to assist the guest master, another for the sub-prior and gardener, the figure rises to 114 which compares with the figure of 110 servants employed at Westminster Abbey at a similar time.[17] This figure does not include the numerous servants who found casual work, or the many who do not feature in the accounts at all. If included, then the notion of about a hundred people increases to a total dependent population of many times that size. As numbers for St Swithun's are taken from a wide range of years, they represent no specific date. The picture portrayed is that the priory offered a significant amount of work to local townspeople. It also drew on a diverse range of skills. Not only did the prior have his own advisory council, attorneys, household and staff but, in addition, the convent used the specialist skills of choir masters, organists and master masons, and relied on the more commonplace, yet vital, services provided by bakers, bath attendants, brewers, candle makers, carpenters, carters, collectors of alms and rentals, glaziers, goldsmiths, horsemen, manorial servants, masons, millers, plumbers, sawyers, servants to serve in the refectory, servants to tend the rabbit warrens or the prior's swans, tailors and tilers. Women also found employment in the priory. Some were paid to clean the entrails of animals, others to do the laundry, to mend or sew the vestments or to make meat puddings or oatmeal. The services rendered assisted the obedientiaries in fulfilling the specific responsibilities with which they had been entrusted.

Table 22 provides information for St Swithun's from *Valor Ecclesiasticus*. It lists and identifies each obedientiary who received an income in 1535, and shows the gross and net income which each received in that year.

The gross income for the priory in 1535 was £1,762 19s. 2d., of which £572 12s. 4d. or 32 per cent was assigned to obedientiaries for the specific purpose of running a monastic department under obedience. By projecting the percentage which benefited lay personnel as calculated in other years, shown on Table 21, on to the 1535 figures for gross income shown on Table 22 it has been possible to estimate to what extent local people gained in 1535 from the prior and the seven obedientiaries, for whom records exist; benefit to clerical and lay personnel, expressed as a percentage of the gross income of known obedientiaries, amounted to 14 per cent. This figure was used to calculate the benefit derived from those obedientiaries for whom no records exist. Total estimated benefit from employment to clerical and lay personnel in 1535 is shown on Table 23.

Residual income, not assigned to a specific monastic department, went to the receiver of the prior's treasury, but appears in *Valor Ecclesiasticus* as income of the prior. This unassigned income in 1535 amounted to £1,190 6s. 9¾d. or 68 per cent of the total gross income. From this, lay servants supporting the prior were also paid, and this amount is included in the total figures which benefited lay personnel.

Table 24 summarises these figures and provides a calculated estimate of priory expenditure on employment of local people, expressed in cash terms, and as a percentage of total gross income of the priory. It indicates that, in 1535, an estimated 14 per cent of total expenditure, or £250 8s. 5d., benefited lay or clerical personnel.

[17] Harvey, *Living and Dying*, p. 164.

Table 22. Income of obedientiaries in 1535 (arranged in descending order of net income)

Office	*Name*	*Gross income*			*Expenses*			*Net income*		
		£	s	d	£	s	d	£	s	d
Prior	Henry Broke	1,190	6	9¾	135	2	6¾	1,055	4	3
Hordarian/kitchener	William Basyng	238	1	11	29	12	7	208	9	4
Chamberlain	John Morton	87	0	9	8	6	6	78	14	3
Sacrist	Richard Petersfield	50	4	0	4	10	0	45	14	0
Master of Works	John Estgate	50	9	2¾	13	13	4	36	15	10¾
†Sub-prior	John Avington	45	6	4	19	15	2½	25	11	1½
Almoner	John Meon	34	17	1½	21	0	6	13	16	7½
†Speciarius	John Andover	16	12	8	5	7	6	11	5	2
Anniversarian	John Guildford	17	14	2	10	6	8	7	7	6
†Guestmaster	Edward Westgate	7	4	3		nil		7	4	3
Infirmarian	John Wodeson	7	6	2	1	5	2	6	1	0
†Precentor	Henry Kyngstone	5	10	0	1	0	0	4	10	0
†Keeper of the altar of BVM	John Burton	6	19	1	2	14	4	4	4	9
†Gardener	John Haycroft	5	6	8	2	7	7½	2	19	0½
		1,762	19	2						

† Those officials for whom no obedientiary accounts survive in *Valor Ecclesiasticus*, ii, pp. 2–3

Table 23. Estimated expenditure on employment of clerical and lay personnel in 1535 (arranged in descending order of gross income)

Obedientiary	*Gross income*			*% expenses on employing lay personnel*	*Cash spent on lay employees*		
	£	s	d		£	s	d
Prior	1,190	6	9¾	13%	154	14	10
Hordarian/kitchener	238	1	11	3%	7	2	10
Chamberlain	87	0	9	8%	6	19	3
Master of Works	50	9	2¾	29%	14	12	8
Sacrist	50	4	0	52%	26	2	1
†Sub-prior	45	6	4	[14%]	[6	6	11]
Almoner	34	17	1½	64%	22	6	2
Anniversarian	17	14	2	33%	5	16	10
†Speciarius	16	12	8	[14%]	[2	6	7]
Infirmarian	7	6	2	7%		10	3
†Guestmaster	7	4	3	[14%]	[1	0	2]
†Keeper of the altar of BVM	6	19	1	[14%]		[19	6]
†Precentor	5	10	0	[14%]		[15	5]
†Gardener	5	6	8	[14%]		[14	11]
	£1,762	19	2		£250	8	5

† Those officials for whom no obedientiary accounts survive, % of those obedientiaries for whom accounts do survive has been used.
Source Valor Ecclesiasticus, ii, pp. 2–3

Table 24. Estimated allocation of income and estimated expenditure on employment in 1535

	£	s	d	
Total gross income for St Swithun's Priory	1,762	19	2	
Amount assigned to obedientaries	572	12	4	
– expressed as % of total gross income				32%
Unallocated income – assigned to prior	1,190	6	10	
– expressed as % of total gross income				68%
Estimated expenditure on employment of clerical and lay personnel	250	8	5	
– expressed as % of total gross income				14%

Source Valor Ecclesiasticus, ii, p. 3

The *Consuetudinary of the Refectory* shows how others gained from the perquisites of office, the left-overs from the table or the cinders from the hearth, both valued commodities. Some servants do not appear in the accounts at all, simply working in return for food and drink. As Barbara Harvey remarked, 'for many in the monastery the principal reward of service was the assured supply of bread and ale whatever the price of these staple foods in the open market'.[18] When similar employment and benefit by the monks of Hyde Abbey, the nuns of St Mary's Abbey, the provost and clerics of St Elizabeth's chantry college, the warden and fellows of Winchester College, as well as the various hospitals and four orders of friars, is also taken into account, it can be seen that the presence of these religious institutions in the town was decidedly to the advantage of the local people.

III

Turning now to consumption; the monastic household was a large-scale institution, an important consumer of food and drink, as well as other commodities. Throughout the period, the priory was responsible not just for feeding the religious community, but also corrodians, guests, servants and numerous others, a large and fluctuating number of people. Food and drink represented a major area of consumption. As Barbara Harvey observed, 'Fish, eggs, cereals and vegetables made up the classic repertoire of monastic refectories',[19] and to this must be added those two fundamentals of any medieval diet, in generous quantities, bread and ale. Eggs were prominent in the monastic diet; the diet roll of 1492–3 revealing that an average of seven hundred eggs were eaten per week. Allowing for Lent, when eggs, like cheese, were excluded from the diet, this represented an average consumption of about seven hundred and fifty eggs per week. By this later period, flesh-meat was widely eaten on 'flesh days', but never on Wednesdays, Fridays and Saturdays, during Lent or on the vigils of important feasts. And it was on special days that the community enjoyed pittances.

The hordarian, an official responsible for the domestic economy, received an income second in size only to the prior, amounting to £208 9s. 4d. in 1535. Subordinate to him was the curtarian/cellarer, whose responsibilities included the acquisition of supplies for the house, stables and outbuildings and for which he was allocated £17 10s. in 1484–5. By 1535, *Valor Ecclesiasticus* reveals that this obedientiary was no longer receiving an income, which suggests that his role diminished or changed in the later years. It was from the hordarian that the monk kitchener received large sums of money each year to feed the community. While not required to keep accounts as such, the diet rolls are his daily record of food purchased, with weekly and quarterly summaries of expenditure. Although they include certain specific items, particularly calves' feet and tripe, which came explicitly from the kitchener's store and for which no charge was made,[20] they do not include supplies which came from priory manors, the monastic garden or those items which the prior was required to provide himself, ale,[21] bread, butter, cheese, salt and wine.[22]

Manorial contributions to the priory larder remained high throughout the

[18] Harvey, *Living and Dying*, p. 172.
[19] Ibid. p. 11.
[20] Kitchin, *Obedientiary Rolls*, p. 335.
[21] Throughout the term 'ale' has been substituted for Kitchin's 'beer' when translating *cervisia/cerevisia*.
[22] Kitchin, *Consuetudinary*, p. 9.

fourteenth century. The abandonment of direct farming and the adoption of a policy of leasing monastic land happened later on the St Swithun's estates than in some other parts of England, such as on the estates of Canterbury, Coventry or Durham Cathedral Priory, where, by 1420, it had become the norm.[23] The extensive estates of the priory included chalkland manors in Hampshire and Wiltshire. Although the monks leased out some of their smaller and outlying estates before 1400, they maintained direct farming on many of these large chalkland manors well into the early fifteenth century. By 1450 most land had been leased.[24] The change had been gradual, and initially on some manors the rent was provided in grain. Thus in 1450, for example, the priory still received a hundred and five quarters of grain in addition to twelve capons, twelve fowl and twelve geese from the Wiltshire manor of Enford,[25] as part of the terms of the lease.

Even after 1450 the monks continued to cultivate on their home farm of Barton.[26] This large estate situated outside Winchester, close to the priory, had been a regular supplier of cereals, dairy products and stock. This continued in 1465 when the arable demesne was temporarily leased,[27] and in 1475 the total quantity of grain produced amounted to forty quarters each of barley and wheat and twenty quarters of oats. By 1479 direct cultivation had resumed on a large scale, so that in 1489 the amount of grain supplied by Barton had risen to 128 quarters of barley and 282 quarters of wheat.[28] Final leasing did not occur here until 1538.[29]

Despite the important role played by the home farm in the core production of food, dependence on the market was significantly greater in this later period than formerly. Joan Greatrex estimated that, in 1400, eighteen priory manors were supplying approximately six hundred quarters of wheat.[30] She also found occasions when the manors could have contributed yet larger amounts to the priory, but chose instead to sell their produce to the local market, leaving the monks to make their purchases close by.[31] Grain, surplus to priory needs, had probably been sold in the local market. Cheese specifically designated to the curtarian almost certainly went to the refectory, the rest of the cheese, sent with quantities of wool to the prior, may well have been intended for sale,[32] consumption in the town or export elsewhere.

By the mid-fifteenth century the quantities of grain, pigs, poultry and sheep sent by priory tenants had been reduced. Pigs had been supplied regularly by priory manors, but in variable numbers. Using evidence from a surviving stock book, Joan Greatrex calculated that a total of 499 and 469 pigs were sent from the manors to the priory in 1390 and 1391 respectively; as late as 1450 a small

23 J. N. Hare, 'The Monks as Landlords: The Leasing of the Monastic Demesnes in Southern England', *The Church in Pre-Reformation Society*, ed. C. M. Barron and C. Harper-Bill (Woodbridge, 1985), p. 93.

24 Ibid., p. 86.

25 Greatrex, 'Administration', app. D1, p. xxii.

26 Hare, 'Monks as Landlords', p. 86.

27 Ibid. p. 86.

28 WCL manorial accounts, Barton, 1475 and 1489.

29 Hare, 'Monks as Landlords', p. 87, n. 32.

30 Greatrex, 'Administration', p. 160.

31 Ibid. p. 164.

32 Ibid. p. 162.

number were still being delivered.[33] The receiver's account of 1335 refers to the monastery's own pig farm, situated in the brewhouse yard. The presence of the piggery and the continuing, though perhaps diminishing, supply of pigs from the manors suggests that some meat was acquired by ad hoc arrangement with demesne tenants, with whom the monks kept a close contact, and some was purchased from local butchers.

Barton not only supplied cereals and stock in 1453, but also cheese, cream and milk, but butter is not mentioned after 1402.[34] Almost certainly, the priory bought some butter, cheese and eggs locally and the receiver's account shows that the prior spent £1 buying bread in the town for distribution to the poor on All Saints' Day 1334;[35] and the account of the anniversarian, 1394–5, indicates that ale was bought in the city for the boys of the choir on Holy Innocents' Day.[36]

Some provisions came from Southampton, the local port. Fish was eaten on Wednesdays, Fridays and Saturdays throughout the year, during Lent and in Holy Week. A wide variety of salt and freshwater fish was consumed, some eaten fresh, but most after being salted, smoked or dried. The receiver's account shows that fish was purchased in Portsmouth and Southampton in 1334–5, and the Southampton brokage book of 1443–4 shows that three carts carried fish from the port to the priory that year,[37] in 1448–9 four cartloads,[38] in 1477–8 eight cartloads,[39] and in 1527–8 twenty-one cartloads.[40] The small quantities taken thence in 1443–4 suggest that fish was also being purchased locally in the town. Deliveries from Southampton make no mention of the cockles, mussels, oysters, periwinkles, shrimps or whelks which the diet rolls show were being eaten at supper or as pittances, so these were probably bought in Winchester as required. In 1334–5, the receiver paid for wine purchased in Southampton. In 1448–9, 693 gallons of wine were delivered to the monastery from the port, 1,575 gallons in 1477–8, and 756 gallons in 1527–8. In 1443–4, no wine was taken to the monastery, but the Southampton records show that it was being taken to Winchester throughout that year. Derek Keene was of the opinion that the religious houses in Winchester did purchase wine from city vintners such as John Coteler.[41] In the absence of other evidence, it is reasonable to deduce that, for years in which wine was not purchased directly from the port, the priory bought it in the city. Similarly, in 1334–5 the receiver paid £3 1s. for forty-five quarters of salt purchased in bulk for the kitchen. The brokage book of Southampton for 1477–8 shows approximately seven hundredweight of salt being taken from Southampton to St Swithun's in that year.[42] In 1527–8, an unspecified quantity was taken from the port to the priory, but on only one occasion.

[33] Greatrex, 'Administration', Appendix D1, p. xxxi; Greatrex, 'Reconciliation of Responsibilities', p. 185.

[34] Greatrex, 'Administration', Appendix D1, p. xix.

[35] Kitchin, *Obedientiary Rolls*, p. 122.

[36] Ibid. p. 204, n. 2.

[37] *The Brokage Book of Southampton 1443–44*, ed. O. Coleman, SRS, 4 (1960).

[38] *The Southampton Port and Brokage Books 1448–9*, ed. E. A. Lewis, SRS, 36 (1993).

[39] *The Brokage Books of Southampton 1477–8 and 1527–8*, ed. K. F. Stevens and T. E. Olding, SRS, 28 (1985).

[40] Ibid.

[41] Keene, *Winchester*, i, p. 272.

[42] Stevens and Olding, *Brokage Books*.

It is difficult to be precise about the extent to which Winchester gained from supplying its religious houses. Fuel appears to have been purchased locally and Winchester itself provided additional supplies of ale, candles and wine and probably bread, cloth and numerous incidental requirements, such as parchment, or the cord for the lantern in the cloister which cost 3d. in 1484–5. Apart from some provisions from the priory manors, other purchases came from further afield. It has already been seen that fish, salt and wine were bought on occasion in Southampton, sometimes in large quantities; the monks were acting here like other great households which made purchases, particularly of wine and fish, direct from their local ports. Heavy commodities – iron, slates and tombstones – were also purchased from the port. The monks considered it economic to buy plaster of Paris from France, despite the cost of transporting it down the Seine and across the Channel. London's influence was also felt during this period. As the capital became the preferred purchasing centre for luxury or expensive goods, so the curtarian, in 1484–5, paid to have wax transported from London to Winchester.[43] It was from London that the hordarian had his new bridle and saddle sent to him at Oxford.[44]

The accounts clearly indicate when goods did originate from London or Southampton, but such occasions are remarkably few. That such information is generally lacking forces the deduction that all other commodities, not specifically designated to a particular place, were purchased in Winchester, and hence to the benefit of the town's retailers and craftsmen.

Table 25 summarises obedientiary purchasing in Winchester for those officials for whom records exist. The amount spent in the town constitutes a major area of expenditure, and is expressed in two ways. Since no commodities were always bought elsewhere, the minimum figure excludes all items which were, on occasion, bought elsewhere. The maximum figure, therefore, includes all those items such as ale, candles, fish or iron, which were sometimes bought in the town, sometimes produced in-house, or sometimes purchased further afield.

IV

Table 26 summarises the amount spent in the town by each obedientiary for whom accounts exist, and expresses the total as a percentage of their expenditure/income for the year of the account. Given the crudity of the figures, expenditure and income differ too little to be of significance for these calculations. By expressing the individual expenditure of all these officials as a percentage of the total, it is possible to calculate the average maximum and minimum percentage of income spent in the town.

Turning to the complete set of figures in *Valor Ecclesiasticus* known percentages for those obedientiaries for whom accounts exist are projected onto their 1535 incomes. The two calculated percentages are used for those

[43] Kitchin, *Obedientiary Rolls*, p. 137.
[44] Ibid. p. 280, n. 1.

Table 25. Obedientiary purchasing within Winchester

Obedientiary/year	A	B	C	D	E	*Amount spent in the town minimum*	F	G	*Amount spent in the town maximum*
	£ s d	£ s d	£ s d	£ s d	£ s d	£ s d	£ s d	£ s d	£ s d
Almoner (1311–12)		7 0 1			17 6 10	24 6 11	0 18 4	0 14 8	25 19 11
Anniversarian (1394–5)		2 4 8	0 5 4		0 3 4	2 13 4	3 6 11	0 7 1	6 7 4
Chamberlain (1416–17)		5 15 5		0 1 8	54 4 1	60 1 2	0 1 6	2 6 6	62 9 2
Curtarian 1484–5	0 1 8	0 11 1	1 14 3	7 18 4	5 3 3	15 8 7		2 1 8	17 10 3
Hordarian [1336]		8 18 6	250 6 2		4 18 0	264 2 8	0 1 3	1 0 8	265 4 7
Infirmarian (1399–1400)		0 9 8		0 1 4	0 7 2	0 18 2	0 3 4	4 10 5	4 13 9
Master of Works (1408–9)	8 19 4	6 6 2		1 8 2	3 11 2	20 4 10	0 0 4	2 12 9	22 17 11
Receiver (1334–35)	15 8 0	135 5 8	155 2 10	18 6 7	55 18 5	380 1 6	6 18 3	224 16 8	611 16 5
Sacrist (1536–7)	6 19 2			1 2 10	1 1 5	9 3 5	0 11 10	11 0 7	20 15 10
	31 8 2	166 11 3	407 8 7	28 18 11	142 13 8	**777 0 7**	12 1 9	249 11 0	**1037 15 2**
Spending in town									
– minimum					**777 0 7**				
– maximum					**1037 15 2**				

Key A = building materials (eg lead, nails); B = cloth, clothing, footwear; C = food; D = charcoal, hearthwood etc.; E = incidentals such as parchment, provender; F = ale, bread; G = fish, candles, iron, salt, and wax

Minimum includes only those items customarily purchased in the town; maximum includes commodities which were, on occasion, bought elsewhere or produced in house.

This table is based only on the accounts of those obedientiaries for whom records exist.

Table 26. Estimated obedientiary expenditure in Winchester (in monetary terms and as percentage of total expenditure of office)

Obedientary/year	*Expenses of office*			*Expenses*			*Spending in town as percentage of expenses of office*	*Expenses directly benefiting the town*			*Spending in town as percentage of expenses of office*
	£	s	d	£	s	d		£	s	d	
Almoner 1311–12	39	17	3	24	6	11	61%	25	19	11	65%
Anniversarian 1394–5	18	1	3	2	13	4	15%	6	7	4	35%
Chamberlain 1416–17	88	9	2	60	1	2	68%	62	9	2	71%
Curtarian 1484–5	23	10	4	15	8	7	66%	17	10	3	74%
Hordarian [1336]	277	11	3	264	2	8	95%	265	4	7	96%
Infirmarian 1399–1400	12	12	8		18	2	7%	4	13	9	37%
Master of Works 1408–9	66	0	2	20	4	10	31%	22	17	11	35%
Receiver 1334–5	1,348	15	7	380	1	6	28%	611	16	5	45%
Sacrist 1536–7	48	4	10	9	3	5	19%	20	15	10	43%
	1,923	2	6	777	0	7		1,037	15	2	
Percentage of income spent in town											
– minimum											40%
– maximum											54%

officials for whom no accounts survive, thus making it possible to estimate the percentage of gross priory income which directly benefited Winchester in 1535, as shown in Table 27.

The figures produced are crude and based on a wide time span. However, they are useful, suggesting that at least £703 1s. 4d. or 40 per cent, or at most £943 15s. 9d. or 54 per cent of total gross income, was spent in Winchester in 1535 (Table 27). Whether commodities originated or were manufactured locally or whether they were imported from further afield, St Swithun's Priory certainly was a very important customer in the town. Add to this the trade generated by priory employees, pilgrims and visitors, and multiply the total to accommodate the purchasing of the other religious institutions, and the major contribution of religious houses to Winchester's economy becomes obvious.

In the absence of a complete set of records, estimates of expenditure devoted to employment or on purchasing in the town are based on composite figures from different periods and are, therefore, somewhat impressionistic. One final set summarises the results. Table 28 estimates the amount of monastic expenditure which directly benefited Winchester.

Table 28 shows that from a total gross monastic income of £1,762 19s. 2d. in 1535, a minimum amount of £953 9s. 9d. or 54 per cent went directly to the

Table 27. Estimated expenditure in Winchester in 1535 (arranged in descending order of gross income)

Obedientiary	*Gross income*	*Amount spent in town minimum*	*% spent in town minimum*	*Amount spent in town*	*% spent in town minimum*
	£ s d	£ s d		£ s d	
Prior	1,190 6 9¾	333 5 11	28%	535 13 1	45%
Hordarian/ kitchener	238 1 11	226 3 10	95%	228 11 5	96%
Chamberlain	87 0 9	59 3 9	68%	61 15 11	71%
Master of Works	50 9 2¾	15 12 10	31%	17 13 3	35%
Sacrist	50 4 0	9 10 9	19%	21 11 9	43%
†Sub-prior	45 6 4	[18 11 7]	[40%]	[24 9 5]	[54%]
Almoner	34 17 1½	21 5 3	61%	22 13 2	65%
Anniversarian	17 14 2	2 13 2	15%	6 4 0	35%
†Speciarius	16 12 8	[6 16 5]	[40%]	[8 19 8]	[54%]
Infirmarian	7 6 2	10 3	7%	2 14 1	37%
†Guestmaster	7 4 3	[2 19 2]	[40%]	[3 17 11]	[54%]
†Keeper of the altar of BVM	6 19 1	[2 17 0]	[40%]	[3 15 1]	[54%]
†Precentor	5 10 0	[2 5 1]	[40%]	[2 19 5]	[54%]
†Gardener	5 6 8	[2 3 9]	[40%]	[2 17 7]	[54%]
	1,762 19 2	703 1 4		943 15 9	

† Those officials for whom no obedientary accounts survive; [ ] % of those obedientaries for whom accounts do survive have been used.

Source Valor Ecclesiasticus, ii, pp. 2–3

town. When, however, those commodities which were sometimes purchased in Winchester and occasionally further afield are included, then the overall expenditure on local purchasing and employment was significantly more, amounting to £1,194 4s. 2d. or 68 per cent of total income.

Unsurprisingly, Table 28 demonstrates clearly how major an employer and consumer the cathedral priory was in the city. It was not the only such religious community. Taken individually and together, Winchester's religious houses were a substantial source of employment and business, perhaps the most substantial one, to one of the major towns in England. It is regrettably impossible to estimate the proportion of total business that they represented. If historians are to determine the economic impact of monasteries as a whole, they can no longer rely solely on those houses with superb records. They must also maximise the potential of the less complete surviving archives of other religious houses. Winchester Cathedral Priory marks a start.

Table 28. Expenditure of St Swithun's Priory on local purchasing and employment (expressed in cash terms and as a percentage of total gross income)

	£	s	d	%
Total gross income for St Swithun's priory in 1535	£1,762	19	2	
Estimated expenditure on employment	£250	8	5	
– expressed as % of total gross income				14%
Estimated expenditure on purchasing in the town (minimum)	£703	1	4	
– expressed as % of total gross income				40%
Estimated expenditure on purchasing in the town (maximum)	£943	15	9	
– expressed as % of total gross income				54%
Total estimated expenditure on local purchasing and employment (minimum)	£953	9	9	
– expressed as a percentage of total gross income				54%
Total estimated expenditure on local purchasing and employment (maximum)	£1,194	4	2	
– expressed as a percentage of total gross income				68%

Source Valor Ecclesiasticus, ii, p. 3

Telling Tales of Oligarchy in the Late Medieval Town

Peter Fleming

The subject of urban oligarchy has inspired a good deal of debate among historians. While there is little argument over the proposition that most urban communities were ruled by a small group of their wealthier citizens, usually drawn from the distributive rather than manufacturing sector, that is from the wholesale merchants, historians are divided over the nature of that rule, and over its acceptability to those over whom it was exercised. To put it crudely, on one side are those, such as Susan Reynolds and Gervase Rosser, who argue for essentially harmonious urban relations, while on the other are historians such as Stephen Rigby and Rodney Hilton who characterise medieval towns as being inherently factious. None deny that there was conflict, but for the former group it usually took the form of protests against individual townsmen who abused their privileges, or against individuals and groups perceived as external threats to civic liberties, such as representatives of ecclesiastical, seigneurial or royal power. Historians in the latter group see conflict as the inevitable product of the steep gradations of power between the ruling elite and the rest, and between employers and employees. Protests may have been sparked by particular abuses, but they were fuelled by an underlying sensitivity to changing power relationships between the constituent groups of urban society: 'class conflict', in other words.[1]

The ability of urban populations to criticise the systems of political authority by which they were governed was dependent on their ability to conceptualise power relations, since a principled critique of systems and structures, as opposed to individual instances of abuse, relies on the process of abstraction, or drawing general conclusions from particular examples. The effectiveness of any group's justification of its opposition is naturally related to its members' sophistication as political thinkers. Reynolds has argued that we should take seriously the political culture of urban elites, and see it in the broader context of medieval notions of just rule and the social order. Not surprisingly, her

[1] A useful summary of this debate is provided by H. Swanson, *Medieval British Towns* (Basingstoke, 1999), pp. 89–96. See also S. Reynolds, *Introduction to the History of English Medieval Towns* (Oxford, 1977), pp. 171–7; Reynolds, 'Medieval Urban History and the History of Political Thought', *Urban History Yearbook* (1982), pp. 14–23, at 20–2; R. H. Hilton, *English and French Towns in Feudal Society: A Comparative Study* (Cambridge, 1992), pp. 134–51; S. H. Rigby, 'Urban "Oligarchy" in Late Medieval England', in *Towns and Townspeople in the Fifteenth Century*, ed. J. A. F. Thomson (Gloucester, 1988), pp. 62–86; Rigby, *English Society in the Later Middle Ages: Class, Status and Gender* (Basingstoke, 1995), pp. 165–76; G. Rosser, *Medieval Westminster, 1200–1540* (Oxford, 1989), pp. 247–8; M. Kowaleski, *Local Markets and Regional Trade in Medieval Exeter* (1995), pp. 96–102; J. Kermode, *Medieval Merchants: York, Beverley and Hull in the Later Middle Ages* (Cambridge, 1998), pp. 53–69.

discussion of urban political culture portrays it largely in terms of a consensus between rulers and ruled: there was general agreement that power should be monopolised by the best, defined as the wisest and most virtuous, qualities which seem to have been possessed to their fullest extent by the wealthiest. How wisdom and virtue was to be identified and exercised was explained in the most conventional, bland terms: 'Much of the advice seems to amount to not much more than being against sin. But it was what people believed in.[2] This paper explores some alternative representations of political power in later medieval towns, and suggests that the constitution of just rule in the discourse of urban authority was more problematic than Reynolds has maintained.

Urban government was ultimately sanctioned from the crown, as was all legitimate authority, in theory. But compared to the lords of the shires – be they titled nobility or gentry – urban governors had fewer resources with which to enforce their rule, not only in terms of such practical matters as retainers, control over tenantry, military training and expertise, but also what might be called the cultural or psychological resources, such as status, a position in local society that could be presented as stretching back for generations, and the other trappings of nobility which engendered the habit of deference among social inferiors. The men who were the mayors, aldermen and common councillors of later medieval towns may have been wealthy and influential within their own communities, but they were not essentially different from those they governed.[3] The two groups lived cheek by jowl, and the patriciate married into and traded with those below them. Mayors were in some degree chosen by their communities, and could, sometimes, be legitimately removed by them. Despite a trend towards more pronounced oligarchy, urban government was still expected to be answerable to its community.[4] The risks of long-distance trade, combined with high mortality among urban populations, meant that enduring concentrations of power within urban dynasties were rare. While the stability of landed elites was often no more than an image, it is probably the case that the average lifespan of a landed dynasty of about three generations in direct succession would have been less often attained in an urban setting. Urban fortunes were generally more volatile than those founded on land. Urban elites took measures to conceal their fragility, many of which drew from the culture of landed elites, developing elaborate civic ritual, giving livery, recruiting retinues of civic officers, building imposing town halls and having elaborate tombs made for themselves, with their merchants' marks taking the place of heraldic achievements. Some went further and acquired knighthoods, coats of arms, and country seats, but these were in the minority, particularly in the provinces.[5] None of this, however, could compensate for the ambiguous nature of the urban elite's political authority.

To what extent did urban governing elites feel themselves to be vulnerable? While it is true that the fifteenth century cannot be characterised by large-scale urban revolts, certainly nothing like the situation in and around 1381, there is

[2] Reynolds, 'Medieval Urban History', p. 23.
[3] Reynolds, *English Medieval Towns*, p. 180.
[4] Rigby, 'Urban "Oligarchy"', pp. 65–6.
[5] Kermode, *Merchants*, pp. 26–7. S. Linenbaum, 'Ceremony and Oligarchy: The London Midsummer Watch', *City and Spectacle in Medieval Europe*, ed. B. A. Hanawalt and K. L. Reyerson (London, 1994), pp. 171–88, at 178–81.

ample evidence of contested authority within the towns.[6] Caroline Barron has anatomised the conflicts in mid-fifteenth-century London between the distributive and manufacturing trades – the drapers and tailors – with the latter led by Ralph Holland.[7] Disputes between gilds, and between burgesses and governing councils over such matters as taxation, alleged financial impropriety, grazing rights, and precedence in civic rituals, were common in provincial towns. Punishment for challenges to the patriciate's authority, or for disparaging the mayor, could be severe.[8] Admittedly, in these fifteenth-century conflicts it is difficult to discern a widespread movement for the dilution of oligarchy through reform of the system, rather than the punishment or control of particular individuals, although there are some instances where this seems to have been the case: Ralph Holland's challenge to what was perceived as growing oligarchy in London is one of these. A provincial example is provided by Leicester in 1489, where two rival mayors were elected on the same day, one by the existing mayor and a small group of cronies, the other by the 'commonalty'. Leicester's schism, throwing up mayor and anti-mayor, was brought about by the attempt to impose a more exclusive system of mayor-making. A similar attempt in early fifteenth-century Lynn aroused similar opposition.[9] York and Beverley also witnessed resistance to the introduction of more restrictive selection processes.[10] For the most part, the protesters' aims were to protect existing structures and practices against attempts to strengthen oligarchy. The copious evidence of dissent within the burgess class must at the very least qualify the view held by some historians that social relations within later medieval towns were essentially harmonious. The evidence deployed in support of this view seems generally to consist of the normative, self-justificatory discourses of the governing elites themselves.[11]

These protests came in the name of the commons. But who were the commons? When individual protesters can be identified, they are usually craftsmen or traders. Such people may have been outside the governing elite, but they were still within the wider elite of burgesses. There is far less evidence for challenges from below this group. But the extant evidence may not tell the whole story. There was little opportunity for those below the burgess class to have their voices heard, still less preserved in the civic record.[12] The strict control of apprentices and journeymen, as seen, for example, in early Tudor Coventry, suggests that the masters perceived the need for a regime of discipline and surveillance that went beyond merely safeguarding their charges' moral

[6] R. H. Hilton, 'Popular Movements in England at the End of the Fourteenth Century', *Class Conflict and the Crisis of Feudalism* (London, 1985), pp. 79–91.

[7] C. M. Barron, 'Ralph Holland and the London Radicals, 1438–1444', *The English Medieval Town: A Reader in English Urban History, 1200–1540*, ed. R. Holt and G. Rosser (London, 1990), pp. 160–83.

[8] Hilton, *English and French Towns*, pp. 123–5, 137–45. Kermode, *Merchants*, pp. 53–66. B. R. McRee, 'Unity or Division? The Social Meaning of Guild Ceremony in Urban Communities', *City and Spectacle*, ed. Hanawalt and Reyerson, pp. 189–207, at 198–200; P. M. Kendall, *The Yorkist Age: Daily Life during the Wars of the Roses* (London, 1962), pp. 121–33. Rigby, 'Urban "Oligarchy"', pp. 67–70.

[9] Ibid. pp. 67–8.

[10] Swanson, *Medieval British Towns*, pp. 100–1.

[11] Kermode, *Merchants*, pp. 54–5. Hilton, *English and French Towns*, p. 126. Rigby, 'Urban "Oligarchy"', p. 67.

[12] Kermode, *Merchants*, p. 27.

well-being.[13] When lower-class opposition is apparent in towns, it is usually harnessed behind a champion or champions from the burgess class, and it is difficult to decide whether such cases represent a genuinely symbiotic relationship or the masters' cynical rabble-rousing among the journeymen for the attainment of their own self-serving objectives.[14] Changes in the organisation of production in later medieval towns, resulting in the greater employment of wage labour and a decrease in the number of journeymen becoming masters, may have encouraged the emergence of some form of class consciousness among the urban proletariat, and there were a number of attempts by journeymen to restrict competition and maintain their wages and conditions of employment.[15]

Urban governors presided over volatile communities. Little wonder then, that obedience to the law, as interpreted and administered by established authority, was the major theme in the discourse of civic elites.[16] This is clearly demonstrated in the account of the Bristol mayor-making recorded by the town clerk, Robert Ricart, in *The Maire of Bristowe is Kalendar* in 1479.[17] There is repeated stress on obedience to the king, and his authority is associated with that of the mayor: obedience to both is portrayed as the measure of virtue of a member of the governing elite. On Michaelmas Day the retiring mayor thanks his brethren, 'for in you hath bene trewe obedience to kepe the king our alther liege lorde is lawes, and my commaundment in his name, at all tymes'. The mayor's authority comes from the king, not from the community, a point made quite clearly by Ricart in his preface to the account of the mayor-making ceremony, which he describes as dealing

> in especiall of the grete hedde Officer, maire of Bristowe, owre souueraigne lorde the Kinges lieftennaunt and oure alther Maistir for the yere beinge, in whome must rest the grete substaunce of poletyk prouisioun, wise and discrete guydinge and surveyeng of all officers and others dependinge, concernynge the comune wele of the hole body of this saide worshipful Toune and procincte of the same. Wherfore we al ar bounde hertilly to praie God for to preserue him, helpe, assist, and counsaille hym, that so diligently with grete instaunt coste and laboure shall apply hym to entende the honoure, welth, and prosperitee of this noble Towne and of al the inhabitauntis of the same.[18]

The mayor, as the king's lieutenant, guides his officers for the common weal of the town; and it is from God that he receives counsel, not from the common council of Bristol. The burgesses must be willing to offer him counsel, when

13 C. Phythian-Adams, *Desolation of a City: Coventry and the Urban Crisis of the Late Middle Ages* (Cambridge, 1979), pp. 74–9, 116–17, 138–9.
14 Hilton, *English and French Towns*, pp. 142–3; Swanson, *Medieval British Towns*, pp. 94–5.
15 Hilton, *English and French Towns*, pp. 145–50; Kermode, *Merchants*, p. 64.
16 Rigby, 'Urban "Oligarchy"', p. 64.
17 R. Ricart, *The Maire of Bristowe is Kalendar*, ed. L. Toulmin Smith, Camden Society, n.s. v (1872), pp. 69–75. For a discussion of the Bristol mayor-making and the meaning of 'community' in the town, see D. H. Sacks, *The Widening Gate: Bristol and the Atlantic Economy, 1450–1700* (California, 1991), pp. 170–7. I do not share Sacks's confidence in the elite's rhetoric of community as a reflection of actual power relations.
18 Ricart, *Kalendar*, p. 5.

required, but there is no requirement on his part to accept it.[19] The divine inspiration behind the institution of the mayor is stressed at the election of the new mayor, where the old mayor exhorts councillors 'to pray the Holly Goste to be at their seid elecion'.[20] The impression given by Ricart is that the mayor rules absolutely under king and God, without even the condition that he take counsel from his immediate inferiors – a position that goes well beyond that recommended by the mirrors for princes as appropriate for a monarch.[21] Nor is it in keeping with the inspiration behind civic practice elsewhere: in Grimsby, appointments not approved by the burgesses were declared invalid.[22] In fact, the mayor of Bristol's absolutism *is* tempered, but only up to a point. As Ricart says, the mayor is to be master of Bristol only 'for the yere beinge': after his term of office he may be called to account for any offences he committed. The speech of the retiring mayor stresses his human frailty and inadequacy for the job he has been undertaking, and invites claims to be made against him:

> Sirs, if that I haue done, of my negligens and wilfulnes, otherwise then right lawe and good conscience wolde to ony man or woman, I will pray theym come to me, and I shal be redy to make theym amendys in that I haue offendid theym.
>
> [The new mayor] shal refourme and amende alle such thinges as I of my sympilnesse haue not duely ne formably executed and fulfilled.[23]

But even this expression of humility actually works to the advantage of the office of mayor, for while it allows for the individual holder of that office to be fallible, those who feel themselves to have been wronged by the mayor must seek redress from the mayor himself or from his immediate successor. Thus, the inescapable fact of human frailty is acknowledged, but without thereby constituting a rival focus of authority to the institution of the mayoralty: a sort of 'mayor's two bodies'.[24] The mayor's monopoly of justice is preserved. The mayor's oath tempers the absolutism a little further, since it makes clear that the mayor will govern for the good of the common weal, observing the laws, and administering them without fear or favour. Such a condition is commonly found elsewhere.[25] However, in Ricart's account, while those laws are made by the mayor, aldermen, sheriffs and common council acting together, there is no doubt that the responsibility for their implementation rests solely with the mayor.[26] The customs described in Ricart's *Kalendar* are not a simple codification of

[19] Similarly, in later fifteenth-century Coventry, the mayor was not obliged to consult with the council, and instead tended to exercise 'cabinet government', taking advice from an informal group which he chose: Kendall, *Yorkist Age*, p. 121; Phythian-Adams, *Desolation of a City*, pp. 122–4.
[20] Ricart, *Kalendar*, p. 70.
[21] For a stimulating discussion of later medieval concepts of kingship, see Watts, *Henry VI*, pp. 16–39.
[22] Rigby, 'Urban "Oligarchy"', p. 66.
[23] Ricart, *Kalendar*, p. 71.
[24] E. H. Kantarowicz, *The King's Two Bodies: A Study in Medieval Political Theology* (Princeton, 1957).
[25] Rigby, 'Urban "Oligarchy"', p. 64; *The Coventry Leet Book or Mayor's Register*, ed. M. D. Harris, EETS, o.s. 134–5 (1907–8), pt 1, p. 224; pt 2, pp. 273–5.
[26] Ricart, *Kalendar*, pp. 72–4.

traditional practice, but a graft onto that existing stock of a set of ordinances drawn from the London customals. The form of the mayor-making ceremony as described by Ricart, including the mayor's oath, may also have been an innovation. As such, the new regime prescribed in the *Kalendar* may represent a stage in Bristol's development towards more exclusive forms of government. This would lead in 1499 to the granting of a charter making Bristol one of England's first closed corporations. Henceforth, Bristol was ruled by a mayor, five aldermen (who also constituted the bench of Justices of the Peace and were appointed for life) and two sheriffs, all chosen from among the forty common councillors; the only vestige of popular election was the shadowy condition that the councillors were to be chosen by the assent of the community.[27] Ricart's description of the mayor-making ceremony may have been a justification of this increasingly oligarchic governance in the guise of a rhetorically neutral record of well-established and accepted practice. If so, it was not the only rhetorical sleight-of-hand being perpetrated in Bristol's civic records.

Bristol's elite could fortify themselves with tales of rebels punished and obedience rewarded. The civic records contain accounts of episodes in the town's recent history which served to highlight the importance of obedience. Three examples are discussed here. The first of these concerns a burgess of Irish origin called Henry May, who in 1456 was discommoned, or ejected, from the freedom of Bristol. Ricart tells the story in this way:

> This yere certein Iressh burgeises of Bristowe began a sewte a yenst the Maire and the Counseile byfore my lorde Chaunceler, with subpenas and prevy sealis, of the whiche Iressh men one Harry May was vaunt parloure and chief labourer; for the whiche he and al his felowes were discomenyd of theyre freedom, til they bought it ayen with the blodde of theyre purses, and with weping Ien, knelyng on their knees, besought the Maire and his brothern of their grace.[28]

Ricart's terse account presents a dramatic tableau of miscreants abasing themselves before magisterial authority; but it also puzzles. No reason is given for the Irishmen's rebellion: it is almost as if their being Irish was explanation enough, and their eventual collapse natural and inevitable.

To make sense of this episode, it must be seen in the context of Anglo-Irish relations. By the 1420s, with effective English lordship restricted to the Dublin Pale and a handful of other townships, the Irish were confirmed in English eyes as enemies and rebels. This estimation extended to the Anglo-Irish as well as to the Gaels. Irishmen living in England became scapegoats for the perceived problems of law and order at home, and in 1422 parliament ordered the expulsion of all Irishmen without visible means of support or a recognised occupation. This measure was repeated in 1430, 1431 and 1432, while the Parliament of 1439–40 included the Irish among those resident aliens required

[27] Bristol 'was a larger, better-established, and more oligarchic place than almost any other city or town in England prior to the Reformation', and 'to the common run of fifteenth-century towns, Bristol represented the wave of the future': R. Tittler, *The Reformation and the Towns in England: Politics and Political Culture, c1540–1640* (London, 1998), pp. 33, 284.

[28] Ricart, *Kalendar*, p. 41.

to pay an annual tax of 1s. 4d., despite their nominal status as subjects of the king of England.[29]

Bristol's close commercial links with Ireland would have made its inhabitants particularly sensitive to the unfolding disaster of Lancastrian rule in the lordship, particularly since Bristol ships were empressed for the transport of troops across the Irish Sea. Predictably, national paranoia found its echo in Bristol. In June 1439 Irishmen were prohibited from membership of the common council, and in the same month were barred from the Hooper's Gild.[30] In 1455, under Mayor Richard Hatter, the common council ordained that those seeking to become burgesses who were born outside the king's allegiance and were not the sons of Bristol burgesses had to pay for their admission a 'redemption' fee of £5, together with 4s. expenses to the chamberlains, who administered the admission of new burgesses. The same ordinance set the fee for native English or Welsh aspirant burgesses at only 40s. plus the chamberlains' expenses. The ordinance specified that the Irish would be counted as aliens, despite the fact that they were technically subjects of the English Crown.[31]

In 1454–5 Henry May, a Bristol burgess of thirty-two years standing, brought a chancery suit against Mayor Hatter and his two chamberlains: this document has not been found, but from the evidence of later chancery records it appears to have been a challenge to the equity of Hatter's ordinance. The dispute remained unresolved at the end of Hatter's mayoralty, but his successor, John Shipward, discommoned Henry May along with four other burgesses of Irish origin.[32] May alleged that Shipward was moved to this action by Hatter in revenge for May's suit against him of the previous year. The ordinance by which they were discommoned talks of 'diuers vntroghtes disseites conuenticules congregacions assemblaunces as of taxes gederyng leyyng and leveyng of the Yeryshemen boron in Yrelond a yenst the goode wele prosperite rewell and gouernance of this Towne of Bristowe' and of their 'diuers disclaundres' and 'vntrewe langage' directed against the mayor, sheriff, common council 'and othour Notabull men'.[33] The text of the ordinance casts the Irish burgesses as conspirators against the commonwealth of Bristol in terms that are hyperbolic even by fifteenth-century standards.

The discommoned burgesses complained to the chancellor.[34] In chancery, Mayor Shipward and his chamberlains defended their discommoning of May with the argument that the town's 1373 charter gave them complete freedom to discommon whomsoever they wished – implying that the chancellor had no legitimate interest in this case. Nevertheless, they went on to explain that they had acted against May because he had broken the town's customs and ordinances by first allowing his apprentice, Richard May, to buy and sell with a stranger (that is, a non-burgess), and then by failing to present his indentures and pay the requisite fee for Richard to be made a burgess. Henry

[29] Griffiths, *Henry VI*, pp. 162–71, 420, 555; A. Cosgrove, *Late Medieval Ireland, 1370–1541* (Dublin, 1981), pp. 29–52.

[30] *The Little Red Book of Bristol*, ed. F. B. Bickley, 2 vols. (Bristol, 1900), i, pp. 86–8; ii, p. 163.

[31] *The Great Red Book of Bristol: Text*, ii, ed. E. W. W. Veale, BRS 8 (1937), p. 49.

[32] PRO C 1/17/213–14. May's associates were named as Thomas Walsh, Nicholas Hoker, Thomas Fraunсis and George Roche. Their names suggest that these were Anglo-Irish rather than Gaels.

[33] *Great Red Book: Text*, ii, p. 54.

[34] The following is based on PRO C 44/31/4.

May's response was that apprentices could trade with strangers provided they had their master's permission – which he had given – and that since the indentures had been lost Henry had sworn to Richard's satisfactory completion of his seven-year term of apprenticeship, as allowed by the customs and ordinances of Bristol. These charges answered, Henry May went on to the central issue. He claimed that until Hatter's ordinance the burgesses' entry fee had remained constant at 2s. There was simply no precedent for the mayor to set a new rate, and so he had refused to pay the 104s. demanded of him on behalf of Richard May as an aspirant burgess of Irish origin.

Chancery's decision was a compromise that avoided the real issue: Henry May was ordered to return to Bristol and place himself under the mayor's obedience, while for his part the mayor was to admit May back into the freedom. This was not the end of the story. May claimed in a subsequent chancery suit that the day after he had submitted himself to the mayor he was summoned to the council house and under great duress forced to sign an obligation in £20 to the use of Mayor Shipward and the sheriff; he had refused to pay the sum when it had become due, and was now asking for a *sub poena* against the mayor and sheriff.

Chancery also ordered the mayor to allow May's fellow Irish burgesses back into the freedom, but this was met with a flat refusal, on the unconvincing grounds that the common councillors had refused to allow the mayor to obey the chancery writ since it conflicted with the town's chartered liberties, and he was unable to overrule them. The dispute rumbled on until at least 1458, when some of the Irish burgesses were examined before the mayor following allegations that they had brought a writ of *sub poena* against one of the chamberlains.[35]

From this reading of the chancery evidence it appears that Ricart's account conceals much that would not redound to the credit of the mayor and common council. The version of events given in the chancery proceedings is a tale of persecution and attempted profiteering on the part of the mayor and his officers, combined with disobedience to the king's chancellor. This rather sordid narrative is in stark contrast to the story told by the civic record, which presents an unprovoked conspiracy by rebellious Irish effortlessly defeated by the authorities.

The next two examples suggest similar manipulations of recent history for the Bristol elite's polemical purposes. On 12 March 1479 Mayor William Spencer and the sheriff were hearing cases in the mayor's court, when Thomas Norton, one of the royal customers, strode into the court, read out an accusation of treason against the mayor and threw down his gauntlet.[36] The mayor denied the charge – the record diplomatically omits the details – but Norton appealed to the sheriff to see that justice be done.[37] The next day Mayor

[35] PRO C 1/26/102.

[36] The following is based on *Great Red Book*: *Text*, iv, ed. E. W. W. Veale, BRS 18 (1953), pp. 57–93. J. Latimer, 'Some Curious Incidents in Bristol History', *TBGAS*, xxii (1899), pp. 272–84, gives an account based on the documents in *Great Red Book*. For more on the Norton family, see J. J. Simpson, 'St Peter's Hospital, Bristol', *TBGAS*, xlviii (1926), pp. 193–210, and Thomas Norton's *The Ordinal of Alchemy*, ed. J. Reidy, EETS, o.s. 272 (1975), pp. xxxvii–li.

[37] For the suggestion that Norton's accusation was connected to Spencer's support for Warwick in 1471, see *Calendar of the Charters etc. of the City and County of Bristol*, ed. J. Latimer (Bristol, 1909), p. 121.

Spencer resigned his office and presented himself to the town gaoler, insisting that he should be shown no special favours. The case was heard before the king, who learned from the common council's attorneys that Norton was a highly disreputable individual: he had robbed and ruined members of his own family, and spent his nights in taverns and his mornings in bed, and played tennis and other immoral sports when he should have been in church. More to the point, he retained a gang of thugs, and had been prosecuted by the mayor for illegal retaining. Norton's response was that the mayor's prosecution was unjust, and had been motivated by the latter's desire for private vengeance. Norton claimed that as customer he had seized some cloths for which Spencer had attempted to evade paying customs duties, and that the accusation of illegal retaining had been brought after he had refused the mayor's bribe of a hogshead of wine to turn a blind eye to the smuggling operation. Norton's defence was not accepted, and the king exonerated the mayor. Norton's fate is not recorded. Mayor Spencer was released from prison, amid scenes of great popular rejoicing, at least according to the account given in *The Great Red Book*.

The theme of rebels humiliated is also prominent in the account of sheriff William Dale's failed attempt to persuade star chamber to moderate the financial demands made by the mayor and common council upon the shrievalty.[38] In 1518 Dale complained to star chamber that the expenses of the shrieval office were unreasonable, and petitioned that the mayor and common council be forced to reduce them. Star chamber was not convinced by Dale's argument, but nonetheless the sheriff's expenses were renegotiated on the orders of Chancellor Wolsey. However, the account given in Ricart's *Kalendar* and *The Great White Book* of Dale's humiliation is not imbued with the spirit of compromise, and has definite echoes of Ricart's handling of the May incident. Accompanying Dale at Westminster were 'many evyll disposed persons of thaffinytie of the fornamed Wyllyam Dale confedrators with hym to sett division in the said Towne and to menteign hym in his symple opynyon and sedicous purpose'.[39] On the orders of the chancellor, Dale submitted himself to the mayor and common council in the council house. Like Henry May, Dale is described as having had to beg for forgiveness, coming before the councillors 'and then and there in right obedient manner with watery tears submitted himself'.[40] The Bristol council house must have been a pretty lachrymose place at times.

These accounts read rather like political fables, particularly that of the stoical mayor Spencer and his dastardly opponent. The weeping recalcitrant burgesses seem more like rhetorical tropes than accurate descriptions of events. Whatever their value as documents of record, these stories undoubtedly functioned as morality plays, imbedded within the civic record, in which men of some wealth and local influence, who have wandered from the true path of obedience, are corrected and humbled before the triumphant mayor, the lieutenant of both God and king. The purpose and rhetorical intent behind these accounts is made plain by the opening lines of the record of the Norton affair in *The Great Red Book*:

[38] The following is based on PRO STAC 2/6/78–85, 18/265 (partly printed and discussed in *Select Cases before the King's Council in the Star Chamber*, ii, ed. I. S. Leadam, Selden Society 25 (1910), pp. cii–cxviii, 142–65); *The Great White Book of Bristol*, ed. E. Ralph, BRS, 32 (1979), pp. 3–4, 72–86; *Great Red Book: Text*, ii, pp. 153–5; Ricart, *Kalendar*, pp. 49–50.
[39] Ibid.
[40] *Great White Book*, p. 81.

> Here followeth a Remembraunce Nevir to be put in oblyvion but to be hadde in perpetuell memory of all the trewe Burgeises and lovers of the Towne of Bristowe of the Innaturall demeanyng and the Inordinate behavyng of Thomas Norton of Bristowe Gentleman against the noble famouse and trewe merchaunte William Spencer beinge the thirde tyme Maire of the Towne of Bristowe.[41]

This discourse shows the Bristol elite as triumphant, but in doing so it has to concede that this authority had first been contested. While in each of these three examples the mayor and common council are vindicated, the necessary exposition of their opponents' complaints does at least raise the possibility that their accusations are true: it was certainly not unthinkable that mayors could be corrupt, profiteering and vindictive.

Presumably, mayoral annals and civic memoranda books would have had a limited circulation, and so the tales recorded in them would have been read only by the burgesses. Accounts of the humiliation of May, Norton and Dale admonished their peers of the strength of the governing elite and the dire consequences of disobedience. These representations of authority are part of an elite discourse, and as such are relatively visible. What those below the burgess class thought about their governors is less easily reconstructed.

Wilkinson, and more recently Harvey, have suggested that the common people of fifteenth-century England were better informed, more opinionated, and of greater importance to the conduct of politics at all levels than is usually assumed.[42] Harvey points to the lower ranks' growing literacy, their awareness of the crucial part they played in the defence of the realm and the financing of government through taxation, and the accumulating memories of previous instances of direct political action, such as the revolts of 1381. The all-too-apparent inadequacies of royal government in the middle years of the century encouraged debate and action among those denied participation in the formal mechanisms of government. The sophistication of the rebels in 1450 is attested by their manifestos, and to a lesser extent by the satirical verses current in that year.[43] Justice has emphasised the political sophistication and confidence of the rebels of 1381.[44] Elements of social protest are also apparent in the Robin Hood ballads, among other popular verses.[45]

Such political awareness and assertiveness was not confined to the rural population.[46] Indeed, it is likely that town dwellers, presumably enjoying higher standards of literacy and better communications with the outside world, would have had more developed political opinions and the wish to express them. Some polemical material was produced in the context of specific urban disputes, such

[41] *Great Red Book: Text*, iv, p. 57.

[42] B. Wilkinson, *The Constitutional History of England in the Fifteenth Century, 1399–1485* (London, 1964), *passim*; I. M. W. Harvey, 'Was there Popular Politics in Fifteenth-Century England?', *The McFarlane Legacy: Studies in Late Medieval Politics and Society*, ed. R. H. Britnell and A. J. Pollard (Stroud, 1995), pp. 155–74. I owe to Mr Keith Dockray the suggestion that Wilkinson had anticipated several points raised by more recent 'constitutional' historians.

[43] I. M. W. Harvey, *Jack Cade's Rebellion of 1450* (Oxford, 1991), pp. 80, 83, 88, 186–91; V. J. Scattergood, *Politics and Poetry in the Fifteenth Century* (London, 1971), pp. 369–70.

[44] S. Justice, *Writing and Rebellion: England in 1381* (Berkeley, 1994).

[45] Scattergood, *Politics and Poetry*, pp. 362–7.

[46] This paragraph is based on ibid. pp. 367–8, 370–6.

as the verses associated with the student riots against the mayor of Cambridge in 1418, and Laurence Saunders' challenge to the governing elite of Coventry in 1495–6. The former is mainly a series of verses threatening the mayor and his cronies, but the Coventry examples, pinned up on church doors by Saunders' supporters, offer a sophisticated critique of oligarchic abuses of power. They criticise the oligarchy's manipulation of customs and taxation, apprentice fees, and enclosure, and insist on the collective power and importance of the 'cominalte'. These examples are likely to have been produced from within the broader elite of urban society. Some verses dating from the early 1460s, on the other hand, may have been penned by a member of the proletariat. They denounce the exploitation of cloth workers by their employers in terms which Scattergood describes as 'the earliest extant to bring into opposition capital and labour in an urban context in anything like modern terms'. They were probably produced as part of a campaign that in 1463–4 resulted in limited statutory regulation of employment relations in the textile industry. The author had a detailed knowledge of the cloth trade, and had also read *The Libelle of Englyshe Polycye*: if a cloth worker, he was exceptionally well-read; if a merchant, unusually sympathetic to the workers, and unusually willing to break ranks with his own class.

All of the above were occasional pieces, created in response to particular conflicts and grievances. By contrast, the mystery cycles of Corpus Christi provided a regular forum in which urban communities could engage with ideas about power and authority. For historians, the interest of civic drama and pageantry has tended to lie mainly with its organisation, patronage, production, and sometimes with its audience. Numerous studies have shown how the staging of civic processions could reflect changing power relationships between different gilds, between governors and governed, and between the town and exterior authorities, while often at the same time attempting to present an image of harmony and stability.[47] Consideration of the texts of the plays has largely been left to literary scholars. This may be to miss valuable evidence for the political attitudes of late medieval townspeople below the governing elite. The play cycles, like every other aspect of civic pageantry, were controlled by the elite, either the ruling body or the gild masters, and so it could be argued that any subversive messages in their texts were sanctioned by the elite as a form of safety valve for the populace, rather in the fashion of the festivals of the Lord of Misrule and the Boy Bishop.[48] On the other hand, control could not have

[47] D. Palliser, 'Civic Mentality and Environment in Tudor York', *Northern History*, xviii (1982), pp. 78–115; M. Berlin, 'Civic Ceremony in Early-Modern London', *Urban History Year Book* (1986), pp. 15–27; M. James 'Ritual, Drama and Social Body in the Late Medieval English Town', *Past and Present*, 87 (1983), pp. 3–29; D. H. Sacks, 'The Demise of the Martyrs: The Feasts of St Clement and St Katherine in Bristol, 1400–1600', *Social History*, xi (1986), pp. 141–69; C. Phythian-Adams, 'Ceremony and the Citizen: The Communal Year at Coventry, 1450–1550', *The Medieval Town*, ed. Holt and Rosser, pp. 238–64; A. J. Fletcher, 'Playing and Staying and Staying Together: Projecting the Corporate Image in Sixteenth-Century Dublin', *Civic Ritual and Drama*, ed. A. F. Johnston and W. Hümsken (Amsterdam, 1997), pp. 15–37; D. Mills, 'The Chester Mystery Plays: Truth and Tradition', *Courts, Counties and the Capital in the Later Middle Ages*, ed. D. Dunn (Stroud, 1996), pp. 1–26; Mills, *Recycling the City: the City of Chester and its Whitsun Plays* (Toronto, 1996); Kermode, *Merchants*, pp. 65–6. *City and Spectacle*, ed. Hanawalt and Reyerson, is a valuable collection of essays on this subject.

[48] Sacks, *Widening Gate*, pp. 180–3: 'the festivity not only criticized the mayor and his brethren for

been total, and so it was not necessarily the case that the plays' authors were never able to challenge the dominant ideology. Censorship is a blunt instrument, and censors usually possess blunt intellects. The censorship which the lord chamberlain imposed on Elizabethan and Jacobean playwrights was at least the equal of that with which the authors of mystery plays may have had to work, but no one would suggest that *King Lear* simply reflects the accepted social and political mores of its time. In addition, neither the censors nor the plays' authors could control how their audiences interpreted the images with which they were presented: playwrights lose control of their texts once they are performed.

The political sophistication of at least one mystery play has been proposed by Squires, who suggests parallels between the 'parliament of heaven' sequence in the 'Coventry', or N-Town Cycle and *Somnium Vigilantis*.[49] In the play, fallen Mankind is put on trial before it is decided that Christ should be incarnated for its redemption. In the *Somnium* it is the Yorkists whose fate hangs in the balance, and the decision goes against them.[50] In the play, Mankind is defended by Mercy and Peace and accused by Righteousness and Truth; their analogues in the *Somnium* speak for and against the Yorkists. However, what Squires does not take into account is the well-established literary and rhetorical tradition from which both of these works spring.[51] In this light, the case for any direct link between the two works appears considerably weakened, but that they share common antecedents does suggest that the creator(s) of this play were familiar with contemporary political concepts.

The theological sophistication of the mystery plays is well known, as is their vivid observation of contemporary society. The latter could easily shade into political comment. The Towneley/Wakefield *Second Shepherds' Play* opens on a cold winter's night, where two shepherds, Coll and Gyb, are bemoaning their lot. Coll's analysis of the evils of 'bastard feudalism' would gladden the heart of the inventor of the term, Charles Plummer:

> We ar so hamyd,
> Fortaxed and ramyd,
> We ar mayde handtamyd
> With thyse gentlery men.
>
> Thus thay refe us oure rest, oure Lady theym wary!
> These men that ar lord-fest, thay cause the ploghe tary;
> . . . . .
> For may he gett a paynt slefe or a broche now-on-dayes,
> Wo is hym that hym grefe or onys agane says!
> Dar no man hym reprefe, what mastry he mays;

their inevitable failings but purged them of their official sins. It also emphasized that the civic authorities served the community and thus were subject to the chastisement and the approbation of those they governed.'

[49] 'Law and Disorder in Ludus Coventriae', *The Drama of the Middle Ages: Comparative and Critical Essays*, ed. C Davidson *et al.* (New York, 1982), pp. 272–85.

[50] 'A Defence of the Proscription of the Yorkists in 1459', ed. J. P. Gilson, *EHR*, xxvi (1911), pp. 512–25.

[51] M. L. Kekewich, 'The Attainder of the Yorkists in 1459: Two Contemporary Accounts', *BIHR*, lv (1982), pp. 25–34.

And yit may no man lefe oone word that he says –
No letter.
He can make purveance
With boste and bragance,
And all is thrugh mantenance
Of men that ar gretter.[52]

Needless to say, this is not in itself subversive: the object of Coll's criticism is the retainer who abuses the system, not the system itself. His objection to livery was shared by the governments of Northampton, Newcastle-on-Tyne and York, all of which banned the wearing of lords' livery within their towns.[53] And indeed, the metanarrative of these cycles demonstrates the fundamental importance of obedience to divine authority, and the awful consequences of its opposite: the Fall, Cain and Abel, Noah's Flood, Abraham and Isaac, the Annunciation, Incarnation, Crucifixion, Harrowing of Hell, Resurrection, Last Judgement – every important stage of the story is decided by a choice between obedience and disobedience to the divine will, and demonstrates the consequences of that choice.[54] For God read his lieutenants, king or mayor, and one has a powerfully persuasive call to obey temporal authority. This is very much in line with the view that the organisation and staging of the plays was a contribution to – and expression of – civic harmony: each limb and organ in the civic body working together to commemorate – and recreate – the Corpus Christi. The fact that these stagings were also the occasion for dissent – for disputes over precedence and individual gilds' unwillingness to contribute, and for hostile take-overs of other gilds' plays – need not detract from the overall validity of this view.[55] But the subtext of these plays may have been liable to more subversive readings.

Repeatedly in these plays, God's purpose is resisted by those enjoying worldly authority: from Pharaoh, through Caesar Augustus to Herod and Pilate, the godly are scorned, enslaved, tortured and killed by evil tyrants, often with the connivance of clerical henchmen, but the Word of God is always triumphant, and the evil get their come-uppance.[56] The plays have contemporary settings and references. As we have seen, a biblical shepherd can decry the evils of retaining, while the mob which takes Jesus prisoner is presented *vi et armis*, demons travel down Watling Street to the Day of Judgement, and a

[52] 'We are so crippled/ Overtaxed and oppressed,/ We are made submissive,/ By these gentry./ Thus they deny us our rest, Our Lady curse them!/ These lords' retainers, they cause the plough to tarry . . . / For he who gets a coloured sleeve or badge nowadays,/ Woe is him that him grieve or once gainsays!/ Dare no man him reprove, whatever force he employs;/ And yet may no man believe one word that he says – no letter./ He can make purveyance/ With boasting and bragging,/ And all is through maintenance/ Of men that are greater.': *The Second Shepherds' Play* (Towneley/Wakefield), lines 15–20, 28–36. All play references are to the editions in *Medieval Drama*, ed. D. Bevington (Boston, 1975). For a discussion of the contemporary context of this passage, see Scattergood, *Politics and Poetry*, pp. 360–2.

[53] R. Horrox, 'The Urban Gentry in the Fifteenth Century', *Towns and Townspeople*, pp. 22–44, at p. 24; Kermode, *Merchants*, p. 27.

[54] 'Law and Disorder in Ludus Coventriae', pp. 274–5.

[55] James, 'Ritual', pp. 3–29. For a critique of the view of the integrative power of *Corpus Christi*, see M. Rubin, 'Small Groups: Identity and Solidarity in the Late Middle Ages', *Enterprise and Individuals in Fifteenth-Century England*, ed. J. Kermode (Stroud, 1991), pp. 132–50.

[56] A. Williams, *The Characterisation of Pilate in the Towneley Plays* (Michigan, 1950), p. 37.

stage direction in *The Woman Taken in Adultery* describes how, during the Pharisees' raid on a brothel, *Hic juvenis quidam extra currit, in deploydo, calligis non ligatis et braccas in manu tenens.*[57] In scenes concerning the workings of the law the parallels with fifteenth-century practice are particularly close. In the N-Town play *The Trial of Joseph and Mary* Mary's denial of allegations that her pregnancy is the result of fornication is given before what is recognisably an ecclesiastical court, presided over by a bishop, who is notably hostile to the Virgin.[58] In the N-Town *Passion*, the costumes for the Jewish priests Caiaphas and Annas are intended to depict 'a busshop of the hoold lawe', and are topped out with mitres. They are accompanied by doctors of law wearing furred cloaks, hoods, and caps, and Rewfyn and Lyon, who wear rayed tabards and hoods, similar to those worn by serjeants-at-law. The hoods also seem to indicate that these costumes are intended to suggest legal costume, while the 'caps' may in fact be coifs.[59] Caiaphas and Annas are repeatedly described as bishops and prelates of the Church:

> As a primat most preudent, I present here sensible
> Buschopys of the lawe, with al the circumstawns.
> I, Caiphas, am jewge with powerys possible
> To distroye all errouris that in oure lawys make variawns.[60]

Christ is accused of treason and heresy, the latter encompassing witchcraft and necromancy: 'He is an eretik and a tretour bolde'; 'Shewe forth thy wichecrafte and nigramansye!'[61] His accusers call for the standard fifteenth-century punishments for these offences:

> Let him first ben hangyn and drawe,
> And thanne his body in fire be brent.[62]

The court presided over by Caiaphas and Annas find Christ guilty of heresy, but in accordance with canon law they are unable to impose the death penalty:

> It is not lefful to us, ye seyn,
> no maner man for to slen.[63]

So they pass him on to the temporal arm, represented first by Pilate and then, after it is revealed that Christ was born outside his jurisdiction, to Herod.[64] In

[57] 'Here a young man runs out in his doublet, his boots untied and holding up his breeches with his hand': *Medieval Drama*, pp. 464, 642. 'Law and Disorder in Ludus Coventriae', pp. 273–4.
[58] Unless otherwise stated, this paragraph is based on 'Law and Disorder in Ludus Coventriae', pp. 272–84.
[59] *Medieval Drama*, pp. 486–8. E. W. Ives, *The Common Lawyers of Pre-Reformation England: Thomas Kebell: A Case Study* (Cambridge, 1983), pp. 358–9 and n. 9.
[60] *Passion Play i* (N-Town), lines 45–8.
[61] Ibid. lines 145, 1,006.
[62] Ibid. lines 155–6.
[63] *Passion Play ii* (N-Town), lines 301–2. See also *The Buffeting* (Towneley/Wakefield), lines 269–70, 276–9.
[64] *Passion Play ii*, lines 325–32, 341–52.

broad terms, the procedural details of the trials of Christ are in accord with fifteenth-century practice.[65]

Needless to say, such contemporary references served to ground the biblical story in the present, thereby making it more vivid and immediate. The identification of Christ's tormentors with contemporary lawyers and prelates need have had no more significance than this. The same applies to the corrupt and sadistic knights with whom the biblical tyrants surround themselves.[66] There are some more precise targets of criticism. The Towneley Cycle's Pilate proclaims how

> . . . all false enditars,
> Quest-gangers, and jurars,
> And thise outridars,
> Ar welcom to me.[67]

A similar equation between wickedness and the law is made in the same cycle's *Last Judgement*, in which demons are portrayed as lawyers, having to handle their brief as carefully as a peer in parliament.[68] Among those listed in their rolls of the damned are 'false quest-ditars' and:

> That rasers of the fals tax,
> And gederars of greyn wax.[69]

However, none of this need be more than conventional pot-shots at the usual objects of criticism familiar from medieval social satire.

More striking is the explicit and repeated association between tyranny and the law. Each of the great tyrants, Pharaoh, Herod and Pilate, associate themselves with the law.[70] Their law is usually described as belonging to Mohammed, who is practically interchangeable with Satan.[71] What this law amounts to is made clear by Pilate's boast:

> For, like as on both sidys the iren the hamer makith playn,
> So do I, that the law has here in my keping.
> The right side to socoure, certys, I am full bain,
> If I may get therby a vantage or wining;

[65] Squires perhaps goes too far in equating the court of Caiaphas and Annas with Henry VII's Council Learned: 'Law and Disorder', pp. 280–1.

[66] For example, in *The Resurrection* (Towneley/Wakefield), lines 190–1, Pilate addresses his retainers thus: 'Sir knightys, that ar of dedys dughty,/ And chosen for chefe of chevalry'.

[67] 'All false accusers/ inquest-chasers and jurors,/ And these summoners,/ Are welcome to me': *The Scourging* (Towneley/Wakefield), lines 23–6.

[68] Lines 118–19: 'It sittys you to tente, in the mater to mell/ As a pere in a parlamente, what case so befell.'

[69] Lines 185, 283–4. In 1450 the Cade rebels also complained of exchequer writs sealed in green wax (Harvey, *Jack Cade's Rebellion*, p. 83), as did the early fourteenth-century author of *The Song of the Husbandman*: Scattergood, *Politics and Poetry*, pp. 351–2.

[70] In, for example, the following Towneley/Wakefield plays: *Pharaoh*, lines 9–10, 'All Egypt is mine awne/ To leede aftyr my lawe'; *Herod the Great*, line 38, where Herod is described as, 'Chefe leder of law'; and Pilate in *The Scourging*, line 15, declares himself to have 'the law . . . in my keeping'.

[71] For example *Passion Play ii*, line 6; *The Scourging* (Towneley/Wakefield), line 3.

Then to the false part I turne me again,
For I se more vaill will to me be rising.
Thus every man to drede me shal be full fain,
And all faint of thare faith to me be obeying,[72]

This law, arbitrary and corrupt, is repeatedly challenged by the servants of God, from Moses to Christ himself.[73] The tyrants' reactions to opposition, real or imagined, are uncompromising:

Full low he shall be thrawne
That harkyns not my sawe –
Hanged by and drawne!

Under my feete I shall thaym fare,
Those ladys that will not lere my lore
Thus shall I tech knavys ensampyll to take,

In thare wittys that ravys sich mastre to make
All wantones wafys! No langage ye crack![74]

With equal regularity, the tyrants announce their arrival on stage by commanding the silence of everyone else, on pain of death:

Pease at my biding, ye wightys in wold!
Looke none be so hardy to speke a word bot I,
Or by Mahowne most mighty, maker on mold,
With this brande that I bere ye shall bitterly aby.[75]

This may be more than simply a theatrical device to get the attention of the audience. The association of tyranny with attempts to silence opposing views is sometimes combined with attempts to conceal the truth, as when Pilate, after the Resurrection, bribes his knights to spread the story that Christ's body had been stolen.[76]

In the mystery plays, temporal wickedness is personified in the chief magistrate, be he Pharaoh, Herod or Pilate. To some extent, this is the stock villain: bullying, cruel, self-regarding and, ultimately, cowardly, but there are other features which give him greater individuality. He insists on the unques-

[72] Lines 14–21: 'For, as the hammer flattens the iron on both sides,/ so do I who has the law in his keeping,/ The right side to assist, certainly, I am quite willing,/ If I may thereby get an advantage or profit;/ Then to the wrong side I turn me again,/ For I see more gain will be coming to me./ Thus every man shall be ready enough to fear me,/ And all those weak in their faith shall truly obey me.'

[73] *Pharaoh* (Towneley/Wakefield), lines 230–1, 234–9. *Ten Commandments* (Chester), lines 201–88. *Woman Taken in Adultery* (N-Town), lines 41, 47. *Passion Play i*, lines 14–16. Williams, *Characterisation of Pilate*, pp. 37–44.

[74] *Pharaoh* (Towneley/Wakefield), lines 13–15; *Offering of the Magi* (Towneley/Wakefield), lines 31–2. *Herod the Great* (Towneley/Wakefield), lines 496–8: 'Thus shall I teach knaves to take example,/ In their wits who rave to claim such authority./ Cease all insolence, do not make any boasts!'

[75] *The Scourging* (Towneley/Wakefield), lines 1–4. See also *Pharaoh* (Towneley/Wakefield), lines 1–24; *The Offering of the Magi* (Towneley/Wakefield), lines 1–6.

[76] *The Scourging* (Towneley/Wakefield), lines 542–61.

tioning obedience of those he rules, but he is not, in theory, an arbitrary ruler: his authority is founded on his claims to be upholding the law of his god, although his corrupt exercise of power flouts that same law by which his rule is justified. While he occasionally takes advice from such as Caiaphas and Annas, he operates independently of any counsel. He attempts to stifle dissent, insisting that only his voice and his version of events be heard, and misrepresents the truth. Had Henry May, Thomas Norton or William Dale seen such a character strutting across the stage, would they have felt a certain thrill of recognition? For these men, and for other burgesses who had fallen foul of their ruling elite, such portrayals may have had a passing resonance, but this would always have been counterbalanced by the knowledge that in different circumstances they too might have shared in the exercise of that authority which was being parodied.

But it is surely less controversial to suggest that such portrayals, unwitting or not on the part of their creators, would have struck a particular chord with those townspeople excluded from the urban elite. The mystery-play tyrant could be seen as the evil *alter ego* of Ricart's benignly autocratic mayor. Ricart's mayor, ruling under the king, expected to administer the law fairly and for the benefit of the common weal, is nevertheless described as a free agent within his town. The crucial point is that Ricart's mayor *is* benign, and he is benign because it is in his nature so to be. This is the gist of the guidance for mayors copied into London's *Liber Custumarum*, adapted from *Li Livre dou Tresor* by the thirteenth-century Florentine magistrate, Brunetto Latini.[77] The mayor is counselled to secure his rule upon the three pillars of justice, reverence and love. There is little more offered by way of constitutional safeguards against tyranny, apart from the equally conventional advice that governors should be wealthy, mature, and chosen for their virtues, not their family connections.[78] Was this enough, in the eyes of *all* townspeople, not just those within the charmed circle of oligarchy, to ensure that urban government was fair and honest? Being against sin, the 'official line' on urban government appears even more anodyne when considered in juxtaposition to the trenchant critique of temporal power in the mystery cycles. To those living at the sharp end of patrician authority it may have seemed that their governors all too often better resembled Pilate than Latini's benign governor. In the mystery plays, the equity of government rests on the fragile foundation of individual moral character. It has been claimed that such was not the case in the later medieval town, where there were structures in place to minimise the risks of corrupt and arbitrary rule. In the words of Reynolds, 'most of the consultative and electoral arrangements of the later middle ages' were intended 'to allow such participation by the body of respectable and solid citizens as would equally avoid corruption, domination by cliques and the disorders of mob rule'.[79] But it was the patrician elite who decided who was 'respectable and solid'. Pharaoh, Herod and Pilate, all three men of means with solid administrative careers behind them, might have qualified, Coll and Gyb the shepherds certainly would not.

77 *Liber Albus*, ii(2), pp. 16–25.
78 Reynolds, 'Medieval Urban History', pp. 22–3.
79 Reynolds, *English Medieval Towns*, pp. 176–7.

INDEX

Key: abp = archbishop; bp = bishop; c = countess; d = duke, duchess; e = earl; ld = lord; w = wife

Lightning Source UK Ltd.
Milton Keynes UK
UKHW01n0927270918
329569UK00005B/231/P